To Cloyd
From
Dad & Mom

TOWARD A
BETTER WORLD

TOWARD A BETTER WORLD

JAN CHRISTIAAN SMUTS

WORLD BOOK COMPANY

Distributed by

DUELL, SLOAN AND PEARCE

NEW YORK

CONTENTS

INTRODUCTION

No country in the British Commonwealth of Nations has had a more colorful and romantic history than the Union of South Africa and no other country presents so many complexities.

Much of South Africa's history is typified in the almost legendary life of Jan Christiaan Smuts.

Winston Churchill was once this man's prisoner. Churchill, a war correspondent in the Anglo-Boer War, was captured by the Dutch Republican forces in which General Smuts was one of the officers.

Today they are both Prime Ministers.

Smuts once fought the British—today he is one of their greatest leaders.

He is the only British Field Marshal who is not British. Smuts is of Dutch descent.

He has a town in Palestine named after him (Ramat Jochanan Smuts) in recognition of friendship shown to Jews.

He was a friend of President Wilson and helped to found the League of Nations.

He is a soldier, statesman, philosopher, and scientist of world repute.

He is an admirer of Walt Whitman and has evolved a philosophy called "holism."

Today, at the apex of his career, South Africa occupies a worthy place in the ranks of the United Nations because

Smuts's leadership swung South Africa solidly into line against the threat of Axis aggression when the country was offered the alternative course of a pallid neutrality.

I

This is the third war that Smuts has fought for freedom.

The first was the Anglo-Boer War of 1899–1902 when, as a citizen of the Transvaal Republic, he helped to perfect commando warfare against the British and led a long and daring raid deep into British territory at the Cape. He was a Boer General of almost legendary performance when, in 1902, he helped to close this chapter of strife between the Dutch and the British in South Africa.

In the field as a British Army Lieutenant-General in World War I, he broke the German power in East Africa and became a towering figure in the British Imperial War Cabinet.

In World War II he is South Africa's Prime Minister, Minister of Defense, and Commander-in-Chief of the South African Forces. These forces have played an important part in smashing Mussolini's East African Empire and chasing Rommel out of North Africa. Today Smuts's recently created armored divisions are poised, ready to strike anywhere across the seas as Allied strategy demands.

Smuts himself has attended various important military conferences in North Africa, one with Mr. Churchill. In October, 1942, he flew to London and once again consulted with the British Cabinet and the Allied war leaders.

Today, at the age of 73, he has the alert and supple bearing of a young man, a tireless capacity for work, a whipcord resistance. He speaks with his old authority in the councils of the nations.

When Jan Christiaan Smuts was born on May 24, 1870, on a farm not a hundred miles from Cape Town, the Cape of Good Hope and Natal were British Colonies and the Orange Free State and the Transvaal were Dutch Republics. These four states have since 1910 comprised the present Union of South Africa. The Western Province of the Cape, where Smuts grew up, had known a long period of comparative tranquility. The Dutch, who came after 1652, and the British, who came after 1806, were teaming together in building up the colony and Smuts's father, Jacobus Smuts, whose forebears had hailed from Holland, was for many years a member of the Cape Legislative Assembly, where since 1882 Dutch, in addition to English, was recognized as an official language.

Jutting southward into the sea some 7,800 miles from New York and washed by the waters of two great oceans lies the Cape of Good Hope. This jagged, rocky peninsula meant "good hope" to the hardy mariners of the fifteenth century who were seeking the fabled riches of India. "Good hope" this peninsula promises today to the ships of the United Nations. Round the Cape before the Mediterranean became a United Nations lake in the fall of 1943, went practically all of the vast convoys of men and arms from Britain and America to Libya, India, Australia, and other battlegrounds, stopping at Cape Town, the "Tavern of the Seas," to take on supplies or to leave ships and weapons for repair. The Cape has stood as one of the vital bastions of the fight for freedom.

Much of South Africa is like Texas and America's western prairies—land that is fairly high, dry, and covered with sparse foliage. Large tracts of the Northwest Cape are wastelands, barren and waterless. There is, however, an abundant rainfall on the coastal areas and large fertile plains of the "Highveld." The country is something like an overturned saucer, with a narrow coastal belt fringing the sea; thence a steep escarpment and mountainous ridges; and finally a great central plateau. Practically no harbors or ports except Table Bay near the extreme south break the monotony of the western seacoast and only a few—Mossel Bay, Port Elizabeth, East London, and Durban—are to be found along the Indian Ocean side. The climate is temperate and South Africa boasts some of the finest scenery in the world.

South Africa is in some respects still a pioneering country, its farmers and cattle growers living close to the soil. Many of its towns are small and isolated. But Johannesburg, with its skyscrapers reminiscent of New York, the busy wharves of Cape Town, and the urbane English atmosphere of Durban and modern transport and communications throughout the country, reflects the spirit of the twentieth century.

II

In the Eastern Province of the Cape, during the nineteenth century, Dutch and English settlers were still periodically engaged in frontier wars against the black Bantu tribes whose penetration into South Africa from the north coincided with the development of the white settlements in the extreme south.

In 1836 began the migration, mainly from the Eastern Province, into the unknown interior, of dissatisfied Dutch farmers who subsequently, in the middle of the century, founded the Transvaal and Free State Republics. South Africans know 1836 as the year of the Great Trek; the episode had its counterpart in America in the Santa Fé trail and the saga of the Covered Wagon. The two Republics became known as the Boer Republics, "boer" being the Dutch word for farmer.

The relationships between the two Republics and the two British Colonies, the Cape and Natal, developed a strange pattern of friendships and antagonisms. Federation of the four states was more than once mooted on both sides. Annexation of the Transvaal by the British took place in 1877. Jan Smuts, a day-dreaming boy who was born a British subject, was ten years old when the first Anglo-Boer War broke out and the defeat of the British in the Battle of Majuba on February 27, 1881, restored republican independence to the Transvaal Boers. Paul Kruger, whom Smuts was to serve later as State Attorney, became President of the Republic in 1883.

Jan Smuts in his youth seems to have been a shy and introspective bookworm with no great liking for school and college playing fields and by all accounts not as "handy" on the farm as practical South African farmers expect their sons to be. His parents hoped he would enter the Dutch Reformed Church ministry; his own leanings proved to be towards law and philosophy and, later, politics.

From the Victoria College, Stellenbosch, he won a scholarship which took him to Cambridge, England. Here he took little part in ordinary student activities, partly because he did not have the funds, mainly because he was a glutton for learning and determined to exact from the great university all he could during his brief years there.

He took his Law Final with a Double First, was admitted to the Middle Temple, London, in 1894, refused a professorship at Christ College, Cambridge, and returned to South Africa to practice as a barrister in the Supreme Court in Cape Town.

Smuts has always returned to South Africa and the hard way. He has been offered great honors and posts of great distinction elsewhere in the world but he has always remained loyal to South Africa. Today South Africa returns this loyalty. He regards that as his greatest triumph and the greatest of all the honors bestowed upon him, since South Africa is a cruel taskmistress to her national leaders; her favors are not easily won.

As a young barrister in Cape Town in the eighteen nineties, Smuts did not readily gain a foothold. People found him cold, aloof, unsympathetic. He was perhaps more shy than aloof, and he has retained this trait of shyness to this day. His lack of warmth did not encourage clients and he resorted to part-time journalism to compensate for the meager returns of his law business. At that time he was a gaunt, pale young man, clean-shaven, sandy-haired, angry-eyed. He emerged from the commando rigors of the Anglo-Boer War tanned, broadened, and toughened. The resistance built up on the open veld during those years of campaigning probably accounts for Smuts's amazing vitality today. South Africa was the first to teach the world that commando work is tough, enterprising work demanding stamina and resourcefulness. Smuts today is a mellowed, kindly personality, rejoicing in the simple pleasures of his farm, when he has time to relax there, in the company of lifelong friends who respect his moods, and especially in the companionship of a growing brood of grandchildren. But on occasion he still assumes a mantle of bleak inaccessibility and his eyes flash cold blue steel as of old.

Political journalism in his young barrister days turned "Advocate" Smuts's thoughts, not unnaturally, to participation in politics. He became deeply interested in the far-sighted expansion schemes of Cecil John Rhodes, the diamond magnate and politician who added Rhodesia to the British Empire. He began to speak on Rhodes's behalf.

In the Transvaal Republic (better known then as the South African Republic) events were beginning to shape for the second Anglo-Boer War. Johannesburg, today the largest city in Africa south of Cairo, was then still in its infancy, a mere mining camp founded in 1886. But this, the world's greatest goldfield, became a magnet for strangers from all parts of the world and their presence created vexing problems for President Paul Kruger's Government. The Boers called these foreigners "Uitlanders" and looked with disfavor on their mode of life and their insistence on franchise and other citizen rights. The Republic was not ready to assimilate them and the Calvinist farmers had no desire to share their political power with others or to be in part assimilated.

The "Uitlanders" in Johannesburg created a Reform Committee and started planning a *coup d'état*. In the dying hours of the year 1895 Dr. Starr Jameson, Rhodes's close friend and associate, invaded the Transvaal with a mounted force from the border of British Bechuanaland and headed for the goldfields. The commando-trained Boers easily rounded up the invaders and the Reform leaders were arrested.

The Jameson Raid, as it is known in South African

history, caused great indignation among Dutch-speaking South Africans, both inside and outside the Republics, and marked the beginning of rapidly worsening relationships between Britain and the Dutch Republics.

For Smuts, broadmindedly pursuing the ideal of British and Dutch cooperation in building up a Greater South Africa, the raid was a blow. He was disillusioned and angry with Rhodes. His sympathies swung over to the two little Republics. He packed his bags and went north to Johannesburg to become a "burger" (citizen) of Paul Kruger's Republic. With him as his bride went Sybella ("Isie") Krige, friend of his student days at Stellenbosch.

Smuts began to practice law in Johannesburg and soon came to the favorable notice of President Kruger, who appointed the young man as his State Attorney. Smuts threw himself into this task with tremendous energy and devoted a good deal of his time to clearing up undesirable conditions in Johannesburg. His methods had a quality of ruthlessness which he displayed again and again in later years when he felt that the interests of the country demanded a firm hand. This trait has made him many enemies—and many of them have afterwards admitted that Smuts was right and are today among his staunchest supporters.

Smuts was a close spectator of the unfolding drama which reached its climax in the outbreak of the second Anglo-Boer War on October 11, 1899, and accompanied Kruger to the abortive conference with the British High Commissioner, Lord Milner, at Bloemfontein, the capital of the Orange Free State Republic. He was present when the aged President, vainly opposing Milner's brusque de-

mands for Uitlander franchise rights and other conces-
sions, broke down and cried, "It is my country you want!"

The Transvaal's ultimatum demanding the withdrawal
of British troops massing on the Cape and Natal borders
gave the signal for war in which the Orange Free State
sided with its sister Republic. After attending for some
time to administrative affairs in Pretoria, Smuts joined the
Republican forces in the field. Into the field, too, against
the British, went the jovial Transvaal farmer, Louis
Botha, afterwards Commandant-General of the Republican forces, and lawyer James Barry Munnik Hertzog,
then a judge on the Free State Supreme Court Bench.
Each was destined to become Prime Minister of the future
Union of South Africa. Smuts and Hertzog were fated to
become political opponents whose classic differences in
outlook heavily colored the South African political scene
for a quarter of a century.

The Boers met with a number of initial successes which
staggered England. Then, when the tide of war started
running strongly against the outnumbered Republican
forces, Smuts undertook a characteristically bold enterprise. At the head of a commando of some two hundred
and fifty young Boers he crossed over the Orange River
into British territory, carrying the "fiery cross" among the
Boers resident in the Cape Colony and recruiting rebels
wherever he went. In his saddlebags, it is recorded, he carried a Greek Testament and Kant's *Critique of Pure
Reason*.

His "task force" of two hundred and fifty men grew to
three thousand. Thrusting, side-stepping, retreating, advancing, raiding and foraging, blowing up bridges and
blockhouses, always doing the bold and unexpected thing,

Smuts and his men for many months led the British forces a pretty dance over the plains and mountain chains of the Cape. Often he escaped capture by a mere handbreadth; today when he motors across the South African veld he will often point out a landmark and recall with a smile what a close call he had had there from a British bullet or how nearly he had walked into a trap. Ten thousand British troops trekking hither and thither failed to bring Smuts and his men into the net and his "invasion" was still actively in progress when the summons came for Smuts to attend the peace negotiations at Vereeniging, a village (today a flourishing industrial town) on the Transvaal-Free State border. He had entered the war a man virtually unknown outside the official circle. He emerged a national leader.

The Peace Treaty of Vereeniging was signed on May 31, 1902, and the two Republics lost their independence. It was a bitter moment for the Boer leaders, some of whom were in favor of continuing the war. Smuts, strongly influenced by Lord Kitchener's opinion that a Liberal Government would shortly come into power in England and that generous treatment could be expected for the two ex-Republics, threw his weight, as did General Louis Botha, on the side of making peace. Having, however, been called direct from his commando headquarters in the Cape, and not being officially delegated by the Transvaal, he was not a signatory to the treaty.

Smuts bought himself a farm, "Doornkloof" (Thorn Valley), at Irene, a few miles outside Pretoria. For his house he erected a wood and corrugated-iron building that had been used in a Transvaal village as a mess for British officers. It is an unpretentious but commodious

building. Visitors complain that it is a little cold in win-
tertime, but Prime Minister and Mrs. Smuts, as simple,
home-loving folk, infinitely prefer it to their magnificent
official residences in Pretoria and in Cape Town. Smuts
is happiest today when he can relax as Farmer Smuts,
looking at the cattle breed in which he specializes, or
striding briskly across the veld, staff in hand, informally
dressed in khaki slacks with shirt open at the neck. Great
and famous people from all parts of the world have visited
the wood-and-iron home at Irene and have felt honored
to enjoy the Smutses' simple Boer hospitality.

Their Republican independence gone, the Transvaal
and the Free State became Crown Colonies with the sign-
ing of the Treaty of Vereeniging. Gone, too, was Smuts's
job as State Attorney and he started practice again as a
barrister at Pretoria, while the young university men
whom Lord Milner had imported from England took up
the administrative reins where Smuts had dropped them
when he went into the field.

These were years of frustration for Smuts and of deep
resentment and sullenness in the war-scourged Transvaal
and Free State. But there was a credit as well as a debit
side to the war. More than ever before the English and
the Dutch learned to respect each other as brave and
chivalrous opponents. There had been many remarkable
acts of chivalry on the field of battle and many enduring
friendships were formed between men who had first
sighted each other down the barrel of a rifle. In the Transvaal, General Louis Botha began laying the foundations
of a conciliation policy; this has survived the political
storms which for forty years swept and sometimes rocked
South Africa. Despite severe differences, however, cooper-

ation between Boer and Briton was not a new phenomenon in South Africa. For nearly a century they had often
made common cause in the Cape in whose administration
they shared. They had fought side by side in the long
series of frontier wars with the Bantu races. Various attempts during the latter half of the nineteenth century
to bring about some form of political unity between the
Cape and Natal and the two Dutch Republics had been
favorably regarded by both races. The Boers writhed
under the humiliation of defeat but they were also
proudly conscious of the fact that they had fought a hard,
clean fight and that for nearly three years they had defied
one of the world's mightiest nations.

Botha wasted little time in repining; instead, he sought
the most practical way to hasten the rehabilitation of his
people and the day when they would again have an
authoritative voice in their own government. Setting as
his ideal cooperation between the two races and full participation of the Boers in administrative affairs, he
founded Het Volk Party (the People's Party). Smuts supported him. Still under Botha's leadership, Het Volk
Party in 1910 became merged into the South African
Party which by this time embraced many English-speaking
adherents. Smuts assumed its leadership in 1919 when
Botha died. In 1921 he brought into the South African
Party fold the predominantly English-speaking Unionist
Party. Still running under the banner of racial cooperation and a united nationhood of Afrikaans (Dutch) and
English-speaking peoples, the South African Party in 1933
itself stepped into the wider portals of the United Party
under the joint leadership of General Hertzog and General Smuts. The solid core of the United Party stood by

General Smuts when the country decided the issue between war and neutrality in September, 1939, and in the
general election of July, 1943, the United Party, with its
Coalition friends, the small Dominion and Labour Parties,
won 107 out of 150 contested seats comprising the South
African House of Assembly. Thus, Smuts is still following
the path of united South African nationhood and of a
stronger and greater South Africa which he and Botha
pointed out forty years ago.

For him they have been forty years of strain and stress,
of humiliations and triumphs which have been the very
warp and woof of South Africa's own history pattern during this period. Neither frustrations nor great honors
have caused him to deviate from his path. He is Kipling's
man, equipped to meet both triumph and defeat.

When a strong Liberal Government came into power
in Britain at the close of 1905 under the premiership of
Campbell-Bannerman, Smuts was sent to London by Het
Volk Party to state the case for self-government for the
ex-Republics and for a place for the Boers in its administration. He convinced the British Government that co-
operation and partnership between the Dutch and the
English was practicable and desirable. Full responsible
government for both the Transvaal and the Free State
came within a year. Botha became Prime Minister of the
Transvaal with Smuts in his Cabinet as Colonial Secretary
and Minister of Education.

Once more, Smuts was able to see in practical outline
the ideal of the greater, united South Africa he had
glimpsed before the war, and he devoted his great influence and all his prodigious energy to the task of realiz-
ing that ideal. Some of his fellow Afrikaners felt that he

was traveling too far and too fast along the road of conciliating Dutch and English. They said he reminded them of Rhodes's ideal, which they had not liked, and that he had assumed the mantle of Rhodes the Empire-builder. For many years he was derided by some of his own people as "Rhodes redivivus."

Less than eight years after the conclusion of the Anglo-Boer War the four South African colonies, each having responsible government and its own Parliament, decided for closer cooperation and called a National Convention to weigh the advantages of a Federal or a Union form of government for the ex-Republics and the Cape and Natal. The Convention chose the latter and Smuts, laboring day and night, played a dominating role in shaping the new Constitution. This was contained in the South Africa Act of the British Parliament. It is today an enactment of South Africa's own Parliament, the country's sole and sovereign legislative authority.

The union of the four states became an accomplished fact on May 31, 1910, on the anniversary of the Peace of Vereeniging. Botha, Britain's enemy in the field only eight years before, became the Union's first Prime Minister. Smuts, the invader of the Cape, was given three important portfolios in the new Cabinet—Defense, Mines, and Interior. In the new Government, too, was another Boer General, Hertzog, already well in the political picture for his advocacy of Dutch language rights when he was Minister of the Free State Cabinet. Smuts, the conciliator of the two races and protagonist of cooperation within the British Empire, and Hertzog, the exponent of Afrikaner national sentiment, were destined to cross political swords for many years to come. For many years voters in South

Africa classed each other as "Hertzog men" and "Smuts men."

General Botha re-formed his Cabinet in 1912 to exclude General Hertzog, whose boldly expressed sentiments against Great Britain and the "foreign fortune-seekers" in South Africa gave grave offense to the leaders of the South African Party and especially to the English-speaking section in the Union. Hertzog went into the political wilderness and founded the Nationalist Party whose policy, in general terms, envisaged eventual secession from the British Empire and non-participation in any war in which Britain happened to be involved. The Nationalist Party, slowly but steadily growing in strength, bitterly opposed General Botha and made Smuts the target of their bitterest barbs. When Smuts assumed the leadership of the South African Party and the premiership on Botha's death in 1919 he inherited a political crown of thorns.

Meanwhile he had played a leading role in epoch-making events and his name had become world-famous. He rapidly became an outstanding figure in South African affairs and the *bête noire* of the Labour Party because of his handling of industrial troubles. He directed with Botha the suppression of the armed rising of a section of the Orange Free State and Transvaal Boers who saw an opportunity in the outbreak of World War I to strike a blow for restoration of Republican Government. As Minister of Defense he played a major role in organizing the campaign against the Germans in South West Africa. In this campaign Botha personally took command of the South African forces. Smuts was also in the field for some time and developed with Botha an enveloping movement which forced the Germans to capitulate early in 1915.

The first of many signal honors was then bestowed upon Smuts. Only fourteen years earlier he himself was carrying arms against Britain. He now became a lieutenant-general in the British Army and was invited to take supreme command of the British and South African forces operating against the German commander, von Lettow-Vorbeck, in East Africa. Smuts's success in that campaign was a prelude to the heavy and responsible work awaiting him in other spheres.

In 1917, Mr. Lloyd George invited him to London to become a member of the Imperial War Cabinet. Smuts arrived in London at the darkest hour of the war. His presence made a tremendous impression and his brilliant mind and his already famous gift for leadership proved an inestimable asset in the councils of the Allied Nations.

The number and variety of the tasks performed by Smuts at this stage was almost legendary. He undertook missions of the greatest delicacy and secrecy. He went to the Western Front to confer with Haig, the President of the French Republic, and the King of the Belgians. He inspected South African troops in France, received French and Belgian decorations, and returned to England to set out his thoughts on the position, conduct, and prospects of the war and profoundly influenced the decisions of the War Cabinet.

He planned the Palestine Campaign, but refused the Palestine command when it was offered to him. He suggested the formation of a War Priorities Committee over which he presided. He was in London when the first air raids began and submitted a plan for the air defense of London and the reconstruction of the old Royal Flying Corps into the Royal Air Force, of which he is thus literally the father. He sat on various committees of the British War Cabinet and came to be known, because of the variety and significance of his work, as "the Empire's handy-man." He even assisted in settling several strikes, notably a strike of Welsh miners. He made a significant contribution to the settlement of Ireland.

He made morale-building speeches. Addressing members of the Commons and the Lords at a banquet given in his honor in London on May 15, 1917, he prophetically outlined the British Commonwealth conception, envisaging the constitutional changes which were to form the basis of the Statute of Westminster of 1931.

His advocacy of a League of Nations began to attract attention. The League concept strongly possessed his mind. "All else I have done in my lifetime," he said once, "is as nothing and as dust and ashes compared with the small effort I have been able to contribute towards the building up of this new organization for the future government of the world." He published his League of Nations Plan in December, 1918, and in the following month he accompanied his Prime Minister, General Botha, to Paris to take part in the peace negotiations there.

The Versailles Peace Treaty was still being shaped when General Hertzog, leader of the Nationalist Party which had made considerable strides in South Africa during the war years, led a deputation to Paris via New York to ask for the return of the old Boer Republics.

Smuts, with General Botha, signed the Versailles Peace Treaty on South Africa's behalf. But he signed under protest. He saw in the Treaty the seeds of future disaster, sensing in it only the threat of future war.

Strong pressure was put on Smuts to remain in England

where, it was argued, his continued presence was urgently needed and where he could play the role in world affairs for which he was so eminently qualified. Posts of great distinction were offered to him, including, it was rumored, the ambassadorship to the United States. But his first duty now lay in South Africa.

He returned home disillusioned and uneasy, but he had little time to worry about Europe's problems and difficulties. Three weeks after their return to South Africa General Botha died and Smuts succeeded to the task of steering South Africa through the post-war years.

From the outset of his premiership, Smuts found himself confronted with the rising tide of Afrikaner nationalism which was making progress in the Cape no less than in the Transvaal and Free State. Leader of the Cape Nationalists was Dr. Daniel François Malan, formerly a minister of religion who, in 1915, assumed the editorship of the Nationalist daily newspaper founded at Cape Town, Die Bürger. The Transvaal Nationalists were led by Tielman Roos, a clever barrister and skillful politician who in the political world had earned for himself the title of the "Lion of the North." General Hertzog was the head of the Free State Nationalists and supreme leader of the party.

Under their steady sniping, Smuts strengthened his position in 1921 by the incorporation of the Unionist Party into his South African Party. In 1922 his allegedly tardy handling of the great strike on the Witwatersrand goldfields, and the swift and decisive measures eventually taken by him to end it, incurred the bitter enmity of both the Labour and the Nationalist parties. These two parties joined forces against Smuts in the General Election of 1924 and the South African Party failed to retain its majority. Smuts was himself defeated in a Pretoria constituency by a Labour candidate, Mr. George Hay, but a seat was immediately found for him at Standerton, in the eastern Transvaal, which he still represents today. He had held Cabinet rank consistently since 1906; now, for nine years after 1924, as Leader of the Opposition, he was merely "the Right Honourable Member for Standerton."

Hertzog, the third of the Boer generals to hold this post, became Prime Minister of the Union in 1924 and, somewhat incongruously, governed the country with the aid of the English-speaking Labour Party which was represented in his Cabinet.

In Opposition Smuts led his South African Party of Afrikaans and English-speaking followers through some of the bitterest years of party politics in South Africa. Racial politics flourished. Smuts was continually execrated by his political opponents for his adherence to the British Commonwealth ideal and his defense of South Africa's continued association with Great Britain. He was reviled because of his services during the Great War and for the measures he had taken for the preservation of law and order in South Africa. He was abused by the Nationalists who saw in him the chief obstacle to their secessionist ideal and by the Labour Party for his handling of labor disputes during his premiership. His detractors harried him year after year. Hertzog himself led many virulent attacks against Smuts both in Parliament and from the political platforms of the rural districts.

In spite of the inherent opposition, the picture also had its credit side for Smuts. He found leisure time during those years to follow those wider intellectual pursuits which have gained him fame in the fields of science and philosophy. As a young man he had been a profound student and admirer of Walt Whitman, and wrote a philosophical treatise on Whitman which was never published. In 1925 he expressed his philosophy in a book called *Holism and Evolution,* which may be briefly if inadequately described as a study of the unifying forces in nature. His opponents said that Smuts's thoughts on "whole-making" forces embraced the imperialist dreams of Cecil Rhodes, especially when he talked about a "greater South Africa."

In 1929 Smuts presided at the meeting of the British Association for the Advancement of Science which took place at Cape Town. He delivered the Rhodes Memorial lecture at Oxford and was made honorary D.C.L. of the university. He was elected Lord Rector of St. Andrews University, Scotland, and was given the freedom of London and various other cities. He toured America and presided over the tenth anniversary meeting of the League of Nations. In 1931 he presided in London over the centenary meeting of the British Association. He has honorary degrees from more than a score of universities in England, Scotland, Ireland, the United States, Canada, and South Africa. He is a Fellow of the Royal Society and a Bencher of the Middle Temple. In 1942 he was awarded the Albert Medal of the Royal Society of Arts, a distinction which he shares with President Roosevelt.

Events have laid stronger emphasis on Smuts as a soldier and statesman than on Smuts as a scholar, philosopher, and scientist, but if it were not for his compelling preoccupation with the affairs of government, his contributions to science and philosophy alone may well have brought him renown.

During the great depression which in 1930 overtook
South Africa in common with the rest of the world the
power and prestige of General Hertzog's Nationalist Government steadily dwindled. To a large extent also the political parties wearied of their own racial recriminations
and more and more the Afrikaans and English-speaking
sections discovered an identity of interests which made the
continuation of the Party divisions a barren and a futile
thing. In 1933 General Hertzog and General Smuts buried
the political hatchet. The Nationalist Party and the South
African Party fused into the United South African National Party (the United Party, for short).

His followers claimed at the time that if Smuts had ap-
pealed to the country, he would have been returned to
power at the head of the South African Party, to assume
once more the premiership which he had held from 1919
to 1924. He chose, however, the course which promised
the country the greatest measure of progress and of freedom from political strife. He entered the new United
Party Government as Minister of Justice and as Deputy to
Premier Hertzog.

It was not an easy role. Many matters cropped up under
Hertzog's leadership which, no doubt, tried Smuts's patience. Under their joint leadership, however, the country
enjoyed a period of development and prosperity such as it
had never known before, and it became possible to em-
bark on great national undertakings which the country's
young and troubled history had not up to then made possible. The goal of a united South Africa nationhood of
Afrikaans and English-speaking people also loomed steadily nearer, and many of the old racial prejudices slipped
rapidly into the background.

One issue, however, remained which was destined once more to split South Africa into two clear-cut political camps, and that was whether, if Britain became involved in a war, South Africa should participate in that war as well. On this issue General Hertzog and General Smuts had agreed to differ when they joined forces in 1933. General Hertzog stood for a policy of neutrality for South Africa in any war in which the country itself was not directly threatened. General Smuts, while himself affirming South Africa's complete autonomy—a right to declare herself neutral if she wished to do so—held that any threat to the safety of Britain was a threat to the safety and the freedom of South Africa.

When war broke out in September, 1939, an immediate Cabinet crisis developed in Cape Town where Parliament had just assembled for a special session. General Hertzog in the House of Assembly introduced a motion which amounted to a policy of benevolent neutrality for South Africa. He was immediately challenged by General Smuts, whose amendment that the Union should sever relations with Germany was carried by eighty votes to sixty-seven. Smuts saw the German threat as a direct threat also against South Africa.

"We are all in the same boat," he told Parliament. "To my mind this new phase of German policy is not a mere affair of Danzig and the Corridor, but is part and parcel of this whole course on which the new Germany has set out to dominate the world by force and to annex as much as she can under threat of war. We have had due notice that the next demand, after Danzig has been wiped off the slate, is going to be the return of the German colonies, and so far as South Africa is concerned and its special interests, apart from the wider world issues raised, the question we have to face in this country is what our position is going to be within some months or some years when we are treated as Austria has been treated, as Czechoslovakia has been treated, and as Poland is now being treated, when we are faced with superior force and we have to surrender what we consider to be vital in the interests of the Union at the point of the bayonet. That is the issue before us."

Having defeated Hertzog, Smuts formed a new Government with the aid of the small Dominion Party (comprising English-speaking members) and of the equally small Labour Party. Hertzog went into opposition, associating himself for a time with Dr. Malan, who, since 1933, had led that remnant of the Nationalist Party which had not followed General Hertzog into the United Party.

After fifteen years Smuts was once again Prime Minister of South Africa, with the backing not only of the English-speaking section in South Africa, but also in a very great measure of the Afrikaans-speaking section who could see no freedom in the future for South Africa in a Nazi-ridden world.

Smuts also became Commander-in-Chief of the South African forces. He faced a colossal task. Not only was the country almost totally unprepared for war so far as trained manpower was concerned, but also her industries were not geared for wartime production.

The country had become a happy hunting ground for Nazi agents financed from Germany, and among his own people Smuts faced a strong isolationist sentiment which inevitably embarrassed the Government in the prosecution of the country's war effort. Smuts stamped out Hitler's spy cells in the Union, and interned a number of people who, if left at large, might have become active fifth-columnists. In Parliament he handled his opposition with tact and patience and slowly built up a sound working majority in the House of Assembly which enabled him to get on with the war without much distraction from the political front.

Political dissension within the opposition camp itself contributed in no small measure to his strong position.

After some hesitation, General Hertzog rejoined Dr. Malan in the Herenigde Party (Reunited Nationalist Party) but the reunion was unhappy and of short duration. After a few months General Hertzog felt compelled to re-sign the chief leadership of the Herenigde Party and re-tired from Parliament and from active politics. His death took place in November, 1942. A handful of his old fol-lowers continued in Parliament as the Afrikaner Party. A "New Order" group of about seventeen members sat in Parliament under the leadership of Mr. Oswald Pirow, former Minister of Defence who had declared himself an adherent of National Socialism. These three groups had a common platform in their opposition to South Africa's participation in the war but clashed with each other in many other respects.

Two or three by-elections and resignations of Opposi-tion Members from their own parties to join the Govern-ment gave Smuts a sound working majority of about twenty in a House of one hundred and fifty members (ex-cluding three representatives of the natives). In the Gen-eral Election of July, 1943, the country abundantly justi-fied the Government's claim that its relatively small ma-jority in the House did not reflect the feeling in the coun-try which, in proportion to the size of its white population, had sent a higher percentage of its manpower into the field as volunteers than any other of the United Nations. The pro-war parties were returned with one hundred and seven members, the Opposition with forty-three—a sensational triumph for Smuts.

The Union's white population numbers less than two and a quarter million of whom approximately sixty per cent are of Afrikaans (Dutch) and the remaining forty per cent of British descent. Smuts's army—the biggest that has ever been built up in South Africa—is fully representative of both sections of the white population, and Afrikaans and English-speaking boys have fought side by side in East Africa, North Africa, and in Madagascar. Some units, according to the area from which they are recruited, are nearly ninety per cent Afrikaans-speaking. Others, again, are mainly English-speaking. But it is one of the most arresting facts of the war, so far as South Africa is concerned, that the Springboks, as South African soldiers are known, are not concerned with questions of race or language. They are fighting side by side as South Africans who realize that the freedom of South Africa, of a united nation of Afrikaans and English-speaking South Africans, is an ideal worth the great fight. Smuts visits them in the Western Desert and proudly calls them "my boys," and they as affectionately call him the "Oubaas" (the Old Chief).

Every man in South Africa's army is a volunteer, for, though South Africa, under her Defence Act of 1912, has the right to conscript every able-bodied citizen to fight in the defense of South Africa, the policy followed in this, as in the last Great War, has been to rely only on volunteers. Of these there has never been a deficiency. The Springboks have high physical standards. They are strong

individualists on the battlefield, steeped in the tradition
of commando fighting which South Africa knows so well
and, whether they are Afrikaans or English-speaking, with
a splendid fighting tradition behind them. They are, mili-
tarily, almost completely equipped from South Africa's
own factories, for on the whole industrial front, too, General Smuts inspired an organization which in three years
of war has given South African industries a fillip equal to
twenty-five years of expansion under normal conditions.

South Africa still looks to Great Britain and the United
States for some of the specialized equipment, for fighting
planes and bombers and for certain types of armaments,
but in other fields of production she herself has impro-
vised brilliantly, and the stage of wartime production already reached has amazed even the Union.

Smuts keeps his hand firmly on the helm, and his followers claim that the events of the war and his own dominating personality and sure sense of leadership have placed
him politically in an impregnable position. He is a world
figure and his voice is heard with great respect overseas.

He has a wonderful helpmate in Mrs. Smuts, a little
curly-headed old lady of simple tastes who is beloved
throughout South Africa. She is "Ouma" (Grandmother)
to the Springbok troops, and as chairwoman of the South
African Gifts and Comforts Fund she has made several
trips by air to East Africa and North Africa to see that
"my boys" are being well looked after.

Smuts was appointed a Field Marshal on his seventy-
first birthday on May 24, 1941. Sir Patrick Duncan, South
Africa's Governor-General who on behalf of the King
handed Smuts his Field Marshal's baton, described him as
"a great rock in a weary world." Smuts characteristically

accepted the baton not as a personal distinction, but as a great honor shown to his country. Among his multitude of friends he is still "General" Smuts, and it is his own wish to be addressed as Field Marshal only on formal occasions. Today when South Africans refer to "the General," they do so with unbounded respect and affection.

When General Smuts addressed his constituents in the last General Election campaign he said, "The old horse is running his last race." His friends, not only in South Africa but throughout the world, pray that he will be sustained in health and vigor and that his voice will once again be raised in authority at the next peace table.

This selection of speeches by General Smuts has been given the title *Toward a Better World*. Naturally it is for South Africa and for what he visualizes as "Greater South Africa" that most of his plans are primarily intended, but the outlook of this great statesman can never be confined within narrow bounds. The use of the word "greater" does not indicate any aggressive imperialism; it means that South Africa—and the world—must be made greater in spiritual things; it conveys an ethical idea.

In the choice of the speeches that central theme has been kept in mind. As General Smuts himself said, his country has been faced with a "problem in holism" ever since the Boer War. But out of many discordant elements a new South Africa is arising. Since the beginning of the century there has been an advance, and today, as a result of the war they are fighting, it is clear that South Africa must face yet another "problem in holism"—the relation of South Africa to the other states and territories on the African continent which are her allies in the struggle. The ideas which General Smuts propounds in these speeches are fundamental to the solution of that problem.

In these speeches General Smuts speaks for himself. They are, more than any biography, a true index of his character and greatness, of the ideals for which he has fought so consistently ever since his boyhood. That consistency is the most striking feature of all his public utterances. His ideal of progressive cooperation between peoples and states has never wavered. In years of political strife in South Africa events have forced many of her leading politicians to change their opinions and policies repeatedly. In the twenty years between Versailles and the war against Hitlerism, few world statesmen have been consistent.

Not the least tribute which the records pay to General Smuts is that neither in local politics nor in the wider sphere of international relations has expediency or circumstance forced him to change any of his lifelong convictions or opinions. Study a speech he made twenty years ago and you will find that he is expressing the same views today as he did then.

This fine consistency is due to a scientific grasp of fundamental principles and supreme faith in human values and the triumph of the Good. That is why this collection of speeches should be a valuable guide to many future generations of rulers and leaders.

Since General Smuts first groped his way into politics and as an immature member of Hofmeyr's Afrikander Bond expressed the first article of his political faith, a United South Africa, he has had at least three crushing disappointments. The Jameson Raid, the Boer War, and then the Great World War all seemed to make a mockery of

his ideas of racial unity and holism. And where the destructive forces of war were at work fate forced Smuts to
play a leading part as a military leader. But after every
one of these destructive phases General Smuts returned
heroically to work of reconstruction and regeneration.

The bitter years that intervened between the Boer War
and Responsible Government in the Transvaal were a barren period for unity and racial cooperation. Even General
Smuts's buoyant optimism was subdued as the Transvaal
licked its wounds and looked for a generous gesture from
the British Government.

But only temporarily. Once he was convinced that Britain wanted to act liberally, General Smuts returned with
undaunted spirit to his ideal of a United South Africa.

Out of the chaos and bitterness of the Boer War rose
the fine edifice of Union. General Smuts would be the first
to give the credit for that achievement to others, but the
truth is that General Botha and his contemporary Prime
Ministers could never have accomplished this great work
without the energetic assistance of Smuts. His was the driv-
ing force before and during the National Convention.

It is partly due to General Smuts's genius for reconstruction that from the shell-wracked and shell-shocked ruins
of the Great War arose the Palace of Peace at Geneva. The
League of Nations was General Smuts's original conception. At the Peace Conference General Smuts was almost
alone in appealing for a settlement based on reconciliation. He wanted Versailles to be Vereeniging on a vaster
scale. What happened in South Africa he believed was
the only formula on which to base his hope of peace in
Europe. Many times since the war, when clouds loomed
over Europe, publicists wise after the event have torn the

Versailles Treaty to pieces. General Smuts was the only statesman at the conference who strove to deter the treaty-makers from the provisions which were to prove such a potent cause of discord in the future.

South Africa has made General Smuts Prime Minister when the nation is again at war with Germany. There have been hints of the many difficulties which beset the Government when General Smuts so dramatically took office on September 4, 1939. It will surely rank as one of his greatest achievements that in a country of divided loyalties and other racial politics his Government has smoothed down all the obstacles with skill and patience, and has at the same time created such a powerful South African Defence Force.

Through these speeches of General Smuts we come to see the future of South Africa in essential, clear lines. Reading them we become imbued with some of his faith in the future. We will be able to say with him: "This is a good world. This is a friendly universe. We are all inter-related. The one helps the other. It is an idea that gives strength and peace and is bound to give a more whole-some view of life and nature than we have had so far."

HENRY M. MOOLMAN
ERIC ESTORICK

Washington, D. C.

TOWARD A
BETTER WORLD

CHAPTER I

THE WHITE MAN'S TASK

Before South Africa had time to settle down under Union, the country was fighting in the Great War. After the conquest of both German South-West and East Africa, Field Marshal Smuts proceeded to London to join the Empire War Cabinet and to render brilliant services to the Allies. One of his most notable—and prophetic—speeches on African problems was delivered at a dinner given in his honour under the chairmanship of Lord Selborne at the Savoy Hotel on May 22, 1917. In it he gives some of the guiding principles of South African native policy.

I AM DEEPLY grateful to you for the reception you have given me here tonight. I am thankful to you, Lord Selborne, for what you have said. Your words tonight carry me back to that period in our history when I was serving under you and was a fellow-labourer with you in what will probably remain the greatest creative epoch in the history of South Africa. . . .

The various South African societies, together with the Imperial Institute, have combined in order to do me this honour, and I am very glad to have you all together on this occasion. I know that there are many here tonight who have, at one time or another, differed from me. Sometimes the differences have been very acute, but tonight all these differences have been swallowed up and forgotten in the great constructive tasks in which we are all engaged. It is a matter of great gratification to me to think that after all, notwithstanding all those differences in the past, you can say tonight to me: "You have not done so badly after all."

This function, of all the various functions I have so far attended, appeals most to me, because it is really not in honour of me, but in honour of that far-away, dear land, which most of us have served and with which most of us have been associated in the past. Tonight we are really met together here as members of the South African family; some born into it, some married into it, some old servants who have grown grey in her hard service and who have given the best years of their lives to that service— here we can all sit together, forgetting Europe, forgetting the storms raging outside, and our minds can travel back to the sun-filled spaces of Southern Africa, to its amazing history, and its immense tasks. A great historian has said: "On those whom the gods love they lavish infinite joys and infinite sorrows." On that principle surely South Africa must be a special favourite of the gods. She has known joys and sorrows; she has known the deepest abasement and she has known the highest exaltation. The history of South Africa is in many respects one of the true and great romances in modern history.

When I look around tonight and I see all who are sitting here at this table, I feel, and you all feel, that we are lifted out of the world of commonplace into a strange world. We feel that whatever the past has been, whatever mistakes we have made—and we have all made mistakes— whatever services we have been able to render to our South Africa, a kind of Providence has intervened and has woven all those mistakes and all those services into a strange and wonderful texture which we call the history of South Africa and of which we are very proud. When we look at that wonderful history we are all cheered and encouraged to move forward in the hope that as our task has not been too difficult for us in the past it may not prove entirely beyond us in the future.

There are very grave questions before South Africa, and these questions will probably increase in magnitude after this war. Now the Ten Plagues are being poured over Europe in this war, and they will be followed by the Exodus in due course. You will see very large numbers of people, after this war, sick of the Old World and looking to the young countries for a new home where they may find peace. I am sure that many of you will find in our large country, our wide spaces, just that repose for body and soul that you desire. We look forward to great times, to great developments in South Africa, and it will be the task of our Governments in South Africa to make the best use of the unique opportunities for a forward move that will be presented by the times that will follow the war.

But in South Africa we always feel that there is something more. With us it is never a question of merely material progress and of prosperity, although we are always very eager to have those good things too; we always feel that under our peculiar historical and racial conditions there are very large political problems in the background which always press for solution. And that is what gives profound interest to life in South Africa. We have made very great progress in recent years. If you remember that it was within seven years of the Boer War that we had all the British Colonies of South Africa united in one great

Union you will see how great and rapid that progress has been. But although we have achieved political union, our aim has always been far•greater; we have aimed not only at political union, but also at national unity; and when you have to deal with very hard-headed races, such as our people in South Africa, both English and Dutch, you can well understand that it takes more than seven years to bring about that consummation. We have grave difficulties in this respect. We have different racial strains, different political tendencies.

We have people in South Africa who prefer isolation, who prefer to stand aside from the great currents that are carrying South Africa to her new and greater destiny. These are not merely Dutch, many of them are English. We have English fellow-citizens who will always remain English, to whom even the sunshine and the wide spaces of South Africa are not sufficient to bring about the great transformation of soul. We look forward patiently in such cases to the next generation. We have also a large section of my own people, the Dutch people in South Africa, who think that the best policy is for them to stand aside and to remain in isolation. They think that in that way they will be better able to preserve their language, their traditions, and their national type, and that they will in that way not be swallowed up and be submerged by the new currents. They point to the precedent of Canada, where French-Canadians are also standing aside from the general current of Canadian life and national development for the same reasons. Now, you know, *that* is the issue which is being fought out now in South Africa, and has been fought out in recent years more acutely than ever before.

The policy General Botha and his associates have stood

for is that we must have national unity in South Africa as the one true basis of future stability and strength—and that national unity is entirely consistent with the preservation of our language, our traditions, our cultural interests, and all that is dear to us in our past. The view we have taken is this, that the different elements in our white populations ought really to be used to build up a stronger and more powerful nation than would have been possible if we had consisted of purely one particular strain. All great Imperial peoples really are a mixture of various stocks. Your own history is one of the completest proofs of that doctrine, and it is only in recent years that this remarkable doctrine of the pure race has come into vogue, and largely in Germany. The man who has preached the doctrine most eloquently is a Germanised Englishman, Houston Chamberlain. The doctrine is to the effect that the governing races of the world are pure races, and that they simply debase themselves and become degenerate if mixed with alien blood. They must remain pure, and in so far as they do so they will play a great part in the world. It is more than hinted at that the German race must guide the world because it is one of these pure races. What arrant nonsense!

We do not pretend in South Africa to listen to these siren voices. We want to create a blend out of the various nationalities and to create a new South African nation out of our allied racial stock, and if we succeed in doing that we shall achieve a new nationality embracing and harmonising our various traits and blending them all into a richer national type than could otherwise have been achieved. The ideal of national unity means a continuous effort towards better relations, towards mutual respect and forbearance, towards co-operation, and that breadth of view and character which will be the most potent instrument for dealing with our other problems. Although in South Africa our national progress is marked by the ox-waggon and not by the train or aeroplane, I am sure in the end we shall achieve success and a new nationhood.

And this is all the more important because in South Africa we are not merely a white man's country. Our problem of white racial unity is being solved in the midst of the black environment in South Africa. Whether we shall succeed in solving that other larger question of the black man's future depends on many factors on which no one could feel very much assurance at present. We know that on the African Continent at various times there have been attempts at civilisation. We read of a great Saracen civilisation in Central Africa, and of the University of Timbuctoo, to which students came from other parts of the world. Rhodesia also shows signs of former civilisation.

Where are those civilisations now? They have all disappeared, and barbarism once more rules over the land and makes the thoughtful man nervous about the white man's future in Southern Africa. There are many people in South Africa—and not very foolish people either—who do not feel certain that our white experiment will be a permanent success, or that we shall ever succeed in making a white man's land of Southern Africa; but, at any rate, we mean to press on with the experiment. It has now been in progress for some two hundred and fifty years, as you know, and perhaps the way we have set about it may be the right way. Former civilisations in Africa have existed mostly for the purpose of exploiting the native populations, and in that way, and probably also through inter-mixture of blood, carried in them the seeds of decay.

We have started by creating a new white base in South Africa and today we are in a position to move forward towards the North and the civilisation of the African Continent. Our problem is a very difficult one, however; quite unique in its way. In the United States there is a similar problem of black and white with the Negro population. But there you have had an overwhelming white population with a smaller Negro element in the midst of it. In South Africa the situation is reversed. There you have an overwhelming black population with a small white population which has got a footing there and which has been trying to make that footing secure for more than two centuries.

You will therefore understand that a problem like that is not only uncertain in its ultimate prospects, but is most difficult in the manner that it should be dealt with. Much experience has been gained, and there are indications that we have come to some certain results. You remember how some Christian missionaries, who went to South Africa in the first half of the Nineteenth Century in their full belief in human brotherhood, proceeded to marry native wives to prove the faith that was in them. We have gained sufficient experience since then to smile at that point of view. With us there are certain axioms now in regard to the relations of white and black; and the principal one is "no intermixture of blood between the two colours." It is probably true that earlier civilisations have largely failed because that principle was never recognised, civilising races being rapidly submerged in the quicksands of the African blood. It has now become an accepted axiom in our dealings with the natives that it is dishonourable to mix white and black blood.

We have settled another axiom, and that is that in all our dealings with the natives we must build our practice on what I believe Lord Cromer has called the granite bedrock of the Christian moral code. Honesty, fair-play, justice, and the ordinary Christian virtues must be the basis of all our relations with the natives. We don't always practise them. We don't always practise that exalted doctrine, but the vast bulk of the white population in South Africa believe sincerely in that doctrine as correct and true; they are convinced that they must stick to the fundamental Christian morality if they want to do their duty to the natives and make a success of their great country. Of course, this doctrine applies to other countries besides South Africa.

If you ask me what is wrong with Europe—although no wise man would express an opinion on such a great matter—I should say the moral basis in Europe, the bedrock of the Christian moral code, has become undermined and can no longer support all that superstructure of economic and industrial prosperity which the last century has built up on it, and the vast whole is now sagging. The same argument applies much more to the natives of Africa. Natives have the simplest minds, understand only the simplest ideas or ideals, and are almost animal-like in the simplicity of their minds and ways. If we want to make a success of our native policy in South Africa we shall have to proceed on the simplest moral lines and on that basis of the Christian moral code. I think we are all agreed on those two points—on what I have called the racial and moral axioms.

I wish we had made more progress and also discovered some political axiom and knowledge how to deal politically with our immense native problem. But although in this regard nothing can be taken as axiomatic, we have gained a great deal of experience in our history, and there is now shaping in South Africa a policy which is becoming expressed in our institutions which may have very far-reaching effects in the future civilisation of the African Continent. We have realised that political ideas which apply to our white civilisation largely do not apply to the administration of native affairs. To apply the same institutions on an equal basis to white and black alike does not lead to the best results, and so a practice has grown up in South Africa of creating parallel institutions—giving the natives their own separate institutions on parallel lines with institutions for whites. It may be that on those parallel lines we may yet be able to solve a problem which may otherwise be insoluble.

More than twenty years ago, as many of you remember, an experiment in native self-government was begun by Cecil Rhodes in the old Cape Colony which gave local institutions to the natives in Glen Grey reserve. That principle has been extended over a large part of the old Transkeian territories, and so successful has it been that when we came to framing the Act of Union an Appendix was added about the future administration of the Protectorates when they should become incorporated into the Union. This Appendix was largely the work of our chairman, Lord Selborne. He fought with extraordinary tenacity for that Appendix, and I am not sure, although I did not see the importance of the matter in those days, whether in the distant future the South Africa Act will not be remembered as much for its Appendix as for its principal contents. This Appendix laid down that the native territories in South Africa should be governed apart from the Parliamentary institutions of the Union and on different lines which would achieve the principle of native self-government. Subsequently Commissions have been appointed in South Africa to inquire into native questions, and more and more the trend of opinion has hardened in the same direction. We have felt more and more that if we are to solve our native question it is useless to try to govern black and white in the same system, to subject them to the same institutions of government and legislation. They are different not only in colour but in minds and in political capacity, and their political institutions should be different, while always proceeding on the basis of self-government. One very important Commission had, I believe, Sir Godfrey Lagden as chairman, and as a result of that and other Commissions we have now legislation before the Parliament of the Union in which an attempt is made to put into shape these ideas I am talking of, and to create all over South Africa, wherever there are any considerable native communities, independent self-governing institutions for them.

Instead of mixing up black and white in the old haphazard way, which instead of lifting up the black degraded the white, we are now trying to lay down a policy of keeping them apart as much as possible in our institutions. In land ownership, settlement and forms of government we are trying to keep them apart, and in that way laying down in outline a general policy which it may take a hundred years to work out, but which in the end may be the solution of our native problem. Thus in South Africa you will have in the long run large areas cultivated by blacks and governed by blacks, where they will look after themselves in all their forms of living and development, while in the rest of the country you will have your white communities, which will govern themselves separately according to the accepted European principles. The natives will, of course, be free to go and to work in the white areas, but as far as possible the administration of white and black areas will be separated, and such that each will be satisfied and developed according to its own proper lines. This is the attempt which we are making now in South Africa to solve the juxtaposition of white and black in the same country, and although the principles underlying our legislation could not be considered in any way axiomatic, I am sure that we are groping towards the right lines, which may in the end tend to be the solution of the most difficult problem confronting us.

As I have already said, we have started in previous times to civilise Africa from the North. All these attempts at civilisation from the North have failed. We now try to proceed from the other end—from South Africa. We have built up a stable white community in the south of the Continent and given them a training for two hundred years, and they have learned the ways of Africa, which are not the ways of other parts of the world. And now we are ready to go forward, and, as you know, in the last few decades enormous progress has already been made in this expansion towards the North. All our people in South Africa, English as well as Dutch, have taken part in this great movement towards the North, which is proceeding ever farther, and the time is coming when it will be almost a misnomer to speak of "South" Africa, because the northern limits of our civilisation will have gone so far that it will be almost impossible to use the word "South" any more except in reminder of our original starting-point.

Great developments have taken place not only in Southern Africa, but in Central Africa in our day. You will remember that only fifty or sixty years ago Central Africa was a place for the explorer and discoverer, a land of mystery, of pigmies and other wonders of which we read in the books of Stanley and others. In a couple of decades Central Africa has marched right into the centre of world politics, and tonight in this great assembly we are not only interested in Southern Africa, but also those other enormous territories farther north, which our troops from South Africa and other parts of the Empire have conquered and occupied. What the future of that country will be no one knows.

I must say that my experience in East Africa has opened my eyes to many very serious dangers that threaten the future, not only of Southern Africa, but also of Europe. We have seen, what we have never known before, what enormously valuable military material lay in the Black Continent. You are aware of the great German scheme which existed before the war, and which no doubt is still in the background of many minds in Germany, of creating a great Central African Empire which would embrace not only the Cameroons and East Africa, but also the Portuguese Colonies and the Congo—an extensive area which would have a very large population and would not only be one of the most valuable tropical parts of the world, but in which it would be possible to train one of the most powerful black armies of the world.

We were not aware of the great military value of the natives until this war. This war has been an eye-opener in many new directions. It will be a serious question for the statesmen of the Empire and Europe whether they are going to allow a state of affairs like that to be possible, and to become a menace not only to Africa, but perhaps to Europe itself. I hope that one of the results of this war will be some arrangement or convention among the nations interested in Central Africa by which the military training of natives in that area will be prevented, as we have prevented it in South Africa. It can well be foreseen that armies may yet be trained there, which under proper leading might prove a danger to civilisation itself. I hope that will be borne in mind when the day for the settlement in Africa comes up for consideration.

You will have further questions in regard to the territorial settlement of Central Africa which will follow the war. We are now, after the conquest of the German Colonies, in the happy position of having a through land route from Egypt to the Cape. We are in the secure position of having no danger on the Atlantic seaboard or on the Indian seaboard to our very essential sea communications as an Empire. What will happen to these communications after the settlement will depend on that settlement itself, but I hope it will be borne in mind that East Africa gives us not only this through land communication from one end of the Continent to the other, but that East Africa also ensures to us the safety of the sea route round the Cape and the sea route through the Red Sea to the East. It is a matter of gratification to us South Africans here tonight that South African troops have taken such a large and leading share in securing these extremely valuable results. I sincerely hope that, whatever settlement is come to, these larger considerations which I have referred to will be borne in mind.

We shall always have a difficult question not only in Central but in Southern Africa. Unlike other British Dominions, our future as a white civilisation is not assured for the reasons which I have given. Many thoughtful people are in doubt about our future, and in any case no cheap and easy victory will be scored in South Africa.

We know we have tremendous problems to contend with. We know we have tremendous tasks before us, and in dealing with these problems and in trying to fulfil these tasks one generation of South Africans after another will brace its nerves and strengthen its intellect and broaden its mind and character. Although these difficulties may seem to us, and indeed are, grave perils to our future, I trust that in the long run these difficulties may prove a blessing in disguise and may prove to have afforded the training school for a large-minded, broad-minded, magnanimous race, capable not only of welding together different racial elements into a new and richer national type, but capable of dealing as no other white race in history has ever dealt with the question of the relations between black and white. . . .

CHAPTER II

THE COMMONWEALTH CONCEPTION

On May 15, 1917, members of the House of Commons and the House of Lords gave a banquet to Field Marshal Smuts. Lord French paid a glowing tribute to the guest of honour. Field Marshal Smuts on this occasion made a speech which was notable for its admirable exposition of the British Commonwealth conception. The constitutional changes Field Marshal Smuts visualised then were to form the basis of the Statute of Westminster fourteen years later.

I CANNOT express to you how deeply I appreciate the honour which you have done me. Ever since I came, two months ago, to this country, I have received nothing but the most perfect and charming kindness and hospitality everywhere, and this hospitality has culminated in the unique banquet at which we are present tonight. I appreciate it all the more because I know it is given at a time when the greatest struggle in the world's history is being decided, and when nobody feels inclined to indulge in festivities. From the Government of the country I have received many marks of confidence, which I have endeavoured to requite in the only way possible to me, by giving them my frank and honest views on every question. When I return home, as I hope shortly to do, I shall be able to tell the people of South Africa that I have been received here by you, not as a guest or as a welcome stranger, but

17

simply as one of yourselves, though speaking with a different accent and laying a different emphasis on many things, as no doubt becomes a barbarian from the outer marches of the Empire.

I am profoundly thankful to you, Lord French, for the words which have fallen from you. The words of eulogy you have expressed in regard to myself are largely, I think, undeserved; but, at any rate, I accept them as coming from an old opponent and comrade in arms. I know they are meant in the best spirit, and I accept them in that spirit even where I feel I do not deserve them. Your words tonight and the great compliment you have paid me by presiding at this gathering recall to my mind many an incident of the stirring times to which you have referred when we were opposing commanders in the last year of the Boer War.

On one occasion, I remember, I was surrounded in a very nasty block of mountains by Lord French. I was face to face practically with disaster. Nothing was left me but the most diligent scouting to find a way out. I did some of the scouting myself, with a small party. I ventured into a place which looked promising, and which bore the appropriate name of "Murderer's Gap." I am sorry to say I was the only man who came out alive from that gap. In an account which I saw subsequently of this incident I saw the remark made that "one Boer escaped, but he probably had so many bullets in him that he would be no further danger."

Well, Lord French, I have survived to be your guest this evening. I was in a very tight corner there. I did get out, and two days afterwards I did break through—blessed words in these times. At night I came out of those mountains to the railway. It was a very dark night, and my small force was just on the point of crossing the railway when we heard that a train was coming. I allowed the train to pass, and we stood alongside and looked on. You can imagine what my feelings were when I heard some time afterwards that the only freight on that train was Lord French, who was moving from one part of his front to the other to find out how I had broken through. If I had not missed that chance Lord French would have been on that occasion my guest. No doubt a very welcome, though a somewhat embarrassing, guest! Now tonight I am his guest, I hope not embarrassing, though very much embarrassed!

Those were very difficult and strenuous days—days in which one learnt many valuable lessons, good for all one's life. One of the lessons I learned was that, under the stress of great difficulties such as we were then passing through, the only things which survived were the simple human feelings, feelings of loyalty to your fellows and feelings of comradeship and patriotism which carried you through danger and privation. We soldiers know the extreme value of these simple feelings.

We know how far they can go, and that in the end they can bear the whole weight of civilisation. . . . You can see how these simple human feelings of loyalty to your comrades and respect for your opponents on both sides have led to a new basis on which to build the larger South Africa we have today.

I am sure that in the present great struggle which is being waged in the world you will see the same causes leading to a like result. Here you have from all parts of the British Empire young men gathered together on the battle-fields of Europe and the other fields of war. While your statesmen may be planning great schemes of union for the future of the Empire, my feeling is that the work is already largely done. The spirit of comradeship which has been born in this war and on the battlefields of Europe among men from all parts of the Empire will be far more powerful than any instrument of government we can erect in the future. I feel sure that in after years, when we or our successors come to sum up what has happened, there will be a good credit balance due to this feeling which has been built up and which will be the best support for the Empire in the future.

Once more, as many ages ago it happened under the Roman Emperors, the German volcano is in eruption and the whole world is shaken. No doubt in this great convulsion you are faced in this country with the most enormous problems which any Government or people has ever been called upon to solve: problems of world-wide strategy, of man-power, of communications, of food supply: problems of every imaginable kind and of such magnitude that it is almost beyond the wit of man to deal with them. It is inevitable where you have so many difficulties to face that one should forget to keep before oneself the situation as a whole; and yet this is very necessary. It is most essential that even in this struggle, even when Europe is looming so much before our eyes, we should keep before us and see steadily the problem of the whole situation. I would ask you not to forget in these times the British Commonwealth of Nations. Europe will not continue to loom so much in view as it does at present.

I want to say a few words tonight on this subject, because I think there is a tendency to forget some of the aspects of the question with which we are now confronted.

This is one of the reasons why I am glad that an Imperial Conference has been called at this time.

It is apparently a very inopportune moment, but the calling together of the Conference has helped to turn attention once more to that aspect of the whole situation which is so important to us. It is not only Europe we have to consider, but the future of the great Commonwealth to which we all belong. This Commonwealth is peculiarly constituted. It is scattered over the whole world. It is not a compact territory, and it is dependent for its very existence on world-wide communications—communications which must be maintained or this Empire goes to pieces.

In the years of peace behind us we see what has happened. Everywhere on your communications Germany has settled down; everywhere on your communications you will find a German colony or a German settlement, small or large; and the day might come when you would be in jeopardy through your lines of communication being cut. One of the by-products of the war has been that the whole world outside of Europe has been cleared of the enemy. Germany has been swept from all the seas and all the continents except Central Europe. While Germany has been gaining ground in Central Europe, from all the rest of the world she has been swept clear. You are now in this position: that once more you can consider the problem of your future as a whole.

When peace comes to be made you have all these cards in your hand, and you can go carefully into the question of what is necessary for your future security and the future safety of the Empire, and can say what you are going to keep and what you are going to give away. I hope that when the time comes—I am speaking for myself and expressing nobody's opinion but my own—when the time comes for peace to be made we shall bear in mind not only Central Europe, but the whole British Empire. As far as we are concerned, we do not wish this war to have been fought in vain. We have not fought for material gain or for territory, but we have fought for security in the future. If we attach any value to this group of nations which composes the British Empire, then in settling the terms of peace we shall have to look to its future security and safety. I hope that no arrangement will be made which will jeopardise the valuable results which have been attained. That is the geographical situation.

There remains the difficult question of the constitutional adjustment and relations of the British Empire. At a luncheon which was given some time back by the Empire Parliamentary Association to the delegates to the Imperial Conference, I said rather cryptically that I did not think this was a matter in which we could follow precedent, and I hope you will bear with me tonight if I say a few words on that theme.

I think that we are inclined to make mistakes in thinking about this group of nations to which we belong, because too often we think about it as one State. We are not a State. The British Empire is much more than a State. I think the very expression "Empire" is misleading, because it makes people think that we are one community, to which the word "Empire" can appropriately be applied. Germany is an Empire. Rome was an Empire. India is an Empire. But we are a system of nations. We are not a State, but a community of States and nations. We are far greater than any Empire which has ever existed, and by using this ancient expression we really disguise the main fact that our whole position is different, and that we are not one State or nation or empire, but a whole world by ourselves, consisting of many nations, of many States, and all sorts of communities, under one flag.

We are a system of States, and not a stationary system, but a dynamic evolving system, always going forward to new destinies. Take the position of that system today. Here you have the United Kingdom with a number of Crown Colonies. Besides that you have a large Protectorate like Egypt, an Empire by itself. Then you have a great Dependency like India, also an Empire by itself, where civilisation has existed from time immemorial, where we are trying to see how East and West can work together.

These are enormous problems, but beyond them we come to the so-called Dominions, independent in their government, which have been evolved on the principles of your free constitutional system into almost independent States, which all belong to this community of nations, and which I prefer to call "the British Commonwealth of Nations."

You can see that no political ideas which have been evolved in the past will apply to this world which is comprised in the British Empire; and any name we have yet found for this group is insufficient. The man who will find a proper name for this system will, I think, do real service to the Empire.

The question is: How are you going to provide for the future government of this Commonwealth? An entirely new problem is presented. If you want to see how great it is, you must indulge in comparison. Look at the United States. There you find what is essentially one nation, not perhaps in the fullest sense, but what is more and more growing into one nation; one big State consisting, no doubt, of separate parts, but all linked up into one big continuous area. The United States had to solve the problem which this presented, and they discovered the federal solution—a solution which provides subordinate treatment for the subordinate parts, but one national Federal Government and Parliament for the whole.

Compare with that State the enormous system which is comprised in the British Empire. You can see at once that a solution which has been found practicable in the case of the United States will never work in the case of a system such as we are, comprising a world by itself.

What I feel in regard to all the empires of the past, and even in regard to the United States, is that the effort has always been towards forming one nation. All the empires we have known in the past and that exist today are founded on the idea of assimilation, or trying to force human material into one mould. Your whole idea and basis is entirely different. You do not want to standardise the nations of the British Empire; you want to develop them towards greater, fuller nationality. These communities, the offspring of the Mother Country, or territories like my own, which have been annexed after the vicissitudes of war, must not be moulded on any one pattern. You want them to develop freely on the principles of self-government, and therefore your whole idea is different from anything that has ever existed before. That is the fundamental fact we have to bear in mind—that this British Commonwealth of Nations does not stand for standardisation or denationalisation, but for the fuller, richer, and more various life of all the nations comprised in it.

Even the nations which have fought against it, like my own, must feel that their cultural interests, their language, their religion, are as safe and as secure under the British flag as those of the children of your own household and your own blood. It is only in proportion as this is realised that you will fulfil the true mission which is yours. Therefore it seems to me that there is only one solution, and that is a solution supplied by our past traditions—the traditions of freedom, self-government, and of the fullest development for all constituent parts of the Empire.

The question arises: How are you going to keep this Commonwealth of Nations together? If there is to be this full development towards a more varied and richer life among our nations, how are you going to keep them together? It seems to me that there are two potent factors that you must rely upon for the future. The first is your hereditary kingship, the other is our Conference system. I have seen some speculations recently in the newspapers about the position of the kingship in this country—speculations by people who, I am sure, have not thought of the wider issues that are at stake. You cannot make a republic of the British Commonwealth of Nations.

If you had to elect a President, he would have to be a President not only here in these islands, but all over the British Empire—in India and in the Dominions—the President who would be really representative of all these peoples; and here you would be facing an absolutely insoluble problem. The theory of the Constitution is that the King is not your King, but the King of all of us, ruling over every part of the whole Commonwealth of Nations; and if his place should be taken by anybody else, that somebody will have to be elected under a process which it will pass the wit of man to devise. Let us be thankful for mercies. We have a kingship here which is really not very different from a hereditary republic. I am sure that more and more in the future the trend will be in the direction of a more democratic kingship, and I shall not be surprised to see the time come when our Royal princes, instead of getting their consorts from among the princelings of Central Europe, will go for them to the Dominions and other portions of the British Empire.

In regard to the present system of Imperial Conferences, it will be necessary to devise better machinery for common consultation than we have at present. So far, we have relied on Imperial Conferences which meet once in every four years or thereabouts. However useful has been the work done at these Conferences, they have not, in my opinion, been a complete success.

It will be necessary to devise better means of achieving our ends. A precedent has now been laid down calling together the Dominion Prime Ministers and representatives from the Empire of India to the Imperial Cabinet. You have seen a statement made by Lord Curzon that it is the intention of the Government to perpetuate this system in the future. Although we shall have to wait for a complete explanation of the scheme from the Government, yet it is clear that in an institution like that we have a better instrument of common consultation than we have in the old Imperial Conference which meets only every four years and which discusses a number of subjects not really of first-rate importance.

What is necessary is that there shall be called together

the most important rulers of the Empire, say, once a year, to discuss matters which concern all parts of the Empire in common, in order that causes of friction and misunderstanding may be prevented or removed. We also need a meeting like that in order to lay down a common policy in common matters concerning the Empire as a whole, and to determine the true orientation of our common Imperial policy. There is, for instance, foreign policy on which the fate of the Empire might from time to time depend. Some such method of procedure must lead to very important results and very great changes.

You cannot settle a common foreign policy for the whole of the British Empire without changing that policy very much from what it has been in the past, because the policy will have to be, for one thing, far simpler. In the other parts of the Empire we do not understand diplomatic finesse. If our foreign policy is going to rest not only on the basis of our Cabinet here, but, finally, on the whole of the British Empire, it will have to be a simpler policy, a far more intelligible policy, and a policy which will in the end lead to less friction and greater safety. No one will dispute the primacy of the Imperial Government in this respect. We shall always look upon the British Government as the senior partner in the concern, as the managing director responsible for our foreign affairs and responsible for carrying on those affairs in the intervals between the meetings of the Imperial Cabinet. But the Imperial foreign policy must always be subject to the principles laid down from time to time at the meetings of the Imperial Cabinet. Such a policy will in the long run be saner and safer for the Empire as a whole. I also think it will lead to greater publicity.

After the great catastrophe which has overtaken Europe, nations in future will want to know more about their foreign policy. I am sure that the after effects of a change like this, although it looks a simple one, are going to be very important and far-reaching not only for our Commonwealth of Nations but for the whole world.

Far too much stress has been laid in the past on instruments of government. People are inclined to forget that the world is growing more democratic, and that public opinion and the forces finding expression in public opinion are going to be far more powerful than they have been in the past. Where you build up a common patriotism and a common ideal, the instrument of government will not be a thing that matters so much as the spirit which actuates the whole.

When I look round this room tonight and see all who are present, I am filled with gratitude to you who have assembled to do me honour; to time, the great judge, the merciful judge, the healer of wounds; and to that "Divinity that shapes our ends, rough-hew them how we will." And then I think of the difficulties that still lie ahead of us, and that are going to test all the nations fighting for liberty far more than they have ever been tested before. And I hope and pray that they all may have clearness of vision and purpose, and especially that strength of soul in the coming days which will be even more necessary than strength of arm. I believe, I verily believe, that we are within reach of priceless and immeasurable good, not only for this United Kingdom and group of nations to which we belong, but also for the whole world. It will depend largely on us whether the great prize is won in this war, or whether the world will once more be plunged into disaster and long years of weary waiting for the dawn. The prize is within our grasp if we have the strength of soul to see the thing through until victory crowns the efforts of our brave men in the field.

CHAPTER III

THE SPIRIT OF THE MOUNTAIN

Whenever Field Marshal Smuts is in Cape Town and can slip away from his Parliamentary duties he finds inspiration by climbing Table Mountain. This oration was made when he unveiled the Mountain Club War Memorial at Maclear's Beacon on the summit of the mountain in May, 1923.

THIS is a very unique occasion, and I am glad to see such a great assemblage to do honour to the memory of our sacred dead. We have gathered here in our thousands, many of us comrades of those who fell. I would especially mention two comrades who were blinded in the war who have taken the trouble to make the ascent of the mountain to take part in this unique ceremony.

Those whose memory we honour today lie buried on the battlefields of the Great War, where they fell. But this is undoubtedly the place to commemorate them.

Nothing could be more fitting and appropriate than this memorial which the Mountain Club of South Africa has erected to the memory of their members who fell in the Great War. And this, the highest point on Table Mountain, is the place to put the memorial. The sons of the cities are remembered and recorded in the streets and squares of their cities and by memorials placed in their churches and cathedrals. But the mountaineers deserve a loftier pedestal and a more appropriate memorial. To them the true church where they worshipped was Table Mountain. Table Mountain was their cathedral where they heard a subtler music and saw wider visions and were inspired with a loftier spirit.

Here in life they breathed the great air; here in death their memory will fill the upper spaces. And it is fitting that in this cathedral of Table Mountain the lasting memorial of their great sacrifice should be placed. Not down there in the glowing and rich plains, but up here on the bleak and cold mountain tops. As Browning put it:

> *Here, here's their place,*
> *Where meteors shoot,*
> *Clouds form,*
> *Lightnings are loosened,*
> *Stars come and go.*

Here for a thousand years their memory shall blend with these great rock masses and humanise them. The men and women of the coming centuries, who will in ever-increasing numbers seek health and inspiration on this great mountain summit, will find here not only the spirit of Nature, but also the spirit of man blending with it, the spirit of joy in Nature deepened and intensified by the memory of the great sacrifice here recorded.

Geologists tell us that in the abyss of time Table Mountain was much more of a mountain than it is today. Then it was more than 18,000 feet high, of which barely one-fifth remains today. And in another million years no trace may be left of it. Here there is no abiding city, neither is there an abiding mountain. Human life itself may be but a passing phase of the history of this great globe. But as long as human memory lasts, as long as men and women will remember and be interested in the history of their storied past, so long the Great War—perhaps the greatest in human history—will be remembered, and the memory of the great sacrifice here recorded will endure as part of it.

Standing here today as we do on the summit of Table Mountain, may I add a few words in reference to the spirit of the place?

The attraction of the mountains for us points to something very significant and deep in our natures. May I illustrate the matter by a little story which is not quite true, but neither is it entirely mythical, as it finds some support in the testimony of science.

Once upon a time, in the far-off beginnings of things, the ancestors of the present human race lived far down in deep blue pools of the ocean, amid the slimy ooze from which they had themselves sprung. There they lived and developed a long time, and in the sounds of the sea, in the rhythm of the waters, and of the rising and falling tides, they learnt that sense of music which is so mysterious a faculty in us, and which is in a much smaller degree shared by so many marine animals.

The music in a sea shell pressed on our ear carries us back to the very beginnings of life on this planet. It is a far-off echo of our most ancient experience as living things. As our ancestors thrived and developed they gradually found the pressure of the waters too much for them. They felt stifled and longed for more freedom to breathe. And so they rose slowly on to the beaches, and finally emerged into the air on the seashore. What a blessed relief was there, what an unconscious sense of lightness and exaltation! No longer submerged in the stifling depths, but with full lungs expanding in the invigorating air. The rising from the sea was the most glorious advance in the forward march of terrestrial life. But it was not enough.

The same process of development and advance continued on the seashore. In the course of time the heavy air of the sea levels became too much for the ever-forward movement of the forms of life. The pressure on the lungs was too great, and the forward movement seemed to be arrested in a sort of atmospheric morass, in which a great heaviness hung on the spirit of life. At this stage a new great advance was registered. The rise to higher levels took place. Some animals developed wings with which they could fly upward and for longer or shorter periods remain in the high places and breathe a keener air. And in this rise they shook off their ancient sluggishness and lethargy, and developed a spirit of joy which had hitherto been unknown to them. The skylark, rising in an ecstasy of song high up into the air, is an illustration of the new great advance.

Other forms of life developed other means of locomotion and of ascent from the heavy low levels. As the dull dead-weight was removed from the lungs a new sense of lightness, of progress, of joy and gladness dawned on the ever higher rising forms of life. The great relief was not only of a physical character, but had the most far-reaching and spiritual values. And so it has come about that finally in man all moral and spiritual values are expressed in terms of altitude. The low expresses degradation, both physical and moral. If we wish to express great intellectual or moral or spiritual attainments we use the language of the altitudes. We speak of men who have risen, of aims and ideals that are lofty, we place the seat of our highest religious ideals in high heaven, and we consign all that is morally base to nethermost hell. Thus the metaphors embedded in language reflect but the realities of the progress of terrestrial life.

The Mountain is not merely something externally sublime. It has a great historic and spiritual meaning for us. It stands for us as the ladder of life. Nay, more, it is the great ladder of the soul, and in a curious way the source of religion. From it came the Law, from it came the Gospel in the Sermon on the Mount. We may truly say that the highest religion is the Religion of the Mountain.

What is that religion? When we reach the mountain summits we leave behind us all the things that weigh heavily down below on our body and our spirit. We leave behind a feeling of weakness and depression; we feel a new freedom, a great exhilaration, an exaltation of the body no less than of the spirit. We feel a great joy. The Religion of the Mountain is in reality the religion of joy, of the release of the soul from the things that weigh it down and fill it with a sense of weariness, sorrow and defeat. The religion of joy realises the freedom of the soul, the soul's kinship to the great creative spirit and its dominance over all the things of sense. As the body has escaped from the over-weight and depression of the sea, so the soul must be released from all sense of weariness, weakness and depression arising from the fret, worry and friction of our daily lives. We must feel that we are above it all, that the soul is essentially free, and in freedom realises the joy of living. And when the feeling of lassitude and depression and the sense of defeat advances upon us, we must repel it, and maintain an equal and cheerful temper.

We must fill our daily lives with the spirit of joy and delight. We must carry this spirit into our daily lives and tasks. We must perform our work not grudgingly and as a burden imposed on us, but in a spirit of cheerfulness, goodwill and delight in it. Not only on the mountain summits of life, not only on the heights of success and achievement, but down in the deep valleys of drudgery, of anxiety and defeat, we must cultivate this great spirit of joyous freedom and uplift of the soul. We must practise the religion of the mountain down in the valleys also.

This may sound a hard doctrine, and it may be that only after years of practice are we able to triumph in spirit over the things that weigh and drag us down. But it is the nature of the soul, as of all life, to rise, to overcome, and finally to attain complete freedom and happiness. And if we consistently practise the religion of the mountain we must succeed in the end. To this great end Nature will co-operate with the soul.

The mountains uphold us and the stars beckon to us. The mountains of our lovely land will make a constant appeal to us to live the higher life of joy and freedom. Table Mountain, in particular, will preach this great gospel to the myriads of toilers in the valley below. And those who, whether members of the Mountain Club or not, make a habit of ascending her beautiful slopes in their free moments, will reap a rich reward not only in bodily health and strength but also in an inner freedom and purity in an habitual spirit of delight, which will be the crowning glory of their lives.

May I express a hope that in the years to come this memorial will draw myriads who live down below to breathe the purer air and become better men and women. Their spirits will join with those up here, and it will make us all purer and nobler in spirit and better citizens of the country. . . .

CHAPTER IV

NATIVE POLICY IN AFRICA

In the Michaelmas term of 1929 Field Marshal Smuts delivered the Rhodes Memorial Lectures at Oxford. One of the lectures expressed Field Marshal Smuts's views on the native problem. The Union's native policy, as enacted in the Native Representation Act and the Native Lands Act of 1936, is largely based on Field Marshal Smuts's ideas.

OUR SUBJECT today will be African Native Policy. It bristles with difficult and contentious issues, and I must crave your attention to what may be a tedious discussion. If, owing to the short time at my disposal, I pass lightly over certain points, you must bear in mind that nevertheless I am fully aware of their importance. In our discussion of white settlement in Africa a good deal was said also on native policy, but only incidentally, as bearing on the subject of white settlement. But native policy deserves to be considered by itself, as it is far and away the most important issue which is raised by our European contact with the African continent and its peoples.

The policy or policies which the European peoples are going to pursue towards the natives of Africa will have far-reaching effects, not only for Africa, but for the future of the world. This is the issue of the contact of colours and civilisations, which seems destined to become a dominant issue of the twentieth century. In Asia a similar ques-

tion of the contact of colours and cultures is rapidly coming to the front, and history tells us what these impacts
of Asia and Europe on each other have meant in the past.
These impacts it was which, renewed at various epochs,
set the peoples of Europe going, and launched them on
that career which has led to their domination of the world.

The influence of Europe today on Asia seems to be having a somewhat similar rousing effect on a colossal scale.
Under the stimulus of Western ideas, Asia is being stirred
and shaken from one end to the other. The rise of Japan,
the awakening of India, China, the Near East, and the
Malayan islands of the Pacific seem to herald another of
the great movements or upheavals of history. It will depend very much on the wisdom and far-sighted policies of
the European peoples, and on the growth and the success
of the League of Nations in its pacific world policy,
whether this awakening of the East will be for the good
or the ill of the human race as a whole.

We are concerned today with these racial reactions in
so far as they affect Europe and Africa—a smaller question,
but still a very large human question, fraught with immense possibilities for the future of our civilisation as
well as that of Africa. What is wanted in Africa today is
a wise, far-sighted native policy. If we could evolve and
pursue a policy which will promote the cause of civilisation in Africa without injustice to the African, without
injury to what is typical and specific in the African, we
shall render a great service to the cause of humanity. For
there is much that is good in the African and which ought
to be preserved and developed. The Negro and the ne-
groid Bantu form a distinct human type which the world
would be poorer without.

Here in this vast continent, with its wide geographical variety and its great climatic differences, this unique human type has been fixing itself for thousands of years. It is even possible, so some anthropologists hold, that this was the original mother-type of the human race and that Africa holds the cradle of mankind. But whether this is so or not, at any rate here we have the vast result of time, which we should conserve and develop with the same high respect which we feel towards all great natural facts. This type has some wonderful characteristics. It has largely remained a child type, with a child psychology and outlook. A child-like human cannot be a bad human, for are we not in spiritual matters bidden to be like unto little children? Perhaps as a direct result of this temperament the African is the only happy human I have come across. No other race is so easily satisfied, so good-tempered, so carefree. If this had not been the case, it could scarcely have survived the intolerable evils which have weighed on it like a nightmare through the ages. A race which could survive the immemorial practice of the witch-doctor and the slave-trader, and preserve its inherent simplicity and sweetness of disposition, must have some very fine moral qualities. The African easily forgets past troubles and does not anticipate future troubles. This happy-go-lucky disposition is a great asset, but it has also its drawbacks.

There is no inward incentive to improvement, there is no persistent effort in construction, and there is complete absorption in the present, its joys and sorrows. Wine, women, and song in their African forms remain the great consolations of life. No indigenous religion has been evolved, no literature, no art since the magnificent promise of the cave-men and the South African petroglyphist,

no architecture since Zimbabwe (if that is African).
Enough for the Africans the simple joys of village life, the
dance, the tom-tom, the continual excitement of forms of
fighting which cause little bloodshed. They can stand any
amount of physical hardship and suffering, but when deprived of these simple enjoyments, they droop, sicken and
die. Travellers tell how for weeks the slaves would move
impassively in captive gangs; but when they passed a village and heard the pleasant noises of children, the song
and the dance, they would suddenly collapse and die, as if
of a broken heart. These children of nature have not the
inner toughness and persistence of the European, nor those
social and moral incentives to progress which have built
up European civilisation in a comparatively short period.
But they have a temperament which suits mother Africa,
and which brings out the simple joys of life and deadens
its pain, such as no other race possesses.

It is clear that a race so unique, and so different in its
mentality and its cultures from those of Europe, requires
a policy very unlike that which would suit Europeans.
Nothing could be worse for Africa than the application of
a policy, the object or tendency of which would be to destroy the basis of this African type, to de-Africanize the
African and turn him either into a beast of the field or
into a pseudo-European. And yet in the past we have tried
both alternatives in our dealings with the Africans. First
we look upon the African as essentially inferior or sub-
human, as having no soul, and as being only fit to be a
slave. As a slave he became an article of commerce, and
the greatest article of export from this continent for centuries. But the horrors of this trade became such that the
modern conscience finally revolted and stamped out Afri-

can slavery—peacefully in the British Empire, but in America with the convulsions of civil war and a million dead.

Then we changed to the opposite extreme. The African now became a man and a brother. Religion and politics combined to shape this new African policy. The principles of the French Revolution which had emancipated Europe were applied to Africa; liberty, equality, and fraternity could turn bad Africans into good Europeans. The political system of the natives was ruthlessly destroyed in order to incorporate them as equals into the white system. The African was good as a potential European; his social and political culture was bad, barbarous, and only deserving to be stamped out root and branch.

In some of the British possessions in Africa the native just emerging from barbarism was accepted as an equal citizen with full political rights along with the whites. But his native institutions were ruthlessly proscribed and destroyed. The principle of equal rights was applied in its crudest form, and while it gave the native a semblance of equality with whites, which was little good to him, it destroyed the basis of his African system which was his highest good. These are the two extreme native policies which have prevailed in the past, and the second has been only less harmful than the first. If Africa has to be redeemed, if Africa has to make her own contribution to the world, if Africa is to take her rightful place among the continents, we shall have to proceed on different lines and evolve a policy which will not force her institutions into an alien European mould, but which will preserve her unity with her own past, conserve what is precious in her past, and build her future progress and civilisation on specifically

African foundations. That should be the new policy, and such a policy would be in line with the traditions of the British Empire. As I said on an occasion which has become historic: the British Empire does not stand for assimilation of its peoples into a common type; it does not stand for standardisation, but for the fullest, freest development of its peoples along their own specific lines. This principle applies not only to its European, but to its Asiatic and its African constituents.

It is a significant fact that this new orientation of African policy had its origin in South Africa, and that its author was Cecil Rhodes in his celebrated Glen Grey Act. Rhodes' African policy embodied two main ideas: white settlement to supply the steel framework and the stimulus for an enduring civilisation, and indigenous native institutions to express the specifically African character of the natives in their future development and civilisation. African policies should arise in Africa, from the experience of the men and women who are in daily contact with the living problems. And it is, therefore, significant that the lines on which the new Africa is being shaped are mainly of African origin. When I call Rhodes the original author of the new policy I do not mean that it was his sole, individual inspiration. During the most fruitful and successful period of his public life he was associated with Jan Hofmeyr, who was one of the wisest, most experienced, and farsighted men whom South Africa has ever produced. In evolving his native policy Rhodes collaborated closely and continuously with Hofmeyr; and the policy in the form it took in the celebrated Glen Grey Act was therefore the joint product of Rhodes and Hofmeyr, of English- and Dutch-speaking South Africans. The new orientation therefore rests on a very broad basis of African experience.

Prior to the Glen Grey legislation it had been the practice in South Africa, as it had been the practice in all European-occupied territory in Africa, to rule the natives direct through Government officials—direct rule, as it has been called. Even where natives were left undisturbed in the possession of their tribal lands, the native organs of self-government were broken down and government rule was constituted in their place. The native chiefs were either deposed and deprived of authority, or where use was made of them they were incorporated into the official system and appointed as officers of the Government, from whom they derived all their authority and in whose name that authority was exercised. The principal innovation of Rhodes in his new legislation was, so far as possible, to introduce indirect white rule, and to make the natives manage their local tribal affairs. A system of native councils was inaugurated for the smaller areas, from which again delegates met to form a larger general council under the chairmanship of the resident magistrate of the area. Powers of taxation, of administration, and of recommending legislation to the Government were conferred on these councils. His second innovation was to make it possible for natives in their tribal areas to become possessed of their own separate plots of agricultural land, instead of the traditional communal holding and working of land which is the universal native system throughout Africa. Under the native system the tribe, not the individual, owns the lands, and from time to time the chief and his advisers assign to each head of a family the plot which he may cultivate for himself.

This plot can be and is usually changed, so that there

is no fixity of tenure, and in consequence no incentive to improve the land and to do the best with it or get the most out of it. For this communal social system of land tenure Rhodes substituted individual tenure, under certain reservations and with certain safeguards, designed in the interests of the native holders themselves. A third feature of his system was a labour tax of ten shillings per annum, imposed on all native heads of families who did not go out to work beyond their district for three months in the year. The object of this tax was obvious. The whites wanted labourers, and the natives were supposed to require some inducement to go and work instead of sitting on their holdings and seeing their women work. Both in the interests of the whites and the natives, therefore, this special tax was imposed as an economic experiment. The tax, however, was unpopular with the natives from the start, and soon appeared to be an unnecessary irritation. The native men went to work quite readily or sent their young men to work for the whites. Before many years this special tax was repealed, and in later years a similar tax in the Transvaal met with the same fate. The native, although a slow worker, is not lazy, and does not require any special inducement to play his part in the economic development of the country. His main incentive is the rising scale of his needs in food and clothing, both for himself and for his often large family of children. In addition, he is handicapped in South Africa by want of sufficient land for his requirements, and by the non-economic character of native farming on the whole.

With his rise in the scale of civilisation his needs rapidly develop, and he soon finds it necessary to supplement the scanty proceeds of his farming with the ready cash which he can earn in white employment. His economic lot, therefore, inevitably becomes more difficult, and forms a sufficient incentive to go out and work without any special means taken to force him to do so. The universal experience in Africa is that, although it takes some time at the beginning for the native to enter white employment, his rapidly growing economic needs in a white enviroment, and with a rising scale of living, soon make him take his full share of the burden without any necessity to resort to special measures. The young European communities who in other parts of the African continent are struggling with this labour question as their principal trouble, and who may feel tempted to resort to the unsuccessful experiments which we have tried and discarded in South Africa, may take heart from our experience in South Africa of the native as a continuously improving worker. Dismissing therefore the question of labour tax, we come to consider the other features of Rhodes' Act, and their general bearing on African native policy.

His provision of individual agricultural holdings has been a great success, and has been a principal means of native advance where it has been adopted in the Union. The native system of land socialism is not only primitive but most wasteful in its working. Why should the native farmer improve and render productive what belongs to the community, and may be taken away from him by the community? The result is that these communal farms rapidly deteriorate and become exhausted, and have to be abandoned after a few years' use. Then the farm lands shift to another area of the tribal domain where the same process of uneconomic exhaustion is repeated. And in the course of years this shifting cultivation works havoc with the natural resources of the domain; the soil is progressively exhausted; the forests and trees disappear; the natural vegetable covering is destroyed; soil erosion sets in; the rainfall is lessened, and what water does fall flows off in torrents; arid conditions arise; and the tribal lands become a barren waste.

This sad phenomenon can be seen in one degree or another all over the African continent. Not only in South Africa, but in many other parts of the continent a native area or reserve can be recognised at a distance by the obvious general deterioration of the natural vegetation and the soil. But for the enormous natural resources and recuperative power of the continent, most of Africa would by now be a howling wilderness, because of the wasteful rural economy of its population. Unless the carrying capacity of the land is to be gravely impaired in the future, steps will have to be taken everywhere to preserve the forests and the soil, and to teach the native better methods of agriculture.

Practical agricultural education must indeed become one of the principal subjects of native education. But nothing will have a more far-reaching effect than a general system of individual agricultural holdings under proper safeguards. The economic incentive to use properly, and to improve, what is one's own, is more powerful than any other factor of progress. In a world tending more and more towards general socialism, the vague phrase of "native socialism" may sound attractive, but its practical effects in Africa are everywhere devastating, and it has significantly maintained on that continent the most backward conditions to be found anywhere.

The main object of the Glen Grey legislation was, however, to give the native his own institutions for his self-development and self-government. It marks definitely the abandonment of the older policy of direct rule, according to which the white man's system and culture had to be imposed on the native, and native institutions had to be scrapped as barbarous. The new policy is to foster an indigenous native culture or system of cultures, and to cease to force the African into alien European moulds. As a practical policy of native government it has worked most successfully. Gradually the system of native councils and native self-government through their own tribal chiefs and elected councils has been extended from one native area to another in the Cape Province, until today about two-thirds of the Cape natives, or roughly over a million, fall under this system and manage their own local affairs according to their own ideas under the supervision of the European magistrates.

They impose a small capitation tax of ten shillings per annum for their own local requirements; they look after their own roads and the dipping of their cattle against disease; they teach improved agricultural methods through their own native officers; they amend their customary native law, advise the Government in regard to proposed laws in their areas, and in many other ways they look after their own local interests, find useful expression for their political energies, and get an invaluable training in disinterested public service. A sense of pride in their institutions and their own administration is rapidly developing, and, along with valuable experience in administration and public affairs, they are also acquiring a due sense of responsibility; where mistakes are made they feel satisfied that they have only themselves to blame. After the new system had worked successfully and with ever-increasing efficiency for twenty-five years, I thought the time ripe in 1920 to extend it to the whole of the Union, and in that year an Act was passed which gave increased powers to the councils and authorised the Government to introduce them over the whole Union, wherever the advance of the natives might justify the step. A Native Affairs Commission was at the same time appointed to advise the natives and the Government in regard to the establishment of new Councils, as well as in reference to all legislation affecting the natives. And it is confidently expected that before many years have passed the greater portion of the native population of South Africa will be in charge of their own local affairs, under general white supervision; and in this way they will get on outlet for their political and administrative energies and ambitions which will give them the necessary training for eventual participation in a wider sphere of public life.

The new departure is most far-reaching and has come none too soon. Already the African system is disintegrating everywhere over the whole African continent. Many factors have combined to produce this situation. Missionaries share the blame with governments; the fight against the native social ideas has been no less destructive than the deposition of native chiefs and the institution of European organs of government. Unfortunately the earlier efforts of missionary enterprise were made without any reference to, or knowledge of, the peculiar native psychology, or the light which anthropology has thrown on the past of human cultures. For the natives, religion, law, natural science, social customs and institutions all form one blended whole, which enshrines their view of the world and of the forces governing it. Attack this complex system at any single point and the whole is endangered.

The introduction of the Christian religion meant not only the breakdown of the primitive belief in spirits, in magic and witchcraft, and the abandonment of the practice of polygamy; it meant the breakdown of the entire integral native *Weltanschauung* or outlook on life and the world. A knowledge of anthropology would have been most useful, and would have helped to conserve the native social system, while ridding it of what was barbarous or degrading. The tendency of the Christian mission has therefore on the whole been to hasten the disintegration of the native system, both in its good and its bad aspects. To this has been added the introduction of the white man's administration through his own official organs, the breakdown of the authority of the chiefs and the tribal system, and the loosening of the bonds which bind native society together, with the consequent weakening or disappearance of tribal discipline over the young men and women of the tribe. The general disintegration has been powerfully reinforced by the vast improvement in the means of transport, the opening of communications, and by labour recruitment, which have led to the movement of natives and their mix-up on a scale which would have been impossible before. The events of the Great War on the African continent have also contributed to this general disintegration.

If the bonds of native tribal cohesion and authority are dissolved, the African governments will everywhere sit with vast hordes of detribalised natives on their hands, for whom the traditional restraints and the discipline of the chiefs and the elders will have no force or effect. The old social and religious sanctions will have disappeared, while no new sanctions except those of the white man's laws will have been substituted. Such a situation would be unprecedented in the history of the world and the results may well be general chaos. From time immemorial the natives of Africa have been subject to a stern, even a ruthless, discipline, and their social system has rested on the despotic authority of their chiefs. If this system breaks down and tribal discipline disappears, native society will be resolved into its human atoms, with possibilities of universal Bolshevism and chaos which no friend of the natives, or the orderly civilisation of this continent, could contemplate with equanimity. Freed from all traditional, moral and social discipline, the native, just emerging from barbarism, may throw all restraint to the winds. Such a breakdown should be prevented at all costs, and everything should be done to maintain in the future the authority which has guided native life in the past.

In the interests of the natives as well as those of the European administrations responsible for their welfare, we are called upon to retrace our steps, to take all proper measures which are still possible to restore or preserve the authority of the chiefs, and to maintain the bonds of solidarity and discipline which have supported the tribal organisation of the natives in the past.

This authority or discipline need not be exercised in a barbarous way, and should be shorn of all old-time cruelty and other undesirable features. But in essence it should be maintained, and under the general supervision and check of the European magistrate it should continue to be exercised. Special means should be taken to instruct chiefs in their duties, and the sons of chiefs and headmen should be trained to the proper exercise of the leadership which they may be called upon to fill. Such schools already exist, not only in South Africa, but under the Tanganyika and Uganda administrations, and may prove most helpful in preserving the traditional native chieftainship and headmanship as a vital link in the organisation of native society.

The new policy is in effect enshrined in the Covenant of the League of Nations and in the mandates passed thereunder. Article 22 of the Covenant lays down that in those colonies and territories taken from the defeated powers, which are inhabited by peoples not yet able to stand by themselves under the strenuous conditions of the modern world, there shall be applied the principle, that the well-being and development of such peoples form a sacred trust of civilisation, and that this trust shall be carried out by advanced nations acting as mandatories on behalf of the League of Nations.

The development of peoples not yet able to stand by themselves can only mean the progress and civilisation of these backward peoples in accordance with their own institutions, customs and ideas, in so far as these are not incompatible with the ideals of civilisation. That this was the plain meaning and intention of the article I can state with some authority, as I was in a measure responsible for this mandate principle and for its formulation in Article 22 of the Covenant. This article enshrines a policy and a principle which is not only in consonance with commonsense, but which has already been tested in practice on a fairly large scale, and which in future ought to govern universally the contacts between European and other less advanced peoples.

It may be of some interest to indicate briefly how this policy is being applied in a mandated territory like Tanganyika. The foundation of the system is the maintenance and building up of the authority of the chiefs in their various ranks. Their sons receive special training in a school for the sons of chiefs, intended to fit them for their future duties. Their office is hereditary, but disposition and popular election are both possible in accordance with native ideas. The chief is responsible for the administration of his tribe, maintains order and good government within its area, and prevents the commission of offences. The heads of families pay an annual tax of ten shillings, which goes into the tribal treasury, from which a fixed amount is paid to the chief for his maintenance, the balance being devoted to tribal purposes. The chief can issue orders for a large number of purposes, such as prohibiting or controlling the manufacture and consumption of intoxicating liquors, preventing the pollution of the water in any stream, controlling migration of natives to or from his area, and requiring any native to cultivate land in such a way and with such crops as will secure a proper supply of food for him and his family. He may also make rules imposing fines and other penalties for the enforcement of his orders. Native courts are also instituted, administering native law and custom in both civil and criminal cases between natives within a certain jurisdiction; and from their decisions or sentences appeals lie ultimately to a white authority, who has also to confirm certain criminal sentences before their execution.

The white administration remains responsible for the

larger functions of government, such as the combating of human and animal diseases, the organisation of education, the improvement of agriculture, and the construction of public works, and maintains a staff for these and similar purposes. But all the purely tribal concerns are left to the chief and his counsellors, whose actions are supervised by the white officer only in certain cases intended to prevent abuses.

The native system may not be as efficient and incorruptible as direct white rule would be, but a certain amount of inefficiency or even injustice, according to white ideas, is excusable, so long as the natives are trained to govern themselves according to their own ideas, and bear the responsibility for their own small mistakes. In this way they learn to stand by themselves, and will in the long run be trained to do their own local government work. It is not only the training in self-government that will benefit them. They will develop the sense of responsibility which goes with it, and which is in itself one of the most valuable lessons of life. In looking after their own concerns they will, in addition, cultivate a sense of pride in their own system and increase their self-respect. And, above all, they will develop an active interest in their own public affairs, which will be of enormous moral and social value. The white man does the native a grave injury by doing everything for him in the way of government, and thereby depriving his life of all public interest. Gone is the excitement of his petty wars; and if in addition there is the repression of all his former public activities and the suppression of his native values, we must expect a sense of frustration which will take all the zest out of his life. The question has even been raised whether the white man's rule, in taking all the interest out of native life, is not responsible for that decadence, lowered birth-rate, and slow petering out which we see in the case of many primitive peoples. At any rate, the new policy of native self-government will provide the natives with plenty of bones to chew at and plenty of matters to wrangle over—and they do love to talk and dispute *ad infinitum*—and in that way help to fill their otherwise empty lives with interest.

Another important consequence will follow from this system of native institutions. Wherever Europeans and natives live in the same country it will mean separate parallel institutions for the two. The old practice mixed up black with white in the same institutions; and nothing else was possible, after the native institutions and traditions had been carelessly or deliberately destroyed. But in the new plan there will be what is called in South Africa "segregation"—separate institutions for the two elements of the population, living in their own separate areas. Separate institutions involve territorial segregation of the white and black. If they live mixed up together it is not practicable to sort them out under separate institutions of their own. Institutional segregation carries with it territorial segregation. The new policy therefore gives the native his own traditional institutions on land which is set aside for his exclusive occupation. For agricultural and pastoral natives, living their tribal life, large areas of reserves are set aside, adequate for their present and future needs.

In not setting aside sufficient such areas in South Africa in the past we committed a grievous mistake, which is at the root of most of our difficulties in native policy. For urbanised natives, on the other hand, who live, not under tribal conditions but as domestic servants or industrial workers in white areas, there are set aside native villages or locations, adjoining the European towns. In both rural reserves and town locations the natives take a part in or run their own local self-government. Such is the practice now in vogue in South Africa and it is likely to develop still further, and to spread all over Africa where white and black live and work together in the same countries. For residential and local government purposes a clean cleavage is becoming ever more marked, the white portion of the population living under more advanced European institutions, while the natives next door maintain their simpler indigenous system. This separation is imperative, not only in the interests of a native culture, and to prevent native traditions and institutions from being swamped by the more powerful organisation of the whites, but also for other important purposes, such as public health, racial purity, and public good order. The mixing up of two such alien elements as white and black leads to unhappy social results—racial miscegenation, moral deterioration of both, racial antipathy and clashes, and to many other forms of social evil.

In these great matters of race, colour, and culture, residential separation and parallel institutions alone can do justice to the ideals of both sections of the population. The system is accepted and welcomed by the vast majority of natives; but it is resented by a small educated minority who claim "equal rights" with the whites. It is, however, evident that the proper place of the educated minority of the natives is with the rest of their people, of whom they are the natural leaders, and from whom they should not in any way be dissociated.

Far more difficult questions arise on the industrial plane. It is not practicable to separate black and white in industry, and their working together in the same industry and in the same works leads to a certain amount of competition and friction and antagonism, for which no solution has yet been found. Unhappy attempts have been made in South Africa to introduce a colour bar, and an Act of that nature is actually on the Statute Book, but happily no attempt has yet been made to apply it in practice. It empowers the Government to set aside separate spheres of work for the native and the non-native, the object being to confine the native to the more or less unskilled occupations or grades of work. The inherent economic difficulties of such a distribution of industrial functions, the universal objection of the native workers, and the sense of fair play among the whites will make its practical application virtually impossible. No statutory barrier of that kind should be placed on the native who wishes to raise himself in the scale of civilisation, nor could it be maintained for long against the weight of modern public opinion. As a worker the white man should be able to hold his own in competition with the native. Industrial, as distinguished from territorial, segregation would be both impracticable and an offence against the modern conscience.

There remains the big question how far the parallelism of native and white institutions is to go. Is it to be confined to local government, or is it to go all the way, up to the level of full political or parliamentary government? Should black and white co-operate in the same parliamentary institutions of the country? If so, should they have separate representatives in the same parliamentary institutions? Few acquainted with the facts and the difficulties can profess to see clear daylight in the tangle of this problem. In the older practice, embodied in the constitution of the former Cape Colony and in many other colonial institutions, political equality between the different races on the basis of a complete mixture of political rights was recognised. Justice is colour-blind and recognises no political differences on grounds of colour or race. Hence the formula of "equal rights for all civilised men" with which the name of Rhodes is identified, and which represents the traditional British policy.

That policy, however, arose at a time when the doctrine of native parallelism had not yet emerged, when native institutions were proscribed as barbarous, and the only place for the civilised native was therefore in the white man's system and the white man's institutions. The question is whether the new principle makes, or should make, any difference to the old tradition of mixed and equal political rights in the same parliamentary institutions. I notice that the Hilton Young Commission, after having made a powerful plea for separate native institutions for local government purposes, pause when they come up against the question of parliamentary institutions, and in the end leave the question over for the future.

"If" (they say) "the idea of parallel development is accepted, then it follows that it is desirable to keep the way open as long as possible for the maximum measure of political segregation. This suggests that political development for the native and the settled areas should be carried forward on separate lines—native and British respectively—as far as possible."

Lord Lugard, in dealing with the question of equal rights in relation to colour, lays down the following proposition which a former President of the United States of America approved of:

"Here, then" (he says), "is the true conception of the inter-relation of colour: complete uniformity in ideals, absolute equality in the paths of knowledge and culture, equal opportunities for those who strive, equal administration for those who achieve; in matters social and racial a separate path, each pursuing his own inherited traditions, preserving his own race-purity and race-pride; equality in things spiritual, agreed difference in the physical and material."

An admirable statement of the principle to which, I think, all fair-minded men will agree. But you notice once more the silence about political rights.

I do not think there can be, or that at bottom there is, among those who have given the subject serious attention, any doubt that in the supreme legislature of a country with a mixed population all classes and colours should have representation. It is repugnant to our civilised European ideas that the weaker in a community should not be heard or should go without representation, either by themselves or through European spokesmen, where their interests are concerned. There can be but one sovereign body in a country, and that body should represent the weaker no less than the stronger. To that extent there should be agreement. As to the mode of representation of colour in the supreme parliament there can be legitimate difference of opinion.

The older practice was to give equal rights in the sense of mixed representation, the same member of the legis-

lature representing mixed bodies of white and native voters alike. The new policy of segregation of political rights
would seem to point to separate representation for the
colours in the same parliament so that white and native
voters would vote in separate constituencies for separate
representatives. There would still be equal political rights,
and the Rhodes ideal in that sense would not be affected,
but they would be exercised separately or communally.
In South Africa, which, owing to the advanced condition
of its natives, has become a sort of cockpit for race issues,
we started with the older system of mixed constituencies
in the Cape Colony, and this system is embodied and entrenched in the Act of Union which forms our Constitution. The present Government has proposed to scrap
this system for the future, and to give separate representation in Parliament to native and non-native voters. A
policy which might have been easy and, from certain
points of view, even commendable, with a clean slate before us, has become enormously difficult because of what
has been done in the past, and the justifiable fervour with
which the Cape natives cling to their vested rights, which
they have enjoyed for three-quarters of a century. A battle
royal is still proceeding on this and cognate issues affecting the political rights of the natives, and it will require
all the wisdom and patience which we can command in
South Africa if we are to reach a generally acceptable
solution.

If we had to do only with the tribal native voters the
question would not be so difficult, and the application of
the general segregation principle to the particular case of
political rights might be justified. Unfortunately very
large numbers of detribalised natives are spread all over

the Cape, and are no longer resident or registered in the native areas. These urbanised natives living among the whites constitute the real crux, and it is a difficulty which goes far beyond the political issue. They raise a problem for the whole principle of segregation, as they claim to be civilised and Europeanised, and do not wish to be thrust back into the seclusion of their former tribal associations, or to forego their new place in the sun among the whites. With the application of strict education and civilisation tests it would probably be the better course to allow them to exercise their political rights along with the whites. Were it not for this case of the urbanised or detribalised natives, the colour problem, not only in South Africa but elsewhere in Africa, would be shorn of most of its difficulties. And the situation in South Africa is therefore a lesson to all the younger British communities farther north to prevent as much as possible the detachment of the native from his tribal connection, and to enforce from the very start the system of segregation with its conservation of separate native institutions.

In conclusion I wish to refer to an apparent discrepancy between this lecture and my previous one. In that lecture I stressed the importance of white settlement in Africa as a potent means of furthering native progress and civilisation. I pointed out that enduring contact with the white man's civilisation is the surest way to civilise the native. In this lecture I have emphasised the importance of preserving native institutions, of keeping intact as far as possible the native system of organisation and social discipline. It may be thought that there is a clash between those two aims, and that civilisation by white contact must inevitably lead to the undermining and ultimately to the destruction of the native culture and social system. This, however, is not so. So long as there is territorial segregation, so long as the native family home is not with the white man but in his own area, so long the native organisation will not be materially affected. While the native may come voluntarily out of his own area for a limited period every year to work with a white employer, he will leave his wife and children behind in their native home. The family life in the native home will continue on the traditional lines; the routine of the family and of the tribe will not be altered in any material respect. The male adults, father and sons, will no doubt imbibe new ideas in their white employment, but their social system will not suffer on that account.

It is only when segregation breaks down, when the whole family migrates from the tribal home and out of the tribal jurisdiction to the white man's farm or the white man's town, that the tribal bond is snapped, and the traditional system falls into decay. And it is this migration of the native family, of the females and children, to the farms and the towns, which should be prevented. As soon as this migration is permitted the process commences which ends in the urbanised, detribalized native and the disappearance of the native organisation. It is not white employment of the native males that works the mischief, but the abandonment of the native tribal home by the women and children. This the law should vigorously prevent, and the system—whether it is administered through passes or in any other way—should only allow the residence of males for limited periods, and for purposes of employment among the whites. If this is done there will be no serious danger that the indigenous native system will be unduly affected.

At the same time I wish to point out that the prevention of this migration will be no easy task, even where ample tribal lands are guaranteed to the natives. The whites like to have the families of their native servants with them. It means more continuous and less broken periods of labour, and it means more satisfied labourers. It means, moreover, the use of the women and children for such work as they are fit for.

These are considerable advantages, and the white employers will not be very keen to carry out a law against them. On the other hand, the native also very often likes to get away from the jurisdiction of the chief and the discipline of the tribe, and prefers to have his women and his children around him in his daily life. For the native the pressure to break away from the old bonds and live with his white master is thus very great. We have seen the process at work in South Africa. When the white emigrants entered and occupied Natal, they found the entire territory between Zululand and Pondoland unoccupied; it had been laid bare and made a waste buffer between these two powerful native states. But no sooner had the whites settled in this empty area than native deserters, dissatisfied with the harsh rule of their chiefs, began to arrive and settle as servants among the whites. And today, through this wholly voluntary migration, the province of Natal has a very large native population. It was not a case of the natives not having sufficient fertile lands for their own use. Zululand is one of the most fertile parts of South Africa, and it was and remains comparatively thinly populated. White employment, white protection, the freedom of the white man's rule compared to the discipline of the native chief and the jurisdiction of the tribe have been the potent factors in bringing about this migration. And they will continue to operate in all parts of Africa where whites settle down.

In the old Cape Colony one frontier after another was drawn by the Cape governors between the white settlements and the native tribes, and migration from the one to the other was prohibited under stern penalties. But the system was forever breaking down. The whites like to have native servants; the natives prefer to have white masters, and this double economic attraction has proved too much for any prohibitory law.

There is, however, no reason why segregation, although it has broken down in South Africa in the past, should not be a workable and enforceable system in the future. The power of Government and the reach of the law are today very different from what they were under the primitive nomadic conditions of the old Cape frontier. The system of native administration is today so ramified and pervasive, the policeman is so ubiquitous, that segregation can be tried under far more favourable conditions than existed in South Africa in the past. The young countries to the north can start with a clean slate. They can learn from the mistakes which we made in South Africa, and can *ab initio* reserve ample lands for the natives to live and work on. They can check the abuses of the chiefs, and can effectively supervise the working of the native system, both in its administrative and judicial aspects. Witchcraft can be fought, official injustice and corruption can be largely prevented, schools can be established, and the simplest amenities of civilised life can be introduced, in the native villages and tribal areas.

The position is really very different from what it was generations ago, and the inducements for native families to remain on their tribal lands are such, or can be made such, that a segregation law will become comparatively easy to carry out. The women and children will continue to carry on their native life at home, will continue to work in the homes and in the fields as they have done from the immemorial past. The men, instead of lying in the sun, or brawling over their beer, or indulging in the dangerous sport of tribal warfare, will go out to work, and supplement the family income and render tolerable a weight which under the new conditions is becoming more and more difficult for the women and children. They should never be away long, and the physical and moral life of the family and the tribe need not suffer because of the short periods of absence. Theorists may pick holes in such a system, but there is no practical reason why it should not work in practice. There is no break in the communal village life, but among the men the thin edge of the industrial wedge is introduced, and they rightly become the bread-winners which they have seldom or never been. Such a system has great redeeming features, and compares more than favourably with the old ways, which meant absolute stagnation for the men, and virtual slavery for the women. It represents a compromise between the native routine of the past and the white man's industrial system, which may work tolerably well in the future.

Without breaking down what is good in the native system, it will graft on to it a wholesome economic development, which will yet not disturb too deeply the traditional ways of mother Africa. The white man's civilisation and the steadily progressing native culture will live side by side and react on each other, and the problems of their contact will provide a fruitful theme for the statesmen of the future.

CHAPTER V

THE CHALLENGE TO FREEDOM

On October 17, 1934, Field Marshal Smuts was installed as Rector of St. Andrew's University. His address on that occasion was memorable, first, because it expressed his own Credo of individual freedom, and, second, because it dealt with the new tyrannies of Fascism and Nazism.

AFTER expressing thanks for his election and paying tribute to his defeated opponent, General Smuts said:

The Principal's remark carried my mind back to the first occasion I had heard mention of the Scots. My people were small farming folk in the old Cape Colony, and when I was a very small boy I used to frequent the company of an old Hottentot shepherd of my father, who used to delight me with stories from his native folklore. He had also been to several kafir wars, and could tell me of his own wonderful feats of arms in those border campaigns. I listened enthralled. At that time the first Boer War—the one that ended at Majuba—was going on, and I remember asking him whom he thought would win. From his great military knowledge he had no doubt that the British would win. I asked him whether he thought the English were the greatest nation in the world, and he replied "No"; there was one nation still greater who lived in the farthest land in the world; they were the greatest of all nations and even the British were very much afraid of them. They were called the "Scots." That was my first introduction to the Scots—and such was my introducer! Now, 54 years after those historic conversations, I find myself the rector of a famous university of this land—of romance, as the Principal calls it—of the greatest of peoples, as old Adam, the Hottentot, called it.

I shall not venture to flatter you, and so I am bound to confess that in the sense of greatness meant by old Adam, he was wrong about Scotland. I have subsequently learnt that the Scots are, in fact, one of the small nations, although I do not intend to say so outside Scotland. To me and to us in our small beginnings in South Africa you are all the dearer on that account. We small ones of the earth feel mutually drawn to each other in a world which has largely gone crazy with the problems of size and scale. Both of us have learnt from Athens and Jerusalem that the real values were no respecters of dimensions. There are also other ties which link us together in common interests and sympathies of a more intimate character. There are the ties of kinship in the distant past, of a common religious faith, of common moral ideals. John Calvin and John Knox both belong to our invisible foundations, and there remains a community of spiritual outlook and moral values between our peoples which is among the most precious things we bring from our past.

In particular we both cherish and practise liberty as the fundamental rule of life. While inclined by our religious traditions to question the freedom of the will as a metaphysical principle, we both make amends by applying freedom with all the more energy as the practical rule of life. We decline to submerge the individual in the

State or the group, and we base our organisation of the State and society on individual freedom and the free initiative of the citizen. Our outlook remains that of free men in a world in which the tradition of freedom is, alas! steadily weakening.

You in Scotland have a great story behind you while we in Africa are only at the beginning of things. The best I could wish for my own young people, now beginning to set up house on its own account, is that its future story may not be so very different in outline from yours. Like you, we have started in trouble and bloodshed. We still have our tribes just as you have had your clans. We are trying to come and grow together in nationhood, just as you have gloriously succeeded in your own union and internal peacemaking. But more: you have set us an example how, while living your own life and maintaining and developing your own peculiar characteristics, to join in the larger life of a wider group, and thereby to make your contribution to the upbuilding of human civilisation and the establishment of a Commonwealth which today secures peace and opportunities for the good life to one-fourth of the human race. Your success in this wider theatre has gone far to justify old Adam the Hottentot in his high opinion of the Scots. They have overflowed their narrow national boundaries and have reinforced human life and endeavour all over the world, and most of all in undeveloped countries like those on the African continent.

Think of David Livingstone, the struggling Scots lad, the harassed missionary, the penniless explorer, whose monument has just gone up at the Victoria Falls. And he is but a type of many others. All over my continent stand the great beacons of progress, erected by Scots pioneers, in the Christian mission, administration, commerce, industry, transport, mining and engineering. The spoor of Scotsmen is indeed found everywhere, and they are probably the greatest pioneers of the modern world. Our world is the better for their labours. And I am told Scotland is still full of this great breed. What a record! I have continually held it up to my own people as a great example to follow. We in our small way have also started as pioneers, as a nation of Voortrekkers in our continent. We also have suffered at the hands of the English; we also have ended by making the grand compromise with them, which has been so successful in your case. May we have something of your luck in the great experiment!

But, as I said, we are still at the beginnings. At this moment we are trying to lay the enduring basis of peace in our national life. Nowhere in the Dominions has more good blood been shed. Nowhere has the political aftermath of war been more unpleasant and bitter. But we believe we are at last approaching the end of that chapter. In our politics and our racial relations we are at present concluding the grand pact of union and of fusion. The South African people have responded to the lead of their party chiefs in the spirit which is truly wonderful and which shows that the time is ripe for a great change. I am indeed very proud of my countrymen of both races. In a world of racial cleavages, in a world of growing economic nationalism and antagonisms, South Africa is busy closing up her ranks and building an enduring peace. Africa is once more true to her reputation for novelty. The young nations of the world have their own contribution to make to the human causes, and they can best begin to do so by setting their house in order and pledging themselves afresh to the great human principles on which our Western civilisation rests.

In the old world—in the motherlands of our European civilisation—those principles are no longer considered sacrosanct and are being widely challenged and even openly defied. The things which Thomas Carlyle in the past century classed with the eternal verities are today being relegated to his limbo of old clothes. With the cataclysm of the Great War the whole European order threatens to collapse and in the ruins to involve the most precious treasures along with the accumulated rubbish of the 19th century. The catastrophe has been so sudden and unexpected that we have not yet had time to do the necessary sifting, to save the treasures from the waste of the middenheap. There has been no time yet to readjust our viewpoints, to take new bearings.

Mankind stands perplexed and baffled before the new situation and the new problems. There is fear, a sense of insecurity among the nations. The primeval dread of the unknown is once more upon us, and the dark irrational forces of the past are once more stalking forward from their obscure background. We have the paralysing sense of having failed. The fair promise of nineteenth-century progress has ended in defeat and frustration and disillusion. There has been a double failure. There was the failure of the Great War, which seemed to be a negation of the principles on which the comity of our Christian civilisation had been laboriously built up, and there was the no less deep and poignant failure of the peace, when at a vital moment, a critical occasion for Western civilisation, human goodwill appeared to be unequal to its task, and the great hopes for a better ordering of the future were rudely disappointed. Such a chance comes but once in a whole era of history, and we missed it. The politics which is founded on despair or desperation, which covers many European countries today with dangerous political experiments, and in others endangers peace and paralyses disarmament, has sprung largely from this second failure and the slaughter of ideals which it involved—a slaughter no less grievous than that of our millions in the war. There was this double human failure, which has wounded, so to say, the very soul of mankind, and left it with insufficient faith and confidence to sustain the causes and the institutions which are essential to our civilisation.

No wonder there is abroad a spirit of pessimism and even of despair. So many high hopes have been dashed. Science, the proudest product of the human reason, the greatest instrument of human progress, the voice of God to our day and generation, has at the same time become the most dangerous weapon for our self-destruction. Democracy, with its promise of international peace, has been no better guarantee against war than the old dynastic rule of kings. International trade and commerce, which were supposed to pave a sure way to better understanding among the nations and a peaceful world, have instead led to economic nationalism, and thereby opened up new sources of international friction and trouble. One by one the vast expectations born of the progress of the last century have been falsified, and today we face a bleak world, bereft of the vast capital destroyed in the war, even doubting the principles on which our civilisation is built, without confidence in ourselves and our destiny, and with no clear vision of the road before us. We console ourselves with the truism that we are living in most interesting times. But the hard truth is that they are the most anxious and critical times that mankind has faced for many centuries.

Speaking here today to you, the young people of this university, an old hard-bitten campaigner like myself might be asked how to view the prospects before us. What message I have from my own experience, as one who has gone through the immense experience of our generation, to those who now stand on the threshold of this strange new world.

I greatly appreciate the opportunity of giving my impressions—to bear my testimony, as the old evangelicals used to say—to "share" with you, as the Oxford groupers of today say.

My fundamental impression of life I can give you in words which most of you know from your childhood. They occur on the first page of the greatest book in the world. They come from the youth of the world, and today in its maturity they are truer than ever. The world is good. This is a good world. We need not approve of all the items in it, nor of all the individuals in it; but the world itself, which is more than its parts or individuals, which has a soul, a spirit, a pull, a fundamental relation to each of us deeper than all other relations, is a friendly world. It has borne us; it has carried us onward; it has humanised us and guided our faltering footsteps throughout the long and slow advance; it has endowed us with strength and courage; it has proved a real vale of soul-making for us humans, and created for us visions, dreams, ideals which are still further moulding us on eternal lines. It is full of tangles, of ups and downs. There is always enough to bite on, to sharpen wits on, to test our courage and manhood. It is indeed a world built for heroism, but also for beauty, tenderness, mercy.

I have passed through pretty rough passages. I have sampled the world and human nature at many points and I have learnt that it takes all sorts to make a world. But through it all my conviction has only deepened that there is nothing in the nature of things which is alien to what is best in us. There is no malign fatalism which makes fools of us in our dark striving towards the good. On the contrary, what is highest in us is deepest in the nature of things, and as virtue is its own reward, so life carries its own sanctions and the guarantee of its own highest fulfilments and perfections. That is my ultimate Credo; and it is not founded on hearsay, but on my first-hand experience in that cross-section of the world which I have lived through. This is no doubt a slender basis of fact for so large a conclusion. But the final convictions are not inductions from experience, but insights into it. I remain at heart an optimist.

In the events of our times I see much ground for anxiety but none for real pessimism. Human nature is not so one-sided and ill-balanced that we need look on our civilisation as doomed. It has survived great shocks in the past and will survive this one, too. In spite of all its defects, the human mind has already solved most difficult problems in national organisation and even begun to lay the foundations of an international order. These are long-range problems, and the pessimist makes a great mistake in taking a short-range view of them. Looking at the broad human situation today, one gets a very different impression from that of the pessimist.

In spite of the international friction of today there is

today more real good will and good feeling in the world than ever before. Contact with the common people everywhere is sufficient to convince us of that fact. There is no decadence abroad, but everywhere the signs of new life and of new forces on the move. In all our feverish activity I see no spirit of defeatism. Indeed, much in the purely human situation is deeply encouraging. There is surely nothing wrong with youth in its frankness, its sincerity and open-eyed outlook on the world, undaunted by the failures of the past, by the spectres of the future. Mankind is no longer held back by the ancient taboos, but is earnestly, valiantly exploring new ways to a better future.

Science has perhaps made more fundamental progress in the last 30 years than in the preceding 2,000.

In particular, as is today commonly recognised, the problem of food shortage, starvation and famine, the most dreadful spectre of all history, is at last yielding to science, and the most fruitful cause of war in the past is thus being eliminated. Instead we are now oppressed with the novel problems of plenty, the solution of which will in due course mean not only the passing of war, but of grinding poverty and slavish toil for the masses of mankind. In these and other ways the scientific results of the last 20 years will come in the future vastly to overshadow in importance the losses and dislocations of the Great War, which still bulk so large in our view.

I have stressed what I call the human situation because in the last resort that is the only thing that matters. For the time being we may be more impressed by great world-shaking events like the Great War and the vast experiments in government which have followed it. But it is only their human values that survive. Men and women alone matter in the last resort. From this point of view is it not significant that the Great War with all its suffering and disillusion, has not availed to dim the ardour and undermine the courage of the human spirit? The generation that suffered the greatest tragedy of history and knew suffering, sorrow and loss such as no previous generation of men had known, faced the world thereafter with spirit uncrushed, with head unbowed, with a heightened energy and a courage which makes man of our period a sublime figure for all time. During the war he carried a burden and faced up to a situation supposed to be too much for human nature, and after the war, in spite of the loss of millions of his best, he made a spurt in progress to which history shows no parallel. Where is the decadence? There is no reason here for tears. Rather let us be proud and grateful that we have in our generation been privileged to see the human soul stand probably the most awful ordeal to which it has ever been subjected in its long history.

But discounting the serious risk of war in the near future, there still remain other grave dangers facing our civilisation. There is a decay of principles, which is eating at the very vitals of free government, and to me that appears to be a far more serious danger to our future than the risk of war. There is today a decay of the individual's responsibility and share in government which seems to strike at the roots of our human advance.

For me the individual is basic to any world order that is worth while. Individual freedom, individual independence of mind, individual participation in the difficult work of government seems to me essential to all true progress. Yet today the individual seems more and more at a discount in the new experiments in government which are being tried out. The sturdy individualism which inspired progress in the past, which made Rome, which made Scotland, which has created all our best human values, seems to be decaying in the atmosphere of lassitude and disillusion of our day. Men and women have suffered until they are abdicating their rights as individuals. In their misery and helplessness they are surrendering to the mass will which leads straight to autocracy. The feebleness of Continental democracy, its ineffectiveness in a crisis calling for swift and decisive action, has contributed to this defeatist attitude of the individual. And the result is that with this individualist prop of freedom gone, freedom itself seems to be in danger. A new sort of hero worship is arising, very different from that which Carlyle preached, and which saps the very foundations of individuality and makes the individual prostrate himself before his national leader as before a god. That way extreme danger lies.

The disappearance of the sturdy, independent-minded, freedom-loving individual, and his replacement by a servile mass mentality is the greatest human menace of our time. Here we reach what I firmly believe is the heart of the problem, the issue round which the greatest battles of this and the coming generation will be fought—if the cause of our civilisation itself is to be saved. As an old soldier in this cause I hope you will excuse me when I state thus bluntly my views on the dangers ahead as I see them. The issue of freedom, the most fundamental issue of all our civilisation, is once more squarely raised by what is happening in the world, and cannot be evaded.

The danger signals are up in many colours and in many lands. The new tyranny, disguised in attractive patriotic colours, is enticing youth everywhere into its horrid service. Freedom must make a great counter-stroke to save itself and our fair Western civilisation. Once more the heroic call is coming to our youth. The fight for human freedom is indeed the supreme issue of the future, as it has always been in the past.

Although the ancient homelands of constitutional liberty in the West are not yet seriously affected, we have to confess sadly that over large parts of Europe the cult of force—what in the Great War we used to call Prussianism—has for the moment triumphed. Popular self-government and parliaments are disappearing. The guarantees for private rights and civil liberties are going. Minorities are trampled upon; dissident views are not tolerated and are forcibly suppressed. For those who do not choose to fall into line there is the concentration camp, the distant labour camp in the wilds or on the islands of the sea.

Intellectual freedom is disappearing with political freedom. Freedom of conscience, of speech, of the Press, of thought and teaching is in extreme danger. One party in the State usurps power, and suppresses its opponents and becomes the State. The Press is made to write to order, and public opinion is manufactured for the support of the autocracy. Even freedom of religion is no longer safe, and religious persecution, after being long considered obsolete, once more shows its head. In many, if not most, European countries the standard of human freedom has already fallen far below that of the nineteenth century.

Perhaps I do not exaggerate when I say that of what we call liberty in its full meaning—freedom of thought, speech, action, self-expression—there is today less in Europe than there has been during the last 2,000 years. In ancient Athens, in ancient Rome, there was at any rate freedom of thought and speculation and teaching, and generally of religion. Now, in the twentieth century, intolerance threatens once more to become the order of the day. In spite of all our scientific expansion, our essential human rights are contracting.

The new dictatorship is nothing but the old tyranny writ large. I fear the new tyranny more than I fear the danger of another great war. Tyranny is infectious. As Burke said, it is a weed which grows in all soils, and it is its nature to spread. Even in this island home of constitutional freedom, I do not know that you are quite immune. Democracy seems to be going out of favour and out of fashion, and unless its methods can be overhauled, its unpopularity may involve the cause of liberty itself.

Let me state quite clearly that I am not against new experiments in human government. The extraordinary difficulties and complications of modern government call for revised methods and new experiments. What I am here concerned with is the serious threat to freedom and self-government which is involved in the new experiments now being tried out on the Continent. They are all based on a denial of liberty—not as a temporary expedient, but on principle.

The assertion that they aim at the eventual enlargement of liberty is vain in view of the fundamental negation of liberty on which they are based, and the absorption of the individual by a State or group, which is their real objective.

I maintain that such a basis of human government is an anachronism, and a moral impossibility in our Western civilisation. The denial of free human rights must in the long run lead to a cataclysm. The machinery of democracy may call, and does call, for reform, and the methods of enabling the people to exercise in freedom their influence on government may have to be altered from those at present in vogue. But to suppose that in the modern world you can dispense with freedom in human government, that you can govern without the consent of the governed, is to fly in the face of decent human nature as well as the facts of history. Dictatorship can only be tolerated as a temporary expedient, and can never be a permanent substitute for free self-government. Freedom is the most ineradicable craving of human nature. Without it peace, contentment and happiness, even manhood itself, are not possible. The declaration of Pericles in his great funeral oration holds for all time:

Τὸ εὔδαιμον τὸ ἐλεύθερον.
τὸ δὲ ἐλεύθερον τὸ εὔψυχον:

"Happiness is freedom, and freedom is courage." That is the fundamental equation of all politics and all human government, and any system which ignores it is built on sand.

The denial of what is deepest in our spiritual nature must lead to a material mechanist civilisation where economic goods take the place of the spiritual values and where mankind can at best only achieve a distorted and stunted growth, a sort of substitute or "Ersatz" humanity—very different from that which has been our ideal through the ages.

In these days of widespread backsliding, of lukewarmness or downright disloyalty to our fundamental human ideals, the countries which have always been in the forefront of the historic fight for human liberty have a very grave duty imposed on them. They cannot refuse the challenge of the times. They dare not abandon the cause which our forefathers rightly placed along with religion itself as calling for the highest loyalty and the greatest sacrifices. For even more than political principles and constitutions are at stake. The vision of freedom, of liberation of the human spirit from its primeval bondage is, perhaps, the greatest which has yet dawned on our human horizon. It forms the real spur of progress, the lure of our race in its ceaseless striving towards the future.

According to Plato, the movement of the world is from brute force to freedom, from fate or necessity to reason, from compulsion to persuasion. Man's progress through the ages is from a regime of domination to one of understanding, consent and free co-operation. That great moment of liberation of the human spirit is the glory of our past. It is also our inescapable programme for the future. We look to our young men and women to carry forward that programme and to band themselves together for the defence of what is most precious in our civilisation.

In the long run only the spirit of international comradeship can solve the problems of freedom and of peace. But in the meantime the supreme cause has to be kept going and to be safeguarded from all danger till the coming of a new renascence of the European spirit.

More and more will to freedom should be our real motive power. In the uncertainties and paralysing perplexities of today, freedom should not merely be our abstract political ideal, but a creative force, inspiring our young men and women to noble action.

The inner freedom and harmony of the soul; social freedom and equality before the law as the foundation of the State; international freedom in the rule of peace and justice; these should be the creative ideals of the new age, instead of sterilising the repressions of the past and still more sterilising the tyrannies which are forging new shackles for the human spirit. Creative freedom is the watchword of the new order to the realisation of which we should bend our energies. I have no doubt that the present disquieting phase will pass and a new renascence of the European spirit will follow.

What a glorious opportunity to our youth today to live in times when the situation is once more fluid and the world is once more in the re-making. Are we going to leave a free field to those who threaten our fundamental human ideals and our proudest heritage from the past? Or are we going to join in battle—an agelong battle which has been going forward from the dawn of history—for the breaking of our bonds and the enlargement of our range of free choice and free action? Remembering the great appeal of Pericles which rings through the ages, let us seek our happiness in freedom, and bravely do our part in hastening the coming of the great day of freedom.

CHAPTER VI

THE STATUTE OF WESTMINSTER

Field Marshal Smuts has made many brilliant speeches in the Union House of Assembly, but as parliamentary debate deals mainly with controversies of the day only two of the Prime Minister's speeches in Parliament have been selected for this book. It is the speech Field Marshal Smuts, then Minister of Justice in General Hertzog's Fusion Cabinet, made on the Status Bill in April, 1934. It was not only acclaimed as a brilliant peroration, but was notable as a lucid exposition of the constitutional developments which found expression in the Statute of Westminster.

It is of considerable historical importance because it not only set out the constitutional changes of the British Commonwealth of Nations, but the new Status of the Union. And at this stage it is worth recalling that the revolutionary departure from the Empire tradition made by the Statute of Westminster has stood the crucial test of war, as Field Marshal Smuts confidently predicted it would.

IN HIS introductory remarks, Field Marshal Smuts emphasised that the Status Bill had been drawn up simply to put into legal language, as far as human knowledge could do, the actual constitutional position as the Cabinet understood it, and that it represented a common measure of agreement between the two wings of the Government (Nationalist and South African Party).

Field Marshal Smuts proceeded:

What does this Bill say? It begins with a preamble which

deals quite clearly and frankly with, and sets out quite fully, the whole position as it has developed since 1926. It starts with that basic declaration of 1926—the Balfour declaration of 1926—sets forth what happened subsequently, the Statute of Westminster, and in that way the preamble sets forth the whole position under our common law, that we have a system of States equal, autonomous, free, none subject to the other; that we are a free association in the British Commonwealth of Nations, and that we owe common allegiance to the Crown. The matter is followed up by a schedule, which sets out the Statute of Westminster—not only the operative clauses, but even the preamble of the Statute of Westminster so far as it applies to South Africa. This Bill then goes on to make certain provisions, and I am going to mention under these provisions those which seem to be important and ought to be discussed in this House.

In the first place, we have the provision which says who our King is in the constitution. The present King is known and settled, and we extend the provision to his heirs and successors too, to provide for the future. There is no change in that and it has been the practice hitherto, and has been laid down in the South Africa Act of 1910. No change is made there. And surely it is a matter of great importance that we should have this solemn reaffirmation, in what will largely be our constitution in future, of the position of the Crown as existing hitherto, and as was laid down in the South Africa Act. Surely in the light of all the controversies which have raged in this country, it is a matter of profound importance that it should be done. No change is made. We are expressing once more for the present and for the future the existing constitutional position of the Crown. I look upon that as most important. This is the first important provision.

The second provision that is important deals with what is called here "the sovereignty of Parliament." All that we say here on this provision of the Bill is this, that no British Act shall apply to this country unless it is covered by an Act of our own Parliament. There may be some residuary power left in the British Parliament. I do not know. It is not a matter that we need argue upon now, but we make the position perfectly plain as far as we are concerned, that is, that only an Act of our Parliament will bind South Africa in future. If there is a British Act and it has to have any relation to us, we must make it our Act. That is what is laid down here. Surely we are not travelling in the least beyond either the existing practice or the Statute of Westminster.

Now we come to the Executive Government. It is provided that in executive government, both in internal and in external affairs, the King acts on the advice of his South African Ministers. I ask whether that has not been the practice. There is only one answer to that. It has been the uniform and invariable practice in this country ever since we received a constitution in 1910. There has never been any other way of acting. The King or the Governor-General as his deputy has always and invariably acted in the executive government of the country on the advice of his Ministers. It has been our practice, it is the British practice. As long as there is a Government the King acts on its advice, and no innovation whatever is made here on the practice that has existed hitherto. It is the very nature of responsible government.

Responsible government means that the King acts on

the advice of his Ministers, and if he did not there would not be responsible government, there would be autocracy. I am trying to prove my case that we have not travelled an inch beyond the existing practice and the existing law. These are the provisions, the really important and governing provisions, in this Bill—who is our King in South Africa, what is the authority of our Parliament and who is our executive government. And I say that in the provisions laid down here, which were very carefully considered in the Cabinet and drafted and redrafted, over and over again, we have tried to express what is the existing position in practice and what has been agreed to at Imperial Conferences and laid down in the Statute of Westminster. Col. Stallard says we have travelled in two or three respects beyond the existing position. I am going to deal with the exceptions which he says we have made to the existing position. He says that where we use the words "sovereign independence" in the preamble, that is new, and travels beyond the existing position. There may be some difference of opinion as to the wisdom and expediency of using those words, but if you ask me the question whether we have the right and are we right to call our present status by that name, then I have no doubt whatever, and I think there can be no doubt. The whole position rests on that fundamental and governing declaration of the conference in 1926. It is set out here, in the preamble, and to my mind the most important part of that declaration, which is often overlooked. It is what I may call the equation between Great Britain and the dominions. That is the governing thing. That was the most daring part of the declaration of 1926, to equate Great Britain with the dominions. She is mentioned with them, she is lumped together with them, in this declaration. That I call the great equation of our commonwealth, upon which our commonwealth rests. If that equation is fundamental, if that is really what this great declaration of 1926 meant, then how can you conceivably argue that the dominions are not sovereign international independent States, without denying that Great Britain, which is equated with them, has that status in the world? It seems to me an utter absurdity, and it is only the unwillingness of some of my friends to face that situation that makes them boggle over this language.

The British statesmen did not boggle over it. This formula was agreed to by the most powerful conservative government that Great Britain has ever had. This formula was drafted by two of the most able and experienced Ministers that England has ever had. Lord Balfour is especially associated with this declaration. Surely he was not the man to be caught napping, or to use words in absent-mindedness. He wrote down his formula, and the other man who was responsible more than any other was the Lord Chancellor of that day, probably the most brilliant Lord Chancellor England has had in our generation, Lord Birkenhead. These were two of the brilliant men on the British side. Lord Birkenhead stood out amongst the Lord Chancellors of our day and was probably one of the ablest men to have held that position. Then we had Lord Balfour. His experience, wisdom and knowledge of the Empire was such as no one could question. These men were not afraid. These men wrote down the grand equation of the commonwealth which equates Great Britain with the dominions. Do not let us boggle over the words.

If Great Britain is a sovereign international State, then by the laws of Euclid, by the laws of thought, the same thing can be applied to any of the dominions. This was not only great statesmanship, but it was great faith in the future of the Empire, of the commonwealth. These men knew the traditions of their race. They knew the essence of the British constitution, they knew and they had faith in the other members of the Empire and they did not boggle over the formula of equality. Do not let us do it. Although some of us may not like the word, some of us may hark back to the past and to what my hon. friend has somewhat ungenerously called the "Crown colony mentality"—do not let us here in this country do that.

Let us have equal faith and equal pride in British institutions, and in the nature of the great group to which we belong. Freedom, equality are the essence of it. I do not think we have made a departure there, except in the mere form of words. Nothing is implied in the words "sovereign independence" which is not implied by the whole full Balfour formula as written down. It has been pointed out in this debate that sovereign independence in the preamble is defined by those resolutions and declarations of the past. That is so. But I am not labouring that point. I think we are on safe ground by pinning our faith to that grand equation that was laid down in 1926 and which is the very foundation and will continue to be the foundation of the Empire. If there is to be any question of that equation, then it will be a bad day for our whole group.

Now I come to the second point which my hon. friend (Col. Stallard) says is new. He says that in providing that the King in his government in South Africa acts on the advice of his Ministers, we have divided the Crown; he says that we have intended doing it and we have done it. He says that under the Statute of Westminster the possibility arises of divided counsels, and therefore if the Empire has to be kept together on great critical and crucial occasions, there must be some authority to keep the commonwealth together, and he says that we have taken that power away. He says we are binding the King, or his deputy in South Africa, to act on the advice of Ministers here. He says the King can no longer exercise that prerogative of personal decision on critical occasions which will allow him to save the Empire.

Now my answer to that is this. There is no such prerogative. I tried to push my friend for precedents on other occasions where the King had exercised that prerogative of personal action in cases of difference.

There is no such prerogative, and if there were such a prerogative left in England, then the British constitution would be an entirely different thing from what it is. The King would be an autocrat. The argument of the hon. member (Col. Stallard) is this: The Statute of Westminster leaves the opening or creates the opening for divided counsels, and therefore the King must have this prerogative which will make united action possible. He must in the last resort take personal action and make a personal decision. I know my British constitution. I know it from the books, I know it because I have seen it work, and I have actually taken part in its working, and I can assure my friend that there is no such action possible for the King, there is no such prerogative. That prerogative stopped hundreds of years ago; it is a feudal prerogative, which goes back to the Stuart times or earlier. The King has no prerogative of acting on his own without the advice and counter-signature of his Ministers. What is the prerogative of the King today? He has one undoubted prerogative, and that is to appoint his Prime Minister. We have all agreed that that is the King's prerogative.

Mr. Coulter: He can dissolve Parliament and appeal to the country.

Smuts: I am inclined to think so myself, but I just want to tell my hon. friend that there is no agreement about that. There is no agreement that the King can dissolve Parliament and dismiss his Ministry without their being first defeated in Parliament. I qualify my statement on this point. I am quite sure that constitutional lawyers are unanimous in thinking that the King has the prerogative of appointing his own Prime Minister without consulting anyone. Sometimes he does consult, but he need not. There is the celebrated case where Mr. Gladstone resigned in 1893, and Lord Rosebery was appointed by the Queen as his successor without Mr. Gladstone being consulted. That appears from the correspondence which was published since. There is no question about that. It is customary for the King to consult his trained advisers, but he has undoubtedly the prerogative of deciding who the Prime Minister is to be, and the Governor-General here acts in the same way. But it is perhaps questionable whether he has the other prerogative. That is the prerogative of the King.

What else is there? You may say that he has the prerogative to veto a Bill passed by both Houses, but it is more than questionable whether that veto is still part of his prerogative. It has not been exercised, I believe, for more than 200 years, and if it is part of his prerogative, it is a dead prerogative. There is no prerogative on the part of the King to act on great occasions on his own. He cannot declare war on his own, he must act on the advice of his

Ministers, and whatever proclamation is issued must be countersigned by his Ministers. He cannot make peace on his own. It is done on the advice of his Ministers. The King has no prerogative such as my friend there has suggested.

The British constitution rests on common sense, it rests on wisdom, it rests on insight, it rests on great experience and on human nature, and on none of these technicalities of law to which my hon. friend alludes. If the King did otherwise, he might lose his head as has happened before, or he would initiate a revolution.

There is no such prerogative, and if such a crisis were to arise we have only to rely on the innate sense of statesmanship, prudence and deep-seated sentiments that bind together our great group of nations, for there is no prerogative in law but only common sense and human wisdom. These are the points of new departure which my hon. friend has mentioned. There is no such prerogative as he says we take away. I would like to say a few words as to the points made by Mr. Coulter; he took a different line. He was also very strongly opposed to the use of the term "sovereign independence," and he also thought that there should be a central authority for the day of emergency. The King has no such functions in the British Empire and never will have; he is in quite a different position. The hon. member added another argument: that the South African Party has always stood for a clear position. We have fought secession, neutrality and a republic, and all these things he thinks are wrapped up in this constitution. He says we are making a surrender of what we have stood for. I would say to him that I stand absolutely where I stood before. I have said so to the Prime Minister, and he has agreed. We want in this document to lay down that broad basis of a constitution on which 95 per cent. of these people are agreed.

To my mind these things, secession, neutrality and the like, are impracticable and academic. I do not believe that anything we can say in a constitution will settle our attitude or influence it when we come to the day of secession or to the day to declare our neutrality. These events, if ever they come to pass, would shake the whole British Empire and perhaps the whole world to its foundations. It is futile. You may talk about these things in a debating way if you are a debating society, but men who have been through the ordeals we have been through attach no importance to formulae of words. Consider, for example, the position of the United States of America during the war. The United States did her utmost to keep out of the Great War. She fought a presidential election during the war to keep out of it, and everybody was pledged to the full to keep out of the war; but in spite of all in a couple of months she was in the war. She could not maintain her neutrality. Whether it is neutrality or secession or any of these things, they will be decided, not by legal documents or the phraseology of a Bill like this, but by the ordeal of facts, of great events which might shake not only this country, but even the world, to its foundations. But sufficient unto the day is the evil thereof. Wise men leave these things alone.

There is nothing in this Bill which we are offering the people of this country to which I think any legitimate exception can be taken. I know the fears, I know the misgivings of some of my friends, but I give them my solemn assurance that, having studied these documents to the full, having given them as much attention as I can give them after a lifetime of experience in these matters, I find nothing in them that I cannot ask my people to ratify and to agree to. I go further, and I would say this here today, that this is the sort of settlement which, in the light of my experience, I would recommend my party and my people in South Africa to accept, because this is the sort of settlement that seems to me, and that always seemed to me, to make for the abiding peace of South Africa. Full sovereign status, freedom to the utmost without limit, but always in the group of comrades and friends with which we have marched hitherto in our history.

Here you have it. This Bill gives us a full sovereign status and is intended to give that; but it also, at the same time, equally emphasises the other aspect of our position, and that is that we belong to a group of friends, a free world-wide association of States. We may leave it in the ripeness of time, but that is the group to which we belong. The King is the symbol of this free association, and common allegiance to him, right through this great group, keeps it together. It seems to me that this is the sort of settlement which I would, if I were a dictator, dictate to South Africa. So far from betraying the position I have stood for, and the confidence of my friends, so far from doing anything that ought to shake their confidence, this is the sort of solution that, if it were in my power, if I were a dictator, I would prescribe to South Africa.

One never knows in this country what the next phase will be. But I have profound faith in this country, and I would ask my friends who do not quite agree with me to have faith in South Africa. I have quoted to them the case of the British statesmen who had faith in what they call the "British Empire"—not only in their little island people, but faith in the whole group spread over the world; and I ask my fellow-citizens here in South Africa: "Have faith in South Africa." After all, we have come grandly out of the struggles of the past—through all that South Africa has undergone, and it has been tested as no other young nation has been tested in history. In our generation she has been tested to the utmost, and she has always come out with flying colours, and she is still moving forward. There has been no wreckage; there has been no fatal mistake by her people, but they have always been guided by sound sense—a nose, so to say, for the right; and I have the fullest faith that South Africa will continue like that.

Do not fear. Do not look to phrases and to words, but look to the character of the people. They have struggled in the past, and have had controversies which seemed to shake the country. But again they have come together and have co-operated. They have done their duty on great occasions and have not let their country down. And I say, when we deal with a document like this, and launch forward into the dark future—a future which is darker for the whole world than for South Africa—let us have some faith in the people of South Africa—in their innate sense of what is fair and right, and in their wisdom and their practical statesmanship. The past has taught us that in that faith we do not go wrong. I appeal to my friends to accept the Bill in that spirit, and I appeal to the country also to do so. I was profoundly moved the other night by what my hon. friend Dr. Bremer said about "nasie trots" (national pride). I know it goes very deep. To a large section of our people their pride is not only a national pride, but a personal pride.

We shall never have peace in South Africa until we satisfy that. We must settle it once for all. We have had two roots of division in the past: one root was racial and the other was constitutional. The racial root is withering. More and more you see people fraternising and doing away with the dead racial issues of the past. We shall continue to have difficulties and racial questions—all is not yet lovely in the garden. But the root is withering, as I say. Let us now cut the other root. I hope that this Bill will cut the root of the constitutional controversies which, for a generation, have divided South Africa and convulsed it to its foundations. In cutting it we are rendering South Africa the greatest service possible, and laying a sure foundation for the future.

Unless we remove these fundamental causes of difference, we shall have no peace in this country. Do not think you will be able to discuss your economic questions in a fair and proper spirit. Do not talk about that, because over it all will be the poison of this controversy, this feeling that justice has not been done to the people of this country, that their status has not been recognised. Remove that, satisfy that feeling. It is a good and proper feeling, it is a human feeling of national self-respect, which nobody should resent. What we are doing here, and we are asking our friends who have that feeling, also to agree, is to confirm our friendship and our association with our group. I know that my English friends especially are profoundly attached to what is called the British connection. Whatever can be said in human language to affirm the British connection is said in this Bill. That being so, and both sections of our population being satisfied and their aspirations being fairly met, let us accept this Bill. Let us not start a controversy among our people. Do not let us divide them, because we honestly mean to do the right thing by them, and to keep them together, now that we have brought them together. Let us accept this Bill, and give it to South Africa as one of the foundation stones of her future unity and strength.

CHAPTER VII

EUROPE AND THE FAR EAST

In November, 1934, Field Marshal Smuts addressed the Royal Institute of International Affairs on British foreign policy. Field Marshal Smuts hoped then that wise statesmanship would save civilisation from the flowing tide of Nazism and the rising dangers in the Far East. He pleaded for a generous recognition of Germany's equal status, for friendship with Japan and for a strengthening of the moral influence of the League of Nations, then facing the first crucial test of Manchukuo. The origins of the second Great War will be found in the failure of Europe's Statesmen to carry out the policies advocated by Field Marshal Smuts in 1934.

AFTER paying a tribute to the work of the Institute, Field Marshal Smuts said: Looking at the European situation today, as distinct from the wider world situation (to which I shall refer later), I am deeply impressed by the fact that two underlying forces are today creating and shaping policies—the fear complex and the inferiority complex. Both are dangerous complexes, the symptoms of disease and not of healthy growth, and unless they are treated on wise lines they may in the long run produce very serious consequences for the public mind and life of the world. It may seem a humiliating confession to make, but it appears to be a fact that fear is today the real driving-force in our European relations. Fear, the meanest of

human motives, is today the master of us all. The victors
of the Great War, so far from feeling secure in their victory, are, in fact, obsessed with this almost neurotic fear.
And the vanquished are reacting in the obvious and inevitable way by refusing to accept their enforced inferiority and their position as second-class nations in the comity
of civilisation. The victors are actuated not by confidence,
but by fear of the defeated; the defeated are determined
to reconquer their lost equality with the victors. The mental reactions seem, in fact, to be reversing the rôles created
by the Great War.

It is all a very absurd and topsy-turvy state of affairs.
But it is this mental topsy-turvydom which is today driv-
ing Europe forward on the road to chaos. In these obsessions reason is in abeyance, the finer human instincts are
paralysed, and a wrong twist is being given to our future
development as a well-ordered continent. Every urgent
question becomes insoluble in this atmosphere of distor-
tion. Disarmament has almost suffered shipwreck when
every solid reason points to its necessity; and international
co-operation is endangered where every common European interest calls imperatively for it.

If Europe is to get back to the right road again, it seems
to me necessary that the nations, both victors and vanquished, should be cured of their Freudian obsessions,
should recover their commonsense and sanity, and should
once more see things in their right and normal relations.
There is no super-psychoanalyst to do this trick, but it is
at least necessary to diagnose the disease, to recognise that
it is a disease, and not a healthy normal condition. Once
Europeans admit to themselves that they are perhaps a
little mad the cure will come of itself. A sense of humour,

of good humour, and a little laughter at themselves will do the rest. "Know thyself," said the wise oracle. "Know thyself" is the word to be spoken to Europe today in its temporary obsessions and aberrations. There is no doubt that the present spell will pass, but what irreparable mischief is not being done while it is on! Let statesmen become the courageous doctors to their sick peoples, and the spell will soon pass.

One of the symptoms of this fear complex is the war talk which is now so common. It is represented that we are on the brink of another war, that war is waiting just round the corner. This war talk is creating a war atmosphere, and is more likely to lead to war than anything else. To me it seems all a vicious and dangerous mistake. And the curious thing is that pacifists are most responsible for the scaremongering. In their well-meant efforts to frighten people into disarming and to a sense of dangers to come they are actually fomenting the mentality that leads to war. To me it seems that the only shrewd, wide-awake people who indulge in war talk are the manufacturers and vendors of munitions. With all the emphasis at my command, I would call a halt to this war talk as mischievous and dangerous war propaganda. . . .

The remedy for this fear complex is the Freudian way of dragging it out from its hidden depths, bringing it into the open, and exposing it to the light of day. And this is exactly the method of the League of Nations. The League may not be a satisfactory source of security; it may be wanting in that element of sanctions which many consider so necessary. But, at any rate, it is an open forum for discussion among the nations; it is a round table for the statesmen, around which they can ventilate and debate their grievances and viewpoints.

The "Open Diplomacy" for which Woodrow Wilson so ardently pleaded is enshrined in the Covenant, and is today the settled and accepted method of international intercourse in the League. The League was designed to be first and foremost the round table of the nations, and at that table and in open discussion the secret fear complex can be treated along truly human and scientific lines.

There are those who say that this is not enough—that as long as the League remains merely a talking shop or debating society, and is not furnished with "teeth" or proper sanctions, the sense of insecurity will remain, and the fear complex will continue to dominate international relations. It is also felt that the inability of the League to guarantee the collective system by means of force, if necessary, is discrediting it and leading to its rapid decay. It is said that the crucial case of Manchukuo has exposed its real weakness and shown that, unless armed with force to carry out its policies, it is doomed. My answer to this is twofold.

In the first place, I cannot visualise the League as a military machine. It was not conceived or built for that purpose; it is not equipped for such functions. And if the attempt were now made to transform it into a military machine, into a system to carry on war for the purpose of preventing or ending war, I think its fate would be sealed. I cannot conceive the dominions remaining in such a League and pledging themselves to fight the wars of the Old World, and if the dominions leave it, Great Britain is bound to follow.

I cannot conceive anything more calculated to keep the

U.S.A. for ever out of the League than its transformation into a fighting machine, pledged to carry out its decisions by force of arms if necessary. And remember the U.S.A. has still to join the League before it will ever be its real self. Membership of the U.S.A. was the assumption on which the League was founded; defection of the U.S.A. has largely defeated its main objects. And the joining up of the U.S.A. must continue to be the ultimate goal of all true friends of the League and of the cause of peace. A conference room of the nations the U.S.A. can, and eventually will, join; it can never join an international War Office.

Remembering the debates on this point in the League of Nations Commission which drafted the Covenant, I say quite definitely that the very idea of a league of force was negatived there; and the League would be false to its great mission as the board of conciliation and settlement for the nations if it ever allowed itself to be turned into something quite different, something just the opposite to its original idea—into a League of force. The solution of the difficulty does not lie in that direction.

But, in the second place, experience since the inception of the League has in fact taught us the way out. Locarno has been incorporated into the League or the collective peace system. And Locarno establishes the principle of limited sanctions, of a smaller group within the League entering into mutual defensive arrangements under the aegis, and subject to the control, of the League. This does not throw the obligation to use force willy-nilly on all members, but binds only those who on grounds of their special situation and interests, choose to enter into such arrangements. The Eastern Pact or Locarno, which the

late M. Barthou proposed for Eastern Europe, as modified
by the British Government, would, if it does not miscarry,
be another such system of limited sanctions to buttress
peace within the League. Its present prospects are somewhat uncertain, but it may be that eventually some such
pact or pacts may yet be found feasible in Eastern Europe
and in other parts of the world.

[*In fact the Eastern Pact never materialised.*]

If the fear obsession in Europe can be removed only by
sanctions, then let it be on some such limited basis and
within the circumscribed area of those interested, and not
by a departure from the principles of universality and conciliation enshrined for ever in the Covenant. To endeavour to cast out the Satan of fear by calling in the Beelze-
bub of militarism, and militarising the League itself,
would be a senseless and indeed fatal proceeding. Whatever forces are used to support peace must be national,
and not League, forces, and must be assembled and employed by mutual defence arrangements of those concerned, made under the general supervision and sanction
of the League.

I have so far referred only to the fear complex and the
way to deal with it. But the other, or inferiority complex,
is very closely associated with it—in the same way that the
mentalities of victor and vanquished are closely associated.
If we desire peace, it is little use dealing with the one
without courageously tackling also the other. It is no use
piling up sanctions to remove fear if at the same time we
do not strike at the root of the inferiority complex. The
fear increases as the inferiority complex becomes more inflamed and threatening. The inferiority complex again becomes more inflamed as the fear complex arms itself with

defensive weapons. They reinforce and augment each other, and both together lead to a policy of fresh defensive armaments. Unless both are therefore dealt with we shall continue to keep moving in a vicious circle of the two complexes and of increasing armaments. Unless both the complexes are healed, I fear the policy of disarmament will continue to suffer the reverse which it has so far encountered. It is simply a case of cause and effect. The removal of the inferiority complex from Germany is just as essential to future peace as the removal of fear from the mind of France; and both are essential to an effective disarmament policy.

How can the inferiority complex which is obsessing and, I fear, poisoning the mind, and indeed the very soul of Germany, be removed? There is only one way, and that is to recognise her complete equality of status with her fellows, and to do so frankly, freely and unreservedly. That is the only medicine for her disease. And when we have summoned up sufficient courage to treat her in that human way, as our equal in the comity of nations, then, and not till then, will the old wound cease to fester and poison the life of Europe and the world. As long as recognition of her equal position is denied her, the sense of grievance and injury will continue to rankle. This is perfectly human, and it is this human situation which we should face with wisdom and courage.

While one understands and sympathises with French fears, one cannot but feel for Germany in the position of inferiority in which she still remains 16 years after the conclusion of the war. The continuance of her Versailles status is becoming an offence to the conscience of Europe and a danger to future peace. Surely there is sufficient human fellow-feeling left in Europe to see that the position has become intolerable and a public danger. There is no place in international law for second-rate nations, and least of all should Germany be kept in that position half a generation after the end of the Great War. Fair play, sportsmanship—indeed every standard of private and public life—calls for frank revision of the position. Indeed, ordinary prudence makes it imperative. Let us break those bonds and set the captive, obsessed soul free in a decent human way; and Europe will reap a rich reward in tranquillity, security, and returning prosperity.

Some people consider magnanimity out of place in international affairs. I have seen it in my own country change a position of dangerous potentialities into one of everlasting friendship between victor and vanquished. That is the way we humans are built. But if there is no place for magnanimity and generosity in European politics, at any rate here is a case where necessity and prudence point in the same direction and call for the same action.

Let us take that action before it is too late. Only such action can bring healing to the sick souls in Europe and lay the ghost of that inferiority complex which is rapidly becoming a flaming portent of danger to the future of our European system. The time is come to call the halt to these devastating passions and to make peace—to complete that true peace which we admittedly failed to make at Versailles.

Germany's equality of status has already been conceded in principle. This was done in December, 1932, when the Great Powers at the Disarmament Conference agreed to accord Germany "equality of rights in a regime of security." If this declaration had been followed up and acted on in the Conference itself Germany would today still be a member of the League, and not a disturbing factor outside it, and we should probably have had an agreement on a far-reaching measure of disarmament. Now she is out of the League, her armament position is wrapped in obscurity and danger, and the opportunity for a general measure of disarmament seems further off than ever. It is the story of the Sibylline books. The circle of the two complexes and of growing armaments is tightening round Europe. Let us hurry to untie the knot and set the good genius of European civilisation once more free from the bonds which may strangle her in future. The call to Europe is becoming ever more insistent to set her house in order, and not to allow present tendencies and complexes to become chronic. We dare not bequeath to the coming generation a legacy of chronic disorder which may prove more than they can bear. The suffering, fear-driven peoples of Europe, filled with anxieties and forebodings of the future, appeal with outstretched hands to their political leaders for wise guidance and courageous leadership.

Is it too much to hope that, with a great lead from the leaders now, a new atmosphere may even yet be created, and a new situation arise in which we could return to the more hopeful outlook which obtained more than a year ago, and in that friendly atmosphere resume the threads which were then so rudely broken off? A really great gesture even now may avail to dispel the fear and inferiority complexes and to render possible a new start in European relations and a propitious resumption even of the disarmament conversations. Europe may yet be steered into calmer waters and into an era of friendly collaboration. My point is that time is passing, and that what has to be done should be done quickly.

Germany declared at the end of last year that, if she was in principle accorded equality of rights, she was in practice willing to limit her defensive armaments so as to be no danger to her neighbours. The specific proposals in respect of her rearmament which she made were admitted by authoritative opinion, at least in this country, to be a not unreasonable basis of discussion. Why should a great opportunity to secure European peace, and so make a new start in European co-operation, be wantonly jettisoned? Repugnant as the principles of Nazism may be to many other Western peoples, that is no reason why Germany's equal international position should not be recognised and the obsessions which lie at the root of Nazism thereby removed. Russia, in spite of her Communism, has at last been welcomed into the circle of the League. Surely the necessity of recognising Germany's equal international status is no less imperative, whatever her internal political system may be.

Unfortunately, there is a spirit of fatalism and defeatism abroad. People shrug their shoulders and despair of anything being done. This is a spirit which ill becomes those who have learnt the lesson of the Great War. A resolute and determined effort even now may avail to save the situation, to bring Germany back to the Disarmament Conference and the League and probably to lead to a substantial step forward in agreed disarmament. But European statesmanship must clear its mind of obsessions, and screw up its courage and boldly take the necessary step in declaring Germany's equal status. If this is not done by agreement, it may soon come of itself. But with this difference, that, whereas the future armament of Germany could have been a matter of agreement with her neighbours, her self-asserted unilateral equality may lead to complete freedom in the matter of her rearmament. It will be with disarmament as it already is with reparations; in default of reasonable action and agreement while there is yet time both may founder and become obsolete issues in the march of events. Statesmanship will have abdicated and events will then decide.

So far I have confined my remarks to the European situation. Europe, like the poor, is always with us. But in the Far East a cloud is appearing which, although it is at present no greater than a man's hand, may come to overshadow the whole international sky in time. Already on its mere appearance it has severely shaken the League and led to menacing reactions in several directions.

People instinctively realise that there is a phenomenon of first-class order, which may have the most far-reaching effects on the fortunes of peace, and indeed of our civilisation. Manchukuo is perhaps not yet the parting of the ways, but it is the warning that we are coming to the parting of the ways and may soon have to make a very solemn choice in national policy.

I have always looked upon the Washington Treaties of 1922 as probably the greatest step forward yet taken since the peace on the road to a stable future world order. In 1921, at the Imperial Conference of that date, I stated my view that a great change was coming over world politics, and that the scene was shifting from the Atlantic to the Pacific. It was felt, and not by me only, that the future of the world would probably be decided, not in the Atlantic, but the Pacific Ocean and countries. The pot might

continue to boil in Europe for perhaps another generation, but in the end it would simmer down. Europe would
settle her essentially family quarrels in the end, and a state
of more or less peaceful equilibrium would be reached.
That feeling I have still. But for these tiresome and obsti-
nate neuroses to which I have referred, Europe would
probably already be settling down. The storm-centre will
pass away from the countries of Christian civilisation and
shift to the Far East. There the hand of destiny is still
writing in its unknown script—in a language and in ideas
which are scarcely intelligible to the Western mind.

The achievement of the Washington Conference was
just this—that in this new danger-zone of the future a concert or collective system of the Powers concerned had been
built up, a loose conference system, founded on certain
vital issues, which might do for the Far East what the
Geneva League was attempting to do in the West. Comparative naval power, the integrity of China, the open
door in that immense potential market, were agreed in
principle, and in case of any differences or danger arising
the Conference would meet for discussion. Here was the
most promising thing for world peace which had yet taken
place since the Covenant. The question which is now being raised is whether the promise of Washington will be
fulfilled and not prove to be a mere mirage. Manchukuo,
as I said, pointed the danger-signal. Now the treaty on
naval ratios seems to be in danger; and if that goes the
other issues settled at Washington may also be re-opened
and the whole Pacific Concert may collapse.

At present we are very much in the dark as to what is
actually going on. Conversations are taking place here between the parties to the Four-Power Treaty, the outcome

of which is still uncertain. Under these circumstances it would be futile, and may even be harmful, to enter upon a discussion of the merits of the naval questions involved, and I do not propose to do so now, even supposing I had the competence to do so. There is, however, an air of pessimism about the outcome of these conversations which gives food for thought. In view of this, and in view also of the far-reaching issues involved, it may perhaps be permissible to refer to certain broad aspects of the whole question and the fundamental considerations of policy which, I submit, should be steadily borne in mind, without going into the particular naval points which are at present the subject of secret exchanges. I therefore address myself to a few general observations on the underlying policies which strike me as pertinent.

In the first place, this threat to the continuance of the Washington arrangements and the Pacific Concert, with all it may ultimately involve, must be another serious call to Europe to put her house in order without undue delay. It must be plain to everybody that the rift in the lute now beginning in the East may have very disturbing effects on the European Concert as well. Whereas Europe, left to herself, may in the end come to some working equilibrium, the new trouble in the East may easily destroy that prospect. Adversity makes strange bedfellows, and those who have in the past talked loudest of the Yellow Peril may in future be tempted to look for friends in that unlikely quarter. The day when Europe calls in the Far East to redress the balance of the West will be an evil day for Western civilisation and the peace of the world. In view of the situation now developing in the Far East, European statesmen should redouble their efforts to compose Euro-

pean differences before it is too late. The dangers I allude
to are so evident that I need not dilate further on this
point.

In the second place, I would appeal most earnestly and
in the friendliest spirit to Japan as our old friend and
war-time ally, to pause before she puts in motion machinery which will in the end imperil the concert in the
Pacific. She has already given notice of withdrawal from
the League. If, in addition, she withdraws from the Washington Treaties, the whole collective system goes, so far as
she is concerned. For herself this might mean a position
of isolation which experience in the Great War has shown
to be most dangerous, even for the greatest of military
Powers. And for all, the disappearance of the Pacific Concert would be a matter of the gravest concern. The collective system is probably the most beneficent of all post-war
changes in international affairs, and its weakening or destruction might involve dangers the magnitude of which
none can foresee today. I therefore pray for the most serious reflection before the final plunge is taken.

In the third place, everything possible in the power of
diplomacy should be done to avoid even the appearance
of antagonism between the East and West. The potentialities of the situation are inherently serious enough, and
should not be rendered worse by one-sided diplomacy.
Asia is at a curious phase of her awakening. Complexes
there, too, are forming. The old exploitation or ascend-
ancy policies are out of place in such a situation, and
should be carefully avoided for the future. The past record
of the West in the East is not one to be proud of or to be
further copied.

While mindful of our duty and responsibility as trustees

for the greatest civilisation that this earth has ever known, we should avoid the assumption of superiority. Not the mailed fist, but the friendly, helping hand, should be in future the symbol of our association with Asia.

We are facing the greatest, most intriguing, most testing human situation which has probably ever arisen in history. It may well be that Western civilisation will stand or fall in this matter of its contacts with the immense human masses of the East. Here let it put its best foot forward and show that it is a universal system, based on the broadest and highest human principles, and not merely a local system for the European peninsula. In this spirit I would say, even if the present negotiations for naval ratios fail, do not let us depart from an attitude of friendliness and large human good will towards Japan. Good will, good temper, friendship, will solve the hardest problems of statesmanship yet. And they are specially called for as the ultimate instruments of diplomacy in our dealings with Asia. If we cannot and should not be allies, we can at least be friends, and proceed to the unknown dangers of the future in a spirit of understanding and friendliness. The old Japanese alliance may have been, and in my opinion was, a mistake. A policy of friendliness and understanding can never be a mistake, and will keep or make friends without thereby making enemies.

Fourthly, and subject to what I have just said, I wish to make another point which I consider no less important and vital. This is a difficult world, in which we have to walk warily, in which even good will may not be enough, and in which we are called upon to exercise a wise discretion as an insurance for the future. In this spirit I would say that to me the future policy and association of our great British Commonwealth lie more with the U.S.A. than with any other group in the world. If ever there comes a parting of the ways, if ever in the crises of the future we are called upon to make a choice, *that,* it seems to me, should be the company we should prefer to walk with and march with to the unknown future. On that path lie our past affiliations, our common moral outlook, our hopes and fears for the future of our common civilisation. Nobody can forecast the outcome of the stormy era of history on which we are now probably entering. Our best insurance in this unknown territory is to be with those with whom we have an instinctive and historic sympathy.

The British Commonwealth has its feet in both worlds. Through Great Britain its one foot is firmly planted on this old continent. Through the Dominions it has its other foot as firmly planted in the outer, newer world, where the U.S.A. already plays so great a part. The Dominions have even stronger affiliations towards the U.S.A. than Great Britain has.

There is a community of outlook, of interests, and perhaps of ultimate destiny between the Dominions and the U.S.A. which in essence is only the first and most important of them. Through the Dominions British policy is ultimately tied up with the U.S.A. in a very profound sense, which goes much deeper than the occasional jars which, perhaps, are more acutely felt at any particular moment. That fundamental affinity, coming from the past, stretching to the future, is, or must be, the real foundation of all British foreign policy. Any policy which ignores it, or runs counter to it, is calculated to have a disruptive effect on the Commonwealth as a whole. We are here on bedrock, which we ignore at our peril.

While, therefore, our Far Eastern policy should, I submit, be based on friendship with all, and exclusive alliances or understandings with none, the ultimate objectives of that policy should continue to conform to that general American orientation which has distinguished it since our association with the U.S.A. in the Great War. In this way our policy will correspond to the actual general situation of our Commonwealth in the world of today—a situation which goes much deeper than, and underlies, all public policies, and on which alone it is possible to base stable and enduring policies for the future. Any other course would mean building our Commonwealth policy on quicksands and placing the future of this group at the mercy of incalculable accidents.

In saying this I do not wish to import any note of exclusiveness in our policies or our world outlook. The day is surely gone for the old exclusive outlooks of the past, and for the alliances and balances of power which were based on that outlook. In spite of all appearances to the contrary, we have in this respect made progress in the post-war period. The principle of universality on which the Covenant and the new world order are based is slowly making headway. More and more the recognition is winning through that there really is a society, and not merely a collection of nations. The League of Nations in itself implies a society of nations. Not in our separateness and exclusiveness, not in mere nationalism, either political or economic, lies the way out of our present troubles, but in our steadily increasing sociality, in the interweaving of interests, viewpoints and ideas, in the open door and the removal of barriers and restrictions, in the dominance of large human principles transcending national boundaries, and in the recognition that in mankind we are members of one another. More and more we are recognising that, in spite of racial and political barriers, humanity is really a whole.

It is in this steadily-growing mutuality of our relations, in this ever-increasing wholeness of our human relationships, that I see the only possible ultimate solution of our present discords. Here lies the true line of progress for the future. And the more we recognise this wholeness of mankind, this integral character of all our relationships, the surer our success will be in the great adventure of human government, and the brighter the prospects will be for that world of ordered liberty and peace which we are out to build. The driving-force in this human world of ours should be, not morbid fears or other sickly obsessions, but this inner urge towards wholesome integration and co-operation. The drive towards holism, which I have elsewhere pointed to as at the basis of nature and the creative process in this universe, is equally operative in our human society. Unless it is artificially interfered with and thwarted, it will lead us forward to sanity, wholeness and wholesomeness and rid us of the pathological obsessions which are today producing so much friction and dislocation at every step of our adventure.

I thank you for the patience with which you have listened to me, even when you may not have agreed with some of my views. What I have said in all sincerity is simply meant as a plea for understanding by one who has no axe to grind and whose sphere of work lies far from the political battlefront of Europe. Ever since Versailles, where I entered my first protest, I have felt very deeply that the real peace was still to come, and that it would be a peace not merely of mechanical arrangements of the territorial or economic kind, but something psychological, something in the nature of European reconciliation, something reaching down to and resting on our common human and Christian foundations. In that spirit I have once more pleaded for peace tonight. I hope that our statesmen will yet lead us to that peace before it is too late—that is to say, before new, sinister forces have advanced and taken possession of the field and imperilled what centuries of European effort have accomplished for our human advance. I feel the hour of action has come, or is rapidly coming, and we all pray that our leadership, for which we feel the profoundest sympathy, will not fail us in this crisis of our fate.

CHAPTER VIII

THE SOUTH AFRICAN SPIRIT

Field Marshal Smuts was suffering from one of his rare indispositions when the Imperial Press Conference opened in Cape Town in 1935, but on March 22 he spoke at a dinner in Cape Town to the Press delegates on a theme close to his heart—the South African Spirit.

THE PRESS CONFERENCE has been a most welcome event for South Africa. The Conference consists of leaders of the Press from all parts of our Commonwealth, under your distinguished leadership, Mr. Chairman (Major J. J. Astor, of *The Times*).

For South Africa your visit has been a great event. I doubt whether we have ever before had such wonderful publicity as you have given us. At the same time I trust that you have had an interesting time and enjoyed yourselves. The visit has been to our mutual advantage, but I am sure that South Africa has had the best of the bargain. The publicity we so much need, and for which we generally have to pay heavily in your pages, we have now had in the best and most attractive form, and for no expense at all. In your reports and speeches you have meted out praise and blame to us, especially praise, in a way that is best calculated to arrest attention abroad, and we expect a rich harvest as the result of your visit. What we value most is your personal interest in South Africa as leaders of the world Press. After your visit we may now hope to be more than merely a geographical expression to your readers. We may now have a fair chance of becoming a real entity and live community to the outside world.

You have travelled far and wide over the expanses of this country, and have formed your own personal impression of it and its people. We have come close to you, we have in a true sense become real to you, as you have become to us. To the ordinary, casual visitor South Africa is interesting mostly because of two things—our natives and our game. These are the original inhabitants of the country, and I admit their importance and their interest for you. The Europeans of this country, and the Western civilisation they have built, are commonplace and drab in comparison, and yet they are also important, even if they are not particularly interesting.

In this visit round the country you have had the advantage over the ordinary globe-trotter, that you have seen not only natives and game, but also the type of Europeans we are breeding in this new country and the standard of civilisation we are trying to uphold under the difficult conditions of Africa. You have seen our farms and villages and cities, our diamond and gold mines, our mountains and deserts and rivers, with or without water. You have sampled our weather, and you have breathed our great air, surely the finest in all the world.

You will now go back to your own great countries, with most of which South Africa cannot for a moment hope to bear comparison. You will see again the green hills of the British Isles and the great cities with their teeming millions and high civilisation; you will see again Canada and Australia, with their endless wheatfields, and New Zealand, the gem, I am told, of the Commonwealth. But in all that grandeur of your home countries you will think back to this strange, primitive land, its curious history, its unique physical features, its flora and fauna found nowhere else, its human races ranging from the very lowest to the highest, its dark problems, some of the hardest ever offered to us humans to solve.

At a distance and in retrospect you will sometimes think of South Africa, and of its strange fascinations, attractive to some, repellent to others. You will try to picture its unknown past, and you will perhaps speculate on its future, on what fate has in store for this country and its great human experiment.

It is not for me to describe your impressions, but I am sure that one thing must have especially struck you—the optimism, the confident outlook of our people, that must have met you everywhere in your travels. Whatever our difficulties and our problems, there is nothing defeatist about the South African outlook. There is hopefulness, buoyancy, resilience everywhere. Not that we are out of the wood; not that we are not oppressed with difficulties and problems enough, but they do not unduly depress us.

You may say, "Oh, ah, but that is due to your gold mines. How could you be depressed with an annual cheque of over £70,000,000 for your gold? It is the one article in the world today for which there is an unlimited market. Oh, fortunate South Africa, with its gold and other mines!"

Grant you that. Our gold means much to us, and in many ways is seeing us through what might very well have been a most difficult situation. But there is more than gold. The people are more than the gold. The people of this country are really doing their best to set their house in order, to build on sound foundations as a State, and to secure the widest measure of public co-operation among themselves. Their differences of language, race, origin and tradition make this effort at co-operation all the more necessary and all the more difficult. But racial co-operation and good will have at last become the accepted policy of this country.

It is the history of this country that inclines us to optimism. South Africa has passed through dark and difficult passages in her history; more than once she has stood face to face with stark disaster. For generations she has been tried and tested as perhaps no other young country of our day has been tested, but a kind Providence has never quite forsaken her. More than once statesmanship here and in Great Britain has come to her rescue. Here we have seen how in a nation's story good comes out of evil; how good will in the end smooths out the tangles and mistakes; how an era of construction follows the destruction and bitter struggles of races and of war. It is this experience that has given us faith in human nature, and makes us believe that whatever the future may bring we shall not utterly fail. History, sunshine, religion, all combine to make South Africans optimists on the whole. You have seen this temperament for yourselves, and I trust it has been a good and exhilarating experience, and that you will take to your homes this impression of the sunshine in the land and in the soul of South Africa.

I have noticed that many people in England consider me that strangest of all animals in these distraught times —an optimist. You will have learnt here the reason why not only I, but South Africans generally, black as well as white, are on the whole inclined towards optimism. We carry our burdens lightly and with a smiling face. We do not believe in failure, and do not think the end of the world is coming.

Some weeks ago in an address to our local Institute of International Affairs I discussed the present situation, as I see it, and referred to some of the danger-signals in the Far East. A French publicist, in commenting on my speech with some bitterness, said that the shadow over this century is not the danger of the Far East, but the imminent break-up of the British Empire. The movement of the various Dominions towards full nationhood and status appeared to this critic to be threatening the break-up of the Empire, and its weakening as an international factor of first-class importance. That is how I understand his remarks. As South Africa has been one of the foremost among the Dominions in her assertion of her own independent status, you will bear with me if for a few moments I comment on this criticism. There is this to be said for our French critic. Foreigners as a rule find the British Commonwealth a strange and unintelligible phenomenon. To them it is a political and constitutional enigma.

They found the old British Empire of the pre-war type difficult enough to understand, but this strange phenomenon of an association of equal sovereign States under the Crown, which we call the Commonwealth, is to them an utter mystery. Hence this talk of a shadow on the 20th century, which is really nothing worse than a darkness in the mind of the foreign critic. In the years before the Great War these gentlemen were very much concerned about signs of break-up in the British Empire, but the Great War showed how completely they had misunderstood the situation. In the Empire today they are even more deeply puzzled. How can freedom and Empire march together? Surely such a thing has never happened before in history? Surely there must be some great disaster looming in the near future that will cause the greatest international upset in the world? Such is their reading of the situation, as reflected in the French remarks I have referred to.

I need not point out to this gathering what a complete misreading this is of the actual position in our Commonwealth. What holds us together is not force at the centre, as in former empires. If force is the only nexus, then this group of ours would be doomed as all previous empires have been doomed. But our group is founded not on force or compulsion, but on freedom, equality and loyal friendship among its component members.

We have set out to prove that equal sovereign States under a common Crown are a more stable combination in these dangerous times than any other form of political union. That great experiment is enshrined in the Balfour formula and the Statute of Westminster, which we have adopted in South Africa in our own Status Act. How could the U.S.A., in the ripeness of time, have remained in a great commonwealth with Great Britain? How can the Dominions of today, with the great destiny in store for them, remain in an enduring group for the future?

These are the questions we are now trying to answer. We are not afraid of equality, of liberty, of sovereignty. We welcome them as inevitable developments, and on them as a basis and foundation we build our great co-operative group. It has already outlasted the empires of our day, and long may it continue as a bulwark of freedom and progress in the civilisation of the world.

We are trying the greatest, most audacious experiment in human government, and we dare try it because our group is not afraid of liberty and equality. In a system resting on force, liberty and equality may be as explosive as dynamite: in a system such as ours they are the only possible ties.

We plan to continue as a united group when some of the present Dominions may have reached an even greater stature than Great Britain itself. It is only on the basis of full self-determination, and the sovereign status of the component States, that such a situation could be possible and such a group could endure.

Our experience in South Africa is in complete agreement with the spirit of this great Commonwealth experiment. You, gentlemen, have looked with curious and critical eyes at this country. You have watched our sayings and our doings. You must have convinced yourselves that here, indeed, is one of the most loyal supporters and co-operators in our Commonwealth system. But only a generation ago this country was locked in a grim and deadly struggle with the old British Empire. We Boers fought for freedom and independence. We found it in a strange way, where we least expected.

It is, indeed, one of the miracles of these latter days. British statesmanship gave us our freedom as a free gift. We accepted that gift, and with it as a key we then proceeded to help you to unlock the doors of the old Empire and to reconstruct it in the free co-operative system under the Crown which it is today.

Your great gift of freedom to us we returned to you in

the form of the new conception of a freely associated Commonwealth, in the shaping of which South Africa has played a foremost part. It has been a great transaction, a great exchange in freedom, in which we have mutually benefited each other, and the enemies of yesterday are the firm and loyal friends of today and tomorrow; and, one prays, for ever.

South Africa is, indeed, one of the finest, most heartening chapters in this story of freedom. But we can understand that the logical French critic misses all this, and sees only decay where there is, in fact, the most promising new growth for the future government of man. Considering the history of South Africa, can you wonder that we incline to optimism and faith in human nature? I trust you will carry some of this optimism back with you to your countries. . . .

CHAPTER IX

THE THEORY OF HOLISM

We all know and admire Smuts, the soldier-statesman, but to a smaller circle he is respected for his brilliant scientific attainments which received world-wide recognition when he was elected President of the British Association for the Advancement of Science in its Centenary Year. Three chapters in this book place on record Field Marshal Smuts's speeches on science. One of his most important contributions to science is Holism, a theory of philosophy which has a bearing on Field Marshal Smuts's political faith. This theory is explained in his book "Holism and Evolution," but a more simple exposition is given in this chapter, based on the "Star" report of a lecture given by Field Marshal Smuts at the Witwatersrand University on September 21, 1927.

AFTER expressing his surprise at being called upon to address such a mighty audience (there were more than a thousand people present) instead of the few pale-faced, bespectacled students he had expected, Field Marshal Smuts, who spoke *extempore,* said: "I think it is all a mistake. This great gathering looks like a political meeting —(laughter)—but my great consolation tonight is that it will not be broken up—(laughter and applause). It is my experience that the Bolsheviks of philosophy, unlike the Bolsheviks of politics, are really quite mild and harmless and well-behaved."

Field Marshal Smuts recalled Mr. Merriman's denunciation of Johannesburg as "the University of Crime." Johannesburg years ago had been a place merely for the acquisition of wealth; now it was clear that the things of the spirit were cherished among them. The subject on which he was to speak was one that took him off the beaten track he had been following for some time. He had been down in the valley of politics, with all its darkness and its mire; now, in their company, he could rise to the heights again. He would endeavour to give a simple, popular statement of his theory. He was not a trained expositor in philosophy. Philosophy was not a subject he discussed with anybody. He was just a seeker among seekers.

"When I was young I saw a light, and I have followed that light ever since. We all feel we have to be guided by some light through the maze of life. What I have done in philosophy is more from a general standpoint, without any technical thought. I have simply tried to hammer out some rule of thought to carry my action along.

"In our day it is all the more necessary for us to hammer out a new point of view. There is no doubt that we are living in a most extraordinary era, and I think the words of the poet apply here:

> 'The old world dead,
> The new unready to be born.'

"We have left behind us a great era in the history of the world. We do not see it yet, and we are in the transition period between the two. It is one of the most interesting and also one of the most difficult periods for any generation to pass through.

"What we want is some larger synthesis, some concepts that will bring together the vast details with which we have to deal. There has been an immense movement forward in thought, science, philosophy and all forms of human development. We are now running the risk of getting lost, becoming submerged in the details, and it is all-important for us to get some larger view of all this vast mass. We want what Professor Hoernle would call after Plato, the 'synoptic vision' over all these details.

"If we could have that vision much of our present-day perplexities would disappear. I have no 'synoptic vision.' I have only an idea that occurred to me and which may, to some small extent, help to guide us through the surrounding difficulties.

"Holism is an attempt at synthesis, an attempt at bringing together many currents of thought and development such as we have seen in our day. It is not a system of philosophy. I do not believe very much in systems. They are sometimes helpful, but it is most difficult, in matters so complex as life and thought, to take any one concept that might embrace and embrace adequately the whole. Holism—the theory of the whole—tries to emphasise one aspect of thought that has been hitherto a neglected factor. I am trying to hammer out this neglected factor, which is, to my mind, all important in getting the 'synoptic vision.' "

He had come to this point of view, not by abstract speculation, but by experience in life. As a young boy at Cambridge he had turned more to poetry than to philosophy for guidance. Wisdom seemed to be with the poets, and he did not know that he was not right. There was more wisdom with the poets than with politicians.

Poetry brought out the fundamentals of reality, and it was as a student of poetry that he first saw the light.

Goethe and Walt Whitman he had admired most, and in studying the works of these great poets it had seemed to him that there was something greater in them than in their great works; there was something greater behind their works and in their personalities than in their works. It was in studying their personalities that he had come on the concept of the whole; the personality, *sui generis,* underlying their lives and their works; a whole that had its own laws of development and that could be followed from the beginning to the end of their works.

When he returned to South Africa from Cambridge he had found the situation here a problem in holism. This was just before the Jameson Raid. South Africa was torn by huge waves of racial strife. After the Jameson Raid came years of friction, culminating in the Boer War, and the Boer War had left them with a problem in holism.

"We were left the fragments out of which we were to make a whole, and it was the problem of South African statesmen to follow up the ideal in the solution of our political problems. We did so, and I think not without some success. Gradually we have seen emerging out of these discordant elements the lineaments of a new South Africa. We have not yet the whole, we have not yet a really unified South Africa, we have not yet attained to the unity which is our ideal. There is still too much of the old division and separation in our national elements, but still the effort has been made, and you see today in South Africa the biggest problem facing us being solved along holistic lines."

While these things were going on in South Africa— one of the greatest dramas in the recent history of the world—the same conditions were reproducing themselves in the greater world outside. From the Boer War onwards a new spirit seemed to have permeated the nations of Europe. The nineteenth century had been called the century of nationality, but the early years of the twentieth century were years of intense nationalism, morbid nationalism. Nations lost their heads in efforts at self-aggrandisement, and this had become so intense and so selfish that a clash became inevitable.

"Again you see a problem in holism. Where there should have been a united family of nations we saw the elements drifting apart, we saw disunity and disruption, and we saw in the end the greatest crash in the history of the world.

"When the Great War ended there was the same problem in holism. I think the League of Nations is a genuine effort in reconstructing the broken front of European civilisation, of once more reforming unity out of division and discord. The American word 'league' was hardly the correct one. I prefer the French word 'society.' The phrase 'Society of Nations' seems to me to bring out the points essential to the unity of spirit which that 'Society of Nations' seeks to produce."

In the years to come, when people looked back on the changes in our human attitude, they would probably say the greatest change had been wrought, not by these events, but by science. Science had proved the greatest constructive force in the world, but it had also proved to be the greatest destructive agent. Our world of ideas had been practically shattered by the changes in science. What was needed was the elaboration of ideas to help the world to get back once more to a sane and wise road.

If he were asked what had been the most notable change

science had made in our world of ideas he would say it was the idea of creative evolution. That was the most fundamental change in our world outlook. Most of his audience had been brought up in a different world of ideas. They had been brought up to look upon the world as something ready-made and finished and moving forward as a constant, fixed, rigid entity. Science had shattered that idea, and had impressed on them that this was not a fixed universe. It was instead a growing world, a creative universe, a learning world. The world was in a constant state of flux; there was a constant increase in all directions.

Once that concept was grasped it would be seen that it meant an enormous change in the outlook on life. The change was taking place in the world in all its details. There was nothing constant about its parts. Just as a human being changed and grew and learned, so it was with the universe.

Once you grasped that idea you had to depart from the view of things as entities; you realised that the world at bottom was not substance but flexible, changing patterns.

In biology, in the first instance, this change had been brought about in ideas, but more recently the same change had come over the scene in physics. Time and space had changed their character and had become flexible things. The only constant things scientists worked with now were ratios. All this showed how there had been a complete change to the new point of view. Matter had gone; it had disappeared into energy. All we could see now were patterns and structures.

"If you take patterns as the ultimate structure of the world, if it is arrangements and not stuff that make up the world, the new concept leads you to the concept of wholes. Wholes have no stuff; they are arrangements. Science has come round to the view that the world consists of patterns, and I construe that to be that the world consists of wholes."

Practical experience had united with the latest works of the sciences to work round to the new point of view of patterns or wholes. The whole and the parts reciprocally determined, formed and shaped each other. Yet the whole was more than the sum of its parts. Take, for example, human personality—the highest whole. A man shaped all his thoughts, all his actions by the whole in him, his personality. Conversely, the parts had influenced the whole in him. It was all a case of mutual service and mutual adaptation. If there were no whole, a thing like mental discipline could not exist. Man as a personality had a certain power over his actions, and the whole idea of discipline was the proof of the existence of wholes as units. According to the most recent speculation, they must apply the same principle to dead things. They must abandon the idea that matter was determined by its elements.

"The effect of this change in point of view is very far-reaching. In philosophy it is difficult to estimate values: the beauty, the truth, the goodness of things. They seem to be additional to the substance of things. On the other hand, if you adopt the idea of patterns, you get away from substance and get patterns in which truth, goodness, beauty and value become bound up in the nature of things. To be a whole is to be real. To be valuable, to be good—these centre in the idea of being a whole.

"The world consists of a rising series of wholes. You start with matter, which is the simplest of wholes. You then rise to plants and animals, to mind, to human beings, to personality and the spiritual world. This progression of wholes, rising tier upon tier, makes up the structure of the universe."

This reasoning must affect the conception of causality. If this world was a growing universe, if it was growing from less to more, then the conception must affect the whole theory of causes. The present theory was that there was an equality between cause and effect. But they could not apply that conception of cause and effect to the world, for then there would have been no growth in the world. The world would have been just as simple as it had been in the beginning.

His theory meant that just a little more was produced in the effect than was contained in the antecedent causes. If that was correct it would mean that all the laws of logic would have to be re-written. The law of cause and effect was in the melting-pot. Our concepts must suit themselves to facts, and there was no doubt that cause and effect must be challenged.

Hitherto they had looked to the physical universe as a necessity in which there was no room for freedom, and in which the effects blindly followed the causes. But he thought the iron rule of necessity did not bind the universe. In its very construction there was a certain latitude, a certain measure of opportunity, which they could call freedom.

There was no doubt that the less created the more. The universe as it existed today was a bigger thing than the universe of thousands of years ago. By infinite increments the universe was still being built up and created.

A criticism of his theory had been that he looked upon

the wholes as being too independent. It had been said that his conception of the universe was a vast assemblage of wholes of independent character.

That was an entirely unfounded criticism. He conceived the universe as a system of wholes interdependent through and through. Leibnitz had held that the world consisted of monads in a "pre-established harmony." He (Field Marshal Smuts) could not conceive what that meant. Wholes were all interdependent.

"Take yourself—you are a whole. Take myself—I am a whole. We both possess a certain inwardness of spirit and other characteristics that I call personality. But I find that I have a body, and that all the time I am in touch with something more. I have a vision that extends to the farthest stars. I have a memory that takes me back over the ages as far as there are records—and sometimes further. Thus you see that any whole has infinite ramifications. I do not say the sun and the moon and the stars are part of my personality—that would be going too far. There must be limits, and thus I have adapted the physics term 'field' for my theory.

"Every whole has its field, and all these fields interpenetrate each other. Thus we have a great community of wholes, each with its own field interpenetrating into the fields of other wholes. I think it is in the intermingling of the fields that the creative element of the universe enters.

"Is there such a whole as nature? Is there *a* whole? Is the world a whole? I don't think there is. If you look upon this community of wholes you might go the length of saying that nature is a whole in the making.

"If this view is true, you will notice that wholes become the very basis of reality. Instead of taking matter as the basis of the world, we see there is something deeper than life and mind and personality. Matter is more than it appears. In matter there is a pattern, a whole, which is its very inmost nature. That explains how it is possible for matter to blossom into such forms as mind and life."

They had to assume that there was this holistic element from the lowest to the highest, that there was a progression of wholes from the lowest to the very highest. The universe on that theory became holistic, and wholes became the aim and object of the universe's striving. Matter was still being formed in the hottest of the stars from the little electrons.

"What the forms of life will be in the millions of years to come it is impossible to conceive. They will, at any rate, be far higher than they are today. Far greater advances in evolution will be made in the future. Life is only young: it is an infant in this universe, and we are only getting into our stride now. I don't believe that we, the human beings, are the acme of the universe. I believe there will be evolved far higher forms of spiritual wholes than we see before us today.

"There is no doubt that one form of life, one form of wholes, after another has been outstripped in the continual scheme of evolution. We shall not remain in the front rank of creation."

One criticism of his theory was that it had not provided for degeneration. But his theory did provide for that. The universe was a universe of experiment. There were wholes that were weak, inchoate, and these must be eliminated. That explained degeneration. Creative evolution was an experimental evolution, and the universe an experimental universe. In the universe there was no room for the weaklings, for the degenerates.

In conclusion Field Marshal Smuts spoke of the peace of mind the theory of holism produced.

"We find, instead of the hostility which is felt in life, that this is a friendly universe. We are all inter-related. The one helps the other. It is an idea that gives strength and peace and is bound to give a more wholesome view of life and nature than we have had so far.

"Wholeness is the key to thought, and when we take that view we shall be able to read much more of the riddle of the universe."

CHAPTER X

SCIENCE FROM THE SOUTH AFRICAN POINT OF VIEW

Field Marshal Smuts was President of the British Association for the Advancement of Science in its Centenary Year—1931–1932. He delivered the following address on July 6, 1925.

IN DIRECTING your attention tonight to some of our scientific and practical problems considered from a South African viewpoint, I can only do so in the most general way and in the broadest outlines. The subject is so vast and the time at my disposal so brief that I can do no more than sketch the standpoint which I wish to suggest and illustrate it by reference to some South African problems without discussing them in any detail. I shall be satisfied if I can convince this critical audience tonight that there is something valuable and fruitful for science in the South African point of view; that our particular angle of vision supplies a real vantage point of attack on some of the great problems of science; and that, so far from the South African viewpoint being parochial in science, it may prove helpful and fruitful in many ways to our workers in the field of scientific research and investigation.

In the first place, the South African point of view will liberate us from old preconceived ways of looking at many scientific problems. Most of our scientific workers have

134

been trained in the schools of Great Britain and the continent of Europe. They bring to the problems of science in South Africa the attitude, the habits of thought and the viewpoints of the Northern Hemisphere.

The Northern Hemisphere, and in particular the European continent, is the home of nineteenth-century science, its birthplace and the great field of its labours and triumphs. The sciences of inorganic and organic evolution have been most highly developed in their application to European conditions; the European situation is best known, it is the classic ground of science. No wonder that it has come to be considered the centre of the world, perhaps the original seat and centre of all terrestrial evolution. In science we know more of the past record of Europe than of any other continent; its palaeontology has received intensive study for generations, while much less in comparison is known of the evolutionary record of other continents. Northern Europe has partly on this account come to be considered the original centre of Geographical Distribution. It is not my purpose for the moment to call this into question; I only mean to emphasise how intensive European exploration has led to a European viewpoint in evolutionary science. It may well be that deeper and wider knowledge of the past of the other continents may lead to a revision of many points of view now current, and the leading rôle assigned to the European continent, or let me rather say the Northern Hemisphere, may have to be modified in material respects. Already we see the beginning of a tendency to look elsewhere for the explanation of many of the great problems of science. For us in South Africa it is no less a duty than a privilege to explore our own angle of the globe, and to see what light it throws on the past and the present, and what contribution it can make to the sum total of scientific knowledge.

A British politician of some eminence declared the other day that Africa was the continent of the twentieth century, and it may yet be that the future will in some measure justify that proud claim. While for the statesman the problems of the African continent may become all-important during this century, it is more than probable that for the scientist also this continent will assume a position of quite outstanding importance. From many points of view Africa occupies a key position among the continents of the world; it has the most curious affinities with all of them; more than any other continent it has special scientific relationships with all the rest. And the character of these relationships shows that it occupies not only geographically but also scientifically a central position among the rest, a position which may yet supply the key and the explanation to many problems that are at present obscure or unexplained by science. Prospectors on the lookout for minerals and precious ores explore the "divides," the high exposed watersheds which divide great drainage areas. The Witwatersrand is such a great divide in the Union; the Katanga Broken Hill area further north is another such divide; and still farther north is the great rift divide which contains the Kilo gold-bearing areas of the North-Eastern Congo. In many ways Africa is the great "scientific divide" among the continents, where future prospectors of science may yet find the most precious and richest veins of knowledge.

Within the last five years a great impetus has been given to this way of looking at Africa by the Wegener theory, or rather hypothesis, for it is, perhaps, not yet more than an hypothesis. Now let me say at once that I am not tonight going to argue the correctness or otherwise of the Wegener hypothesis. I disclaim any competence or desire to do so. The Wegener hypothesis as an explanation of great groups of problems may be right or it may be wrong. Its profound significance to us is not so much the particular solution it propounds as the attention it focuses on those problems. The Wegener hypothesis purports to explain the origin, the past and the present of all continents and oceans of this globe. But for us in South Africa it has a special interest in its account of the origin and distribution of continents in the Southern Hemisphere. Whether this account is correct or not, the hypothesis has the great merit of focusing attention on many great problems which call for explanation; and it has the further merit of associating these problems and making them parts and aspects of a great common scheme, instead of merely leaving them, as disjointed, unconnected items, scattered haphazard over the various special sciences. There are many most interesting and important problems belonging to many sciences which call insistently for an explanation. And the merit of the Wegener hypothesis is that, for the first time, these problems are faced boldly in a comprehensive scheme of solution.

For us in this part of the world the most interesting feature of the scheme is that in it Africa assumes a central position among the continents; it becomes, in fact, the great "divide" among the continents of the Southern Hemisphere. It appears as the mother-continent from which South America on the one side and Madagascar, India, Australasia and their surrounding areas on the other, have split off and drifted away, have calved off, so to speak. The evidence for all this is strong; but it may well be that the evidence is yet insufficient to account for the whole Wegener hypothesis. It may not be strong enough to prove the actual disruption and separation of the continents in the past which is the essence of the hypothesis. But, even so, it may be right in assigning to the African continent a central determining position in respect of many of the great unsolved problems of Geographical Distribution, and in making that position the key which science will have to use in ever-increasing measure if it wishes to unlock the door to future advances. The value of a hypothesis often depends not so much on its correctness as on its fruitfulness. A hypothesis may in the light of further knowledge prove to have been wrong, but, in the meantime, it may perhaps have suggested new points of view and new methods of attack and thus have cleared the way for real advances. Its value consists in the advances it opens up and the way it thus prepares, perhaps, for its own supersession. The actual truth is a far-off goal to which any hypothesis may be only a step and often a faulty step. The processes of nature are usually very complex and unlike the simple solutions which our hypotheses propose. But the simplest solution does often help us some little distance on the way, and if we take it as a temporary expedient and not as a final explanation, it can be most helpful and suggestive up to a point, when it makes way for a fresh approximation to the truth. For the present I am prepared to look upon Wegener's hypothesis as a fruitful point of view more than a solution, as a suggestive line of thought and research along which useful work may be done in the future.

One important line of research which it suggests to us

is the East-West aspect, in addition to the hitherto prevalent North-South line of orientation. Hitherto, as I have said, it is the European affiliations which have guided our thought and our research; we have looked to the North for explanations as well as our origins. In future, on the lines of Wegener's speculations, we shall look more to East and West—to our affiliations with South America, India and Madagascar and Australasia for the great connections which can explain the problems of our past and present.

We shall look upon Southern Africa as the centre of the Southern Hemisphere and correlate all the relative scientific problems of this hemisphere from that new point of view. The grouping of the southern continents and lands and the intimate connections and interdependence of their scientific problems will be our new point of departure.

It may prove a most suggestive and creative point of view for science in general. This new aspect will establish new contacts, and it is generally such new contacts which prove fruitful and creative for scientific progress. Our workers, in following up the new clues, may reach solutions which will have a far-reaching value for universal science. I hope you will bear with me if I now proceed to indicate in a general and cursory way some of the lines of scientific work which may be usefully followed up from this point of view.

Let me first take the case of Geology, a science in which a very high standard of success and excellence has been achieved in South Africa. A great deal of attention has been devoted to the question of correlation of our geological formations with those of Europe and, although many unsolved problems still remain, the main outlines of the correspondence of our formations with those of the Northern Hemisphere have been successfully worked out. A good deal has been done, yet quite insufficient, to correlate our formations with those of South America, India, or Australasia. Yet it is evident that the subject is one of profound interest, both from a scientific and a practical point of view. Several of our formations at the Cape seem to be continued or paralleled by identical or similar formations in India and South America. A proper correlation of the geological systems may lead to most interesting results, and may also throw great light on the past of the three continents.

We may be enabled thereby to explain just why they are practically the sole producers of the world's diamonds; why the diamond-fields of South-West Africa are situated on the one edge of the Atlantic and those of Brazil on the other; why the coalfields of these three countries and of Australia are confined to the eastern portions of each of these land masses; and why the curious and ancient banded ironstones are so widely spread in South Africa, Brazil, peninsular India and Western Australia, though absent from Europe. The results of such a comparative study for the Southern Hemisphere might be most valuable and might settle many of the problems which still agitate science as to the past of the earth. And correlation of the several geologies of the Southern Hemisphere would decidedly throw a new light on all of them.

But it is when we come to the biological sciences that such a comparative study promises the most fruitful results. Here there are a number of momentous problems still awaiting solution. Consider, for instance, the problems affecting our Botany. We have two distinct floras in South Africa; the one, the South African flora, which covers most of sub-tropical Africa and is clearly of tropical origin; the other, a temperate flora, found only in the south-west of the Cape Province on the seaward side of the first great mountain barrier, with outliers extending to the north along the mountain systems into the tropics.

The two floras are, apparently, quite different and distinct and are engaged in a mortal conflict with each other, in which the temperate or Cape flora is slowly losing ground. This Cape flora forms, indeed, a problem of profound and baffling interest. What is its origin, and what its relation to the South African flora? The South African flora is, as I have said, clearly of tropical origin, and consists largely of sub-tropical derivations and modifications of the tropical forms found farther north in the equatorial regions. Can its origin be traced farther back? In the answer to this question we meet again with what I may call the European fallacy, or the fallacy of the European origin. The current idea among botanists is that Northern Europe is the source and the north temperate flora of Europe the origin of both our South African and Cape floras. The north temperate flora of Europe is supposed to have been driven south by the onset of the last great Ice Age in Europe and in the much cooler climate of the tropics at that time to have migrated southward along the eastern mountain systems of Africa until southern Africa was reached. Sir W. Thiselton-Dyer, summing up the views held on this question of the northern origin of our floras, says:

"The theory of southward immigration is the key to the interpretation of the geographical distribution of plants.

It received enormous support from the researches of Heer, and has now become an accepted commonplace."

This common view of the European origin of our floras will, however, require very careful reconsideration from the viewpoint which I am suggesting here. The correlation of our floras with the other floras of the Southern Hemisphere may profoundly affect this question of origins, and may throw much fresh light, not only on the origin of our floras in Southern Africa, but even on so momentous a question as the origin of the Flowering Plants, and on Geographical Distribution generally. On all these great questions conclusions may yet be reached which may differ from those at present commonly held. It may, for instance, yet be found that our floras are not of northern origin, but come from the ancient lands of the Southern Hemisphere which are covered by the Wegener hypothesis. Even according to our present knowledge, the African floras do not seem to fit in well with the current view of their origin. Apart from the Cape flora in the extreme south and the Mediterranean temperate flora in the extreme north, the African flora—better known as the Tropical African flora or the Palaeotropical African flora— cover the rest of the continent. In this flora an element predominates which is peculiar to this part of the world, but is more or less closely related to the floras of India, Madagascar, Australasia and South America. In other words, the special affiliations of the Tropical African flora are in the Southern Hemisphere. Similarly, the Cape flora has peculiar affiliations with the floras of certain countries in the Southern Hemisphere. The current view of the northern origin may therefore not be the last word so far as Botany is concerned.

Dyer credits Darwin with having been the first to suggest the southward migration of the European flora in the Great Ice Age. But that surely is a very recent age from which to date our floras with all their vast wealth of indigenous forms and their high degree of adaptation. The highly-specialised adaptation of our floras, more especially to conditions of severe drought, would seem to call for a much longer period of development than the comparatively short spell of time which has elapsed since the last Ice Age. Moreover, if Darwin was the author of this theory of the northern origin, it is clear from his letters that an element of doubt remained in his mind on this most important point.

The origin of the Flowering Plants and the existence of the Southern or Cape Flora remained for him to the end of his life problems which had some vague connection, and as late as 1881 we find him writing to his friend Hooker:

"Nothing is more extraordinary in the history of the Vegetable Kingdom, as it seems to me, than the apparently very sudden and abrupt development of the higher plants. I have sometimes speculated whether there did not exist somewhere during the long ages an extremely isolated continent, perhaps near the South Pole."

His surmise and, I may add, Hooker's surmise, about a great isolated continent in the Southern Ocean was to be carried much farther.

Here it is necessary to point out that Darwin, while holding to the northern origin, yet continued to be haunted by the idea of a southern continent whose mystery might, perhaps, hold also the secret of the origin of the Angiosperms.

Since his day the great advances in fossil botany have led to the well-known hypothesis of an ancient continent of Gondwanaland which existed in Permo-Carboniferous times, with a probably semi-arid and cold climate and a peculiar Glossopteris flora. The evidence has been thus summed up by Professor Seward:

"There can be little doubt that the Indian lower Gondwana rocks, in which the boulder beds and the Glossopteris flora occur, must be regarded as belonging to a vast continental area, of which remnants are preserved in Australia, South Africa, and South America. This continental area has been described as Gondwanaland, a tract of enormous extent occupying an area, part of which has since given place to a Southern Ocean, while detached masses persist as portions of more modern continents, which have enabled us to read in their fossil plants and ice-scratched boulders the records of the lost continent in which the Mesozoic Vegetation of the Northern continent had its origin."

Finally, Darwin's wonderful guess has found expression in the great southern continent of Wegener's hypothesis, a continent which existed in Permo-Carboniferous times, of which Africa was the centre and South America, Madagascar, India and Australia, as well as Antarctica, were integral portions, a continent which must have become disrupted somewhere in the Mesozoic period, and the parts of which have gradually drifted away to the positions which they today occupy in the Southern Hemisphere. In his lecture before this Association in 1921, Dr. A. L. du Toit gave a most illuminating account of Gondwanaland, its rise, decline and fall, to which reference may be made for full details.

On the question of the origin of our two floras, we have the following two interesting facts. First, the fact already mentioned that the chief types of the African flora have their affiliations in the Southern and not in the Northern Hemisphere. Second, the fact that the chief types of the present Cape flora, such as the Proteaceae and Restiaceae, today occupy the areas that correspond to the former Gondwanaland, that is to say, exactly the same area which was covered by the Glossopteris flora in Mesozoic times. It is alleged that some fossil types of Proteaceae have been found in Central Europe in lower Cretaceous deposits, but these finds are hotly disputed and cannot be looked upon as substantiated. These two facts would seem to point to the conclusion that the two African floras are probably of southern origin and have not been derived from the northern or European flora.

Nay, more, the suggestion of Seward that the Mesozoic flora of Europe, which is markedly dissimilar from that of its Palaeozoic flora, may have had a southern origin in Gondwanaland, opens up very interesting possibilities. Indeed, in the palaeobotany of the Southern Hemisphere we are only at the beginnings; and who knows whether further discoveries in this largely-virgin field of research may not yet give point and substance to Darwin's surmise that the existence far back in the long ages of an extremely isolated southern continent is somehow to be linked with the mysterious origin of Flowering Plants. I say this, not in order to express any particular opinion as to the northern or southern origin of the Angiosperms, but to point to the necessity of further research in the fossil botany of Southern Africa. Some of the greatest problems of botany, of geographical distribution, and of the past of the earth will have to wait for their solution until palaeobotany has made much further advances in South Africa and the Southern Hemisphere generally. In this connection, a great opportunity lies before science in South Africa, and I trust a step will be taken by the establishment of a Chair of Palaeobotany at one or other of our South African universities. It will be a small step, but its significance will be great and its results may be far-reaching.

So far, I have only referred to the evidence of palaeobotany. But the evidence of our Southern Palaeontology generally is all in the same direction. Still more so is the evidence of the present botanical distribution throughout the Southern Hemisphere. The present distribution is not only strong presumptive evidence in favour either of a great southern continent or great land connections in the south in the past, but also in favour of the independent origin of the African flora. Dr. Otto Stapf, whose knowledge of African grasses is unrivalled, goes even farther in his masterly "Gräserflora Süd-Afrikas," and would seem to suggest that very special importance is to be attached to the unique character of the Cape flora as distinguished from the African flora.

"The Cape Province (that is to say, the province of the South-West Cape flora), which is in a great measure the centre of the temperate South African elements among the grasses, is a narrow corner of the African continent, of smaller size even than Portugal. Its wealth of endemic forms is out of all proportion to its area. Neither climatic nor edaphic relations suffice to give an explanation of this, which must rather be looked for in the geological history of the country. That migrants from the north could have experienced in such a small area so extraordinary a development is hardly thinkable. Is it not more probable that the south-western corner of Africa is the remains of a land which extended much farther in the Southern Ocean?"

In other words, this flora points not only to a southern origin, but to an origin even farther south than the ancient Gondwanaland is commonly supposed to have extended. May we not venture the suggestion that the Cape temperate flora is the survival of an Antarctic and sub-Antarctic flora which has perished in the climatic changes of the past? That, at any rate, would account for its marked differences from our sub-tropical South African flora.

Enough has been said to show how important it is that there should be a regular comparative study of the scientific problems of the countries which lie in the Southern Hemisphere, with South Africa as the centre of the whole group. Such a comparative study promises rich results and will probably give a new direction and a fresh impetus to many branches of scientific work. For this purpose it seems to me not only advisable to devote more attention to palaeobotany at our universities, but also essential that South African students and workers should visit other countries of our hemisphere and familiarise themselves with the scientific conditions and problems which obtain there. Many of the problems of science in South Africa will only find their proper solution after such a comparative study, while others will in that way have a new light thrown on them. And for the same reason everything in our power should be done to encourage the visits and researches of scientific men from these countries to South

Africa. Here more than almost anywhere else will the interchanges of science prove fruitful and beneficial.

In discussing what I call the South African point of view, I have referred merely to questions connected with our Botany and Palaeobotany. The discussion of our Zoology from the same point of view would raise questions of equal if not of even greater interest. The comparative study, for instance, of the present and past distribution of our scorpions and land mollusca in South Africa and in the lands of the Southern Hemisphere generally would give valuable evidence in regard to our zoological origins. But I have no time to do more than merely mention Zoology here, and to add that the study of the Zoology of the Southern Hemisphere will prove a fruitful field for biological science, and will greatly emphasise the importance of the African point of view which I have here suggested.

Let us now pass on from biological questions to the problems of our South African Climate and Meteorology, which, I need hardly point out, are of supreme importance not only in an economic but also in a scientific sense. Here, too, we shall find that the present has its roots deep in the far-off past. Our climate is but a section of universal climate, which in the ages of the earth's existence has passed through the most amazing fluctuations, ice-ages alternating with tropical heat in countries where the local climate is today far removed from both these extremes.

Great ice-ages are known to have occurred far back at the beginnings of geological time before the present sedimentary formations were laid down. To pass to the other extreme, Europe during the Permo-Carboniferous period, when the coal-measures were mostly laid down, possessed the climate of a sub-tropical rain-forest and, at a much later date, the Magnolia and similar tropical plants flourished in Greenland and Spitzbergen. At that time Europe was mostly covered by shallow seas, and its tropical climate was balanced by a cold, dry climate which existed in the contemporaneous Gondwanaland of the Southern Hemisphere. The Glossopteris flora of the latter was the vegetation of a cold, dry climate. And the glaciation of many parts of Gondwanaland of which evidence is visible over a large part of South Africa shows that great ice-masses must have covered its high tableland. Much other evidence points to the fact that the ancient Africa which formed the centre of Gondwanaland was, on the whole, a cold and arid country. Gondwanaland must have been an unpleasant country to live in, not only because of its climate, but because of the vast geological disturbances which were gradually tearing it to pieces. Even if the tearing asunder and drifting apart of the ancient continent according to Wegener did not take place, there must have been submergence and disappearance under the sea of great land connections between the countries of the Southern Hemisphere.

Other indisputable evidence of the severe and long-continued convulsions of Africa during the Tertiary times exists. The vast cracks and fissures which rent it from south to north exist today still in the chains of great lakes and "rift-valleys" which extend across Africa from the Zambesi to the Red Sea, the Dead Sea and the deep valley of the Jordan. Farther north the crust of the earth folded up slowly like a crumpled scroll, and as a result the huge mountain chains of the Atlas and the Alps, the Taurus and the Himalayas were formed. Volcanoes burst forth in Africa in many places along the lines of weakness, while in the south the diamond pipes were formed. During this prolonged period of change the climate of Southern Africa also must have changed considerably, for, instead of the cold of Mesozoic Gondwanaland, we find as far south as Kerguelen Island the remains of Araucarias which must have flourished there in Tertiary times.

Those far-off climatic conditions of the ancient Africa have for us of today only a mild scientific interest. But the remarkable changes in terrestrial climate which set in at the end of the Tertiary period are on a different footing and have produced effects which are still felt by us in the present era. Let me, therefore, briefly refer to them. It is difficult to reconstruct the happenings of that distant era. But the known facts seem to point to the following developments probably having taken place.

It is supposed that equatorial lands in the Pacific were depressed, leaving only the present scattered islands, while the lands in high latitudes both in the Northern and Southern Hemispheres were correspondingly elevated. Europe was raised from the shallow seas which covered most of it until, in the Pliocene, Scandinavia was 1,000 feet above its present elevation, and Great Britain, as well as the bottom of the North Sea, appeared as land and as an annex of the continent. A marked elevation also took place in the lands of the Southern Hemisphere, and South Africa ended considerably farther south and nearer to the Antarctic than today. Then the snow began to fall and the ice to form on Scandinavia and the glaciers and icefields to extend south into Central Europe. Similar conditions ensued in North America and Antarctica. The last great ice-age had begun, with effects which were felt right across the Equator into sub-tropical South Africa. The increasing cold in the Antarctic and the sub-Antarctic islands wiped out the entire south temperate flora with the single considerable exception of its most northern outlier in the South-West Cape, where it still survives as a unique relic of the past. The combined effects of the two northern and southern cold areas were reflected in moister conditions and greater rainfall in Southern Africa during the Pleistocene than we have today. Throughout the half a million to a million years which cover this period, the land level of Northern Europe kept oscillating, and the Scandinavian ice-mantle was growing or dwindling, with mild or even warm interglacial periods between.

It was in the last two interglacial phases that man appeared in Europe, not yet *Homo sapiens,* but earlier species of mankind. To locate ourselves properly in the frame of the geological picture, we have to envisage ourselves as living in a new and mild interglacial period; we have to remember that Scandinavia is once more rising at the present rate of perhaps a metre or more per century, and that in another ten thousand years or more Europe will possibly be once more in the grip of a great ice-age. South Africa is also rising at a rate which has not yet been determined, but is appreciable; our climate will gradually become cooler, until we shall again have more moist and rainy conditions than today; and the voices of the Schwarzes will no longer be heard crying in the wilderness which will have passed away. We may regret that we shall not live to see that day, but that regret will be tempered by the further thought that, hitherto, each interglacial phase has seen the passing away of a lower species of the human genus to make way for a higher one, and that, in all probability, our present human races will, before the next phase, have had to disappear and make way for the higher species of humans which it is hoped will occupy the next age. Let us, therefore, be content and make the best of our time and our corner, which is indeed a most fair and pleasant one, even under present conditions. We can, at any rate, flatter ourselves with the consolation that today there is nothing better or higher than ourselves among the living.

The factors which affect large divisions and periodicities of climate and rainfall are still a matter of controversy amongst scientists. But there can be little doubt that the formation of the great Scandinavian ice-field, partly, at any rate, through land elevation at the end of the Plio-cene, had the most profound effect on the climate and the history of Europe and Asia during the present geological period. A great anticyclonic storm centre was thereupon established, which displaced the rain-bearing cyclonic belts and thereby produced the most far-reaching changes, which were felt even across the Equator of the old world.

The great ice-age in Europe appears to have synchro-nised with a period of greater rainfall in Africa, including South Africa. The remains of great rivers and lakes in all parts of Southern Africa and the gravel terraces in certain regions which are now waterless deserts bear witness to the higher rainfall during the Pleistocene and to the con-sequent accumulation of surplus waters in the sub-conti-nent. The Swedish geologist, de Geer, has by methods of remarkable ingenuity and accuracy determined that the ice-body finally retreated from Sweden about twelve thousand years ago, and this result agrees very well with the corresponding estimates obtained in North America. We may, therefore, take it that during the last ten thousand or twelve thousand years, this sub-continent has been experiencing a lessening rainfall; the run-off of the rivers to the ocean has not been properly compensated for by rain.

There has thus been a progressive desiccation of the land, and the arid or semi-desert conditions of today have probably been in existence for some thousands of years. That is the opinion of Passarge, who made a closer study of this question in the Kalahari region than any other worker. At the same time it has to be admitted that we are still ignorant of, or in doubt about, a number of important matters bearing on the past rainfall of Southern Africa, and very important problems still await the attention of our scientific workers in this regard. Professor Schwarz's writings have focused much popular attention on some of these questions, but in scientific circles the matter as a whole has not yet received the attention it deserves. It is to be hoped that this omission will soon be repaired, for there can be no question either of the scientific interest or the practical economic importance of the subject as a whole.

Meteorology ought to occupy a foremost place in our activities as a State and as a country for scientific investigation. The comparative smallness and seasonal uncertainties of our rainfall make this a matter of the greatest economic importance, while our central position in the Southern Hemisphere carries with it peculiar advantages and responsibilities for meteorological observation and research. Yet very little pure research has so far been done. In his letter to the recent Drought Investigation Commission, Dr. G. C. Simpson, Director of the Meteorological Office, London, makes the following grave charge against us:

"Of the large land surfaces, the meteorological conditions of Africa are probably the least known; for except from Egypt we receive practically no meteorological information from this great continent, and South Africa is probably the largest area having a settled civilised Government which publishes officially little or no meteorological information."

And he goes on to make the following recommendation:

"The most hopeful method of attack on the problem of seasonal forecasts is to compare and correlate the records of various meteorological factors; thus one of the first steps to the attainment of your object will be the formation of a strong meteorological service to gather data of satisfactory reliability from Africa itself, and probably, in connection with other countries in the Southern Hemisphere, from the Antarctic continent. I do not think that one country alone should undertake to place meteorological observatories on the Antarctic continent. There should be international co-operation of the countries interested, and the aim should be to establish one or more observatories, which can be kept in constant activity along a well-planned programme for an indefinite time."

Here, then, is a very valuable suggestion for us to act on. The Argentine Government have already made a start by maintaining two meteorological stations in the Antarctic, one on the South Orkneys and one in South Georgia.

If the Union and Australia could agree each to maintain an Antarctic station opposite or to the south-west of their respective territories, and the work of the four Antarctic stations could be co-ordinated, the results might be of the utmost value. I trust we shall not have long to wait for the adoption and execution of the recommendations of Dr. Simpson, which have been backed by both the former and the present Directors of Irrigation, and which may prove to be of as much value to pure science as to our productive industries. The proper correlation of data, not only from the Antarctic stations, but from South America, India, Madagascar and Australia, with our own African observations, might yield results of great practical as well as scientific value. The round table of Meteorology should become the meeting-place and reunion of the scattered members of the ancient mother continent of Gondwanaland.

The discussion of our climate and meteorology leads me to mention the subject of Astronomy and to refer for a moment to some of the outstanding contributions which have been made to it in South Africa. Here, too, our favourable situation in the Southern Hemisphere and our meteorological conditions, unrivalled for astronomical research, have enabled South Africa to play an honourable part in the advancement of science.

Here it was that, in the middle of the eighteenth century, the Abbé Lacaille made the first scientific catalogue of Southern Stars. Here, too, it was that, early in the nineteenth century, our second Astronomer Royal, Henderson, made the first determination of the distance of a fixed star from the earth. in the case of x Centauri. Here it was that Sir David Gill, the first President of this Association, made the classic determination of the mean distance of the sun from the earth, a determination the accuracy of which has received only additional confirmation from subsequent determinations. Thus South African Astronomy has the distinction of being responsible for the determination of both great astronomical standards of measurement—the distance of the sun and the distance of the fixed stars.

But the Cape is the birthplace of many other lines of astronomical research. It was at the Cape Observatory that celestial photography had its real beginning. Previous to 1882 it was more an amusement in, than an auxiliary to, astronomy. But in that year Gill, while photographing the great comet, was struck with the power of the photographic plate to picture the faintest stars. Forthwith he conceived the idea of photographing the whole heavens, and thus the most efficient and far-reaching arm in stellar research had its beginnings.

From that day photography became the most powerful weapon in the astronomical armoury. The epoch-making departure thus happily initiated will now be further followed up in South Africa with the great resources of the United States of America. We wish the Yale Observatory at Johannesburg under Dr. Schlesinger, and the coming Michigan University Observatory at Bloemfontein under Dr. Hussey, all possible success in the important tasks they have set themselves.

Let me mention a second line of astronomical research where South Africa was responsible for taking the initiative. For many years it was the home of Variable Star research. The first observatory in the Southern Hemisphere for this special branch of astronomy was built at Lovedale in 1891 by Senator A. W. Roberts, a former President of this Association and one of its medallists. It was at this observatory that he made the first estimates of stellar densities, as well as the earliest determinations of close binary systems and their evolution. This pioneer work has led to most important developments in astronomy which are now rapidly revolutionising our views as to the origin and evolution of the material universe. On all these grounds the record of South Africa in astronomical research is indeed one of outstanding distinction. And there is no reason why this record should not be maintained for the future in this land of clear skies, of equable climate, of peaceful days and cloudless nights, where an endless attraction and a rich promise are continually held out to the lover of the heavens.

I now pass on to the last science, which I shall refer to as one to which our country should, from its central position, be able to make a great contribution in the future; I refer to human Palaeontology. And here I wish to congratulate Professor Raymond Dart once more on behalf of our Association for the great service he has rendered both to science and South Africa by his important work in connection with the Taungs fossil skull. This great discovery has brought South Africa right into the centre of the picture. It has focused attention on our scientific possibilities in a way which will, I hope, prove helpful to South African science generally. There is no doubt that recent events have once more turned the gaze of the world on South Africa as a rich field for scientific investigation. Who knows whether South Africa may not yet become the Mecca of Human Palaeontology?

Three finds of outstanding importance have in recent years signalled South Africa as a great field of research into the human past. The first was the discovery of the Boskop skull, which, according to Professor Dart, represents a still existing strain among our native peoples. The second was the discovery of *Homo rhodesiensis* at Broken Hill, which Professor Elliot Smith is reported to have declared to be one of the most significant finds ever made in human palaeontology. Finally, we have *Australopithecus africanus,* which largely breaks new ground in palaeontology.

To show the peculiar significance of this discovery I may point out that palaeontology so far as the apes or monkeys are concerned has hitherto contributed practically nothing to our understanding of the links between the human and the monkey or ape types. Fossil monkeys are by no means plentiful, and what there are throw practically no light on any past connections between the two classes of primates. The obvious likeness between man and ape is due to our knowledge of living anthropoids, not to fossil apes or anthropoids. Professor Boule, after reviewing the whole question and discussing the views of other workers, comes to the following conclusion:

"It must be confessed, however, that palaeontology has not yet revealed any indisputable transitional form, any material proof of a hereditary connection between the ape form and the human form."

It will be seen at once what a change Professor Dart's discovery brings into this situation. For in *Australopithecus africanus* we have just such an anticipated transitional form between the ape and the human; we have a creature which is still indisputably an ape, but with certain facial features and a brain development which take it some way towards the human. Looking upon the human and the ape forms as the two extremes which will have to be bridged by palaeontology, we note that this can be effected in either of two ways.

We may find fossil forms carrying the human farther back into its human or pre-human past. Or we may find fossil forms carrying the ape form forward toward some intermediate point on the road towards the human. The Broken Hill skull has done the first and the Taungs skull has done the second. Together they form an outstanding contribution to the elucidation of a most difficult but most fascinating problem of anthropological science.

It is a remarkable fact that *Homo rhodesiensis,* although apparently a more primitive and simian type than *Homo neanderthalensis,* was found still unfossilised, and among animal remains which belong to still living Rhodesian species. The deduction has been made that *Homo rhodesiensis* was living quite out of his proper geological horizon, and was surviving in South Africa long ages after his compeers in Europe had passed away. In fact, he was probably still flourishing in the south when his European "contemporaries" had been dead for thousands of years. But there is really nothing singular in such an idea. After all, such a situation is typical of South Africa in more respects than one. Our Bushmen are nothing but living fossils, whose "contemporaries" disappeared from Europe many thousands of years ago. The interest of South Africa as a field for anthropological research is partly just this, that it is possibly ten thousand years behind the times, as measured by the standards of European cultures. And in this respect our anthropology does not stand alone, for in botany also we have true "living fossils" like the cycads.

In South Africa, therefore, certain biological problems can still be studied from life which in Europe can only be deduced with difficulty from the fossil records of the past.

But that is by no means the only or the best claim that South Africa can put forward as a fitting place for palaeontological study and research. Discoveries already made point to the possibility that South Africa may yet figure as the cradle of mankind, or shall I rather say, one of the cradles? As we have seen, it is not only one of the oldest land surfaces, but since the end of the Mesozoic period it has generally enjoyed a fairly habitable, though on the whole, dry climate. While in Tertiary and Pleistocene times most of Europe and much of Asia and North America were intermittently under ice or shallow seas, Southern Africa was very much as it is today. No wonder, therefore, that it should contain not only some of the most ancient fossil records of the human race, but that among its living races it should include what are "fossils" in other continents. Its little Bushmen are unique; its little pigmy population that hide in the tropical and sub-tropical forests are the representatives of the long-vanished human past. Going a little farther back, we find in Africa the home of the great anthropoid apes which are nearest to us in the affinities of life. Here, then, we are clearly near to the great origins. Charles Darwin already in 1871 in the "Descent of Man" wrote:

"It is probable that Africa was formerly inhabited by extinct apes closely allied to the gorilla and the chimpanzee; and as these two species are now man's nearest allies, it is somewhat more probable that our early progenitors lived on the African continent than elsewhere."

This suggestion derives added force from Professor Dart's discovery of an ape-like form which seems to be even closer to the human family than any of the living apes. Professor Elliot Smith, commenting recently on this statement of Darwin in the light of the much fuller evidence which we have now, fifty-four years after Darwin's statement was written, says:

"Speculation upon the location of the cradle of mankind is still a hazardous occupation, but it is not wholly useless. Discussion of such matters helps us to define the real issues, and to weigh the balance of probabilities, which still, as in Darwin's time, favour Africa as the original home."

These and other considerations point to the vast importance of Africa from a palaeontological point of view, if not to the possibility that here may yet be found some intimate connection with the far-off beginnings of the human race. The scope for scientific work in South Africa in this department of knowledge is therefore immense; the ground lies literally cumbered with the possibilities of great discoveries.

Our coasts are covered with raised beaches and caves which have never been explored and which probably hold precious secrets. Our limestone and dolomite formations are honeycombed with unexplored grottos. In every direction lie great opportunities of discovery and illuminating work. I venture to express the hope that we shall not stumble with closed eyes and folded hands over all this *embarras de richesses*. Science has in South Africa a splendid field of labour; other nations may well envy us the rich ores of this great "scientific divide" which is our heritage. I trust that South African science will rise to the height of its great opportunities, and that this sub-continent will yet earn for itself that scientific leadership of the

Southern Hemisphere to which its central position and its great scientific assets and opportunities entitle it.

And my appeal is to a wider circle than that of Science. Public opinion has also to be roused to a realisation of our opportunities and responsibilities. The people of this country ought to realise that science holds the key to stable and permanent future progress; that our agriculture, our industries and the rate of our future economic advance depend on science, which is the real pioneer and voortrekker to our future.

A beautiful illustration of this was recently given when Sir Arnold Theiler and his assistants in a piece of brilliant research made this country realise the great importance of phosphate deficiency in its soil and flora, and what this deficiency meant for its economic life and how it could successfully be combated. Our people should learn that money spent on scientific education and research is a permanent and reproductive investment, which sooner or later will yield an enhanced return to the national welfare. Our wealthy citizens who so generously give large sums to art and charity should appreciate that Science is no less deserving a cause than these, and that one of the best ways in which they could contribute to our progress and well-being would be by the endowment of scientific research and, in particular, the establishment of Chairs in our Universities for the young Cinderellas of Science; I refer to the rising sciences of Climatology, Palaeobotany and Palaeontology, for which practically nothing is being done at our Universities. And, finally, I would venture to make an appeal to our Parliament and Government. I appreciate that the Government of this country already does a great deal for science. But certain things are not being done, which it concerns us specially to do. Two years ago, when I was last in London, I discussed with Dr. Simpson the steps which should be taken to place our meteorological service on a proper basis.

Hard times prevented the execution of my plans. But my successors have better luck and a noble opportunity, which I trust they will exploit to the full. The day when scientific progress in the broadest sense becomes a first-class concern for our people and our Government will, indeed, be a red-letter day for the progress as a whole of South Africa. May we look forward to its speedy dawn!

CHAPTER XI

THE SCIENTIFIC WORLD-PICTURE
OF TODAY

The Address to the British Association for the Advancement of Science by Field Marshal the Rt. Hon. J. C. Smuts, P.C., C.H., F.R.S., President of the Association in its Centenary Year, 1931–1932.

AFTER what I said at the opening this afternoon it is unnecessary for me to emphasise further the significance of this Centenary Meeting of our Association. It is a milestone which enables us to look back upon a hundred years of scientific progress, such as has no parallel in history. It brings us to a point in the advance from which we can confidently look forward to fundamental solutions and discoveries in the near future, which may transform the entire field of science. In this second and greater renaissance of the human spirit this Association and its members have borne a foremost part, to which it would be impossible for me to do justice tonight. I shall, therefore, not attempt to review the achievements of this century of science, but shall content myself with the simpler undertaking of giving a generalised composite impression of the present situation in science. The honour of presiding over this historic meeting, which was not of my seeking, and for which I was chosen on grounds other than my personal merits, is indeed an almost overwhelming one, and I confidently appeal for your indulgence in the difficult task which awaits me tonight.

I am going to ask the question tonight: What sort of world-picture is science leading to? Is science tending towards a definite scientific outlook on the universe, and how does it differ from the traditional outlook of common-sense?

The question is not without its interest. For our world-view is closely connected with our sense of ultimate values, our reading of the riddle of the universe, and of the meaning of life and of human destiny. Our scientific world-picture will draw its material from all the sciences. Among these, physical science will—in view of its revolutionary discoveries in recent years—be a most important source. But no less important will be the contribution of the biological sciences with their clear revelation of organic structure and function as well as of organic evolution. And last, not least, the social and mental sciences will not only supply valuable material, but especially methods of interpretation, insights into meanings and values, without which the perspectives of our world-picture would be hopelessly wrong.

Can we from some reunion or symposium of these sciences obtain a world-picture or synoptic view of the universe, based on observation and calculation, which are the instruments of science, but reaching beyond the particular phenomena which are its immediate field to a conception of the universe as a whole?

That was how science began—in the attempt to find some simple substances or elements to which the complex world of phenomena could in the last analysis be reduced. The century on which we now look back, with its wonderful advance in the methods of technique of exact observation, has been a period of specialisation or decentralisation. Have we now reached a point where science can again become universal in its ultimate outlook? Has a scientific world-picture become possible?

Of course there can be no final picture at any one stage of culture. The canvas is as large as the universe, and the moving finger of humanity itself will fill it in from age to age. All the advances of knowledge, all the new insights gained from those advances will from time to time be blended into that picture. To the deeper insight of every era of our human advance there has been some such world-picture, however vague and faulty. It has been continually changing with the changing knowledge and beliefs of man. Thus, there was the world of magic and animism, which was followed by that of the early nature gods. There was the geocentric world which still survives in the world of common-sense. There is the machine or mechanistic world-view dominant since the time of Galileo and Newton, and now, since the coming of Einstein, being replaced by the mathematician's conception of the universe as a symbolic structure of which no mechanical model is possible. All these world-views have in turn obtained currency according as some well-defined aspect of our advancing knowledge has from time to time been dominant. My object tonight is to focus attention on the sort of world-picture which results from the advances of physical, biological and mental science during the period covered roughly by the activities of our Association.

Science arose from our ordinary experience and commonsense outlook. The world of commonsense is a world of matter, of material stuff, of real separate things and their properties which act on each other and cause changes in each other. To the various things observable by the senses were added the imperceptible things—space and time, invisible forces, life and the soul. Even these were not enough, and the supernatural was added to the natural world. The original inventory was continually being enlarged, and thus a complex empirical world-view arose, full of latent contradictions, but with a solid basis of actual experience and facts behind it.

Speaking generally, we may say that this is substantially still the commonsense view of the world and the background of our common practical beliefs. How has science dealt with this commonsense empirical world-view? The fundamental procedure of science has been to rely on sense observation and experiment, and to base theory on fact. Thus the vast body of exact science arose, and all entities were discarded which were either inconsistent with observed facts or unnecessary for their strict interpretation. The atomic view of matter was established. Ether was given a status in the physical order, which is now again being questioned in the light of the conception of space-time. New entities like energy emerged; old entities like forces disappeared; the principle of the uniformity of nature was established; the laws of motion, of conservation, and of electro-magnetism were formulated; and on their basis a closed mechanistic order of nature was constructed, forming a rigid deterministic scheme. Into this scheme it has been difficult, if not impossible, to fit entities like life and mind; and the scientific attitude has on the whole been to put them to a suspense account and to await developments. As to the supernatural, science is or has been agnostic, if not frankly sceptical. Such in very general terms was the scientific outlook of the nineteenth century, which has not yet completely passed away. It will be noticed that much of the fundamental outlook of commonsense has thus survived, though clarified and purified by a closer accord with facts. This scientific view retained unimpaired and indeed stressed with a new emphasis the things of commonsense, matter, time and space, as well as all material or physical entities which are capable of observation or experimental verification. Nineteenth-century science is, in fact, a system of purified, glorified commonsense. Its deterministic theory certainly gave a shock to the common man's instinctive belief in free will; in most other respects it conformed to the outlook of commonsense. It is true that its practical inventions have produced the most astounding changes in our material civilisation, but neither in its methods nor in its world outlook was there anything really revolutionary.

But underneath this placid surface, the seeds of the future were germinating. With the coming of the twentieth century, fundamental changes began to set in. The new point of departure was reached when physical science ceased to confine its attention to the things that are observed. It dug down to a deeper level, and below the things that appear to the sense, it found, or invented, at the base of the world, so-called scientific entities, not capable of direct observation, but which are necessary to account for the facts of observation. Thus, below molecules and atoms still more ultimate entities appeared; radiations, electrons and protons emerged as elements which underlie and form our world of matter. Matter itself, the time-honoured

mother of all, practically disappeared into electrical
energy.

> *"The cloud-capp'd towers, the gorgeous palaces,*
> *The solemn temples, the great globe itself."*

Yea, all the material forms of earth and sky and sea were
dissolved and spirited away into the blue of energy. Outstanding among the men who brought about this transformation are two of my predecessors in this Chair—Sir
J. J. Thomson and Lord Rutherford. Like Prospero, like
Shakespeare himself, they must be reckoned among the
magicians.

Great as was this advance, it does not stand alone. Away
in the last century, Clerk Maxwell, following up Faraday's
theories and experiments, had formulated his celebrated
equations of the electro-magnetic field, which apply to
light no less than to electro-magnetism, and the exploration of this fruitful subject led Minkowski to the amazing
discovery in 1908 that time and space were not separate
things, but constituent elements in the deeper synthesis of
space-time. Thus time is as much of the essence of things
as space; it enters from the first into their existence as an
integral element. Time is not something extra and super-
added to things in their behaviour, but is integral and
basic to their constitution. The stuff of the world is thus
envisaged as events instead of material things.

This physical concept or insight of space-time is our first
revolutionary innovation, our first complete break with
the old world of commonsense. Already it has proved an
instrument of amazing power in the newer physics. In the
hands of an Einstein it has led beyond Euclid and Newton,
to the recasting of the law and the concept of gravitation,

and to the new relativity conception of the basic structure of the world. The transformation of the concept of space, owing to the injection into it of time, has destroyed the old passive homogeneous notion of space and has substituted a flexible, variable continuum, the curvatures and unevennesses of which constitute to our senses what we call a material world. The new concept has made it possible to construe matter, mass and energy as but definite measure conditions of curvature in the structure of space-time. Assuming that electro-magnetism will eventually follow the fate of gravitation, we may say that space-time will then appear as the scientific concept for the only purely physical reality in the universe, and that matter and energy, in all their forms, will have disappeared as independent entities, and will have become mere configurations of this space-time. Einstein has recently indicated that for further advance a modification in our space-time concept will become necessary, and that the additional element of direction will have to be incorporated into it. Whatever change may become necessary in our space-time concept, there can be no doubt about the immense possibilities it has opened up.

I pass on to an even more revolutionary recent advance of physics. The space-time world, however novel, however shattering to commonsense, is not in conflict with reason. Indeed, the space-time world is largely a discovery of the mathematical reason and is an entirely rational world. It is a world where reason, as it were, dissolves the refractoriness of the old material substance and smoothes it out into forms of space-time. Science, which began with empirical brute facts, seems to be heading for the reign of pure reason. But wait a bit; another fundamental discovery of our age has apparently taken us beyond the bounds of rationality, and is thus even more revolutionary than that of space-time. I refer to the Quantum theory, Max Planck's discovery at the end of the nineteenth century, according to which energy is granular, consisting of discrete grains or quanta. The world in space-time is a continuum; the quantum action is a negation of continuity. Thus arises the contradiction, not only of commonsense, but apparently of reason itself. The quantum appears to behave like a particle, but a particle out of space or time. As Sir Arthur Eddington graphically puts it: a quantum of light is large enough to fill the lens of a hundred-inch telescope, but it is also small enough to enter an atom. It may spread like a circular wave through the universe, but when it hits its mark this cosmic wave instantaneously contracts to a point where it strikes with its full and undivided force. Space-time, therefore, does not seem to exist for the quantum, at least not in its lower multiples. Nay, more, the very hitting of its mark presents another strange puzzle, which seems to defy the principles of causation and of the uniformity of nature, and to take us into the realm of chance and probability. The significant thing is that this strange quantum character of the universe is not the result of theory but is an experimental fact well attested from several departments of physics. In spite of the strange, Puck-like behaviour of the quantum, we should not lightly conclude, with some prominent physicists, that the universe has a skeleton in its cupboard in the shape of an irrational or chaotic factor. Our macroscopic concepts may not fit this ultra-microscopic world of the quantum. And our best hopes for the future are founded on the working out of a new system of concepts and laws suited to this new world that has swum into the ken of science. The rapid development of wave mechanics in the last four years seems to have brought us within sight of this ideal, and we are beginning to discern a new kind of order in the microscopic elements of the world, very different from any type of law hitherto imagined in science, but none the less a rational order capable of mathematical formulation.

We may summarise these remarks by saying that the vastly improved technique of research has led to physical discoveries in recent years which have at last completely shattered the traditional commonsense view of the material world. A new space-time world has emerged which is essentially immaterial, and in which the old-time matter, and even the scientific mass, gravitation, and energy stand for no independent entities, but can be best construed as configuration of space-time. And this discovery of the quantic properties of this world points to still more radical transformations which loom on the horizon of science. The complete recasting of many of our categories of experience and thought may ultimately be involved.

From the brilliant discoveries of physical science we pass on to the advances in biological science which, although far less revolutionary, have been scarcely less important for our world-outlook. The most important biological discovery of the last century was the great fact of organic evolution; and for this fact the space-time concept has at last come to provide the necessary physical basis. It is unnecessary for my purpose to canvass the claims and discuss the views represented by the great names of Lamarck, Darwin and Mendel, beyond saying that they represent a progressive advance in biological discovery, the end of which has by no means been reached yet. Whatever doubts and differences of opinion there may be about the methods, the mechanism, or the causes, there is no doubt about the reality of organic evolution, which is one of the most firmly-established results in the whole range of science. Palaeontology, embryology, comparative anatomy, taxonomy and geographical distribution all combine to give the most convincing testimony that throughout the history of this earth life has advanced genetically from at most a few simple primitive forms to ever more numerous and highly specialised forms. Under the double influence of the internal genetic and the external environmental factors life has subtly adapted itself to the ever-changing situations on this planet. In the process of this evolution not only new structures and organs, but also new functions and powers have successively appeared, culminating in the master key of the mind and in the crowning achievement of human personality. To have hammered the great truth of organic evolution into the consciousness of mankind is the undying achievement of Charles Darwin, by the side of which his discovery of natural selection as the method of evolution is of secondary importance.

The acceptance of the theory of evolution has brought about a far-reaching change in our outlook on the universe and our sense of values. The story of Creation, so intimately associated with the groundwork of most religions, has thus come to be re-written. The unity and inter-connections of life in all its manifold forms have been clearly recognised. And man himself has had to come down from his privileged position among the angels and take his proper place in the universe as part of the order of Nature. Thus Darwin completes the revolution begun by Copernicus.

Space-time finds its natural completion in organic evolution. For in organic evolution the time aspect of the world finds its most authentic expression. The world truly becomes process, where nothing ever remains the same or is a duplicate of anything else, but a growing, gathering, creative stream of unique events rolls for ever forward.

But while we recognise this intimate connection between the conceptions of space-time and organic evolution, we should be careful not to identify the time of evolution with that of space-time. There is a very real difference between them. Biological time has direction, passes from the past to the future, and is therefore historical. It corresponds to the "before" and "after" of our conscious experience. Physical time as an aspect of space-time is neutral as regards direction. It is space-like, and may be plus or minus, but does not distinguish between past or future. It may move in either direction, backwards or forwards, while biological time, like the time of experience, knows only a forward flow. Hence cosmic evolution, as we see it in astronomy and physics, is mostly in an opposite direction * to that of organic evolution. While biological time on the whole shows a forward movement towards ever higher organisation and rising qualities throughout the geological ages, the process of the physical world is mostly in the opposite direction—towards disorganisation, disintegration of more complex structures, and dissipation of energy. The second law of thermodynamics thus marks the

* No doubt there are exceptions to this broad generalisation. In astronomy stars and solar systems and galaxies are probably still being formed, while in physics synthesis of elements may possibly still be going on. In the same way we find in organic evolution minor phases of regression, degeneration and parasitism.

direction of the physical time. While the smaller world of life seems on the whole to be on the up-grade, the larger physical universe is on the down-grade. One may say that in the universe we witness a majority movement downward, and a minority movement upward. The energy which is being dissipated by the decay of physical structure is being partly taken up and organised into life structures —at any rate on this planet. Life and mind thus appear as products of the cosmic decline, and arise like the phoenix from the ashes of a universe radiating itself away. In them Nature seems to have discovered a secret which enables her to irradiate with imperishable glory the decay to which she seems physically doomed.

Another striking point arises here. Organic evolution describes the specific process of what we call life, perhaps the most mysterious phenomenon of this mysterious universe. When we ask what is the nature of life we are curiously reminded of the behaviour of the quantum referred to. I do not for a moment wish to say that the quantum is the physical basis of life, but I do say that in the quantum the physical world offers an analogy to life which is at least suggestive. The quantum follows the all-or-nothing law and behaves as an indivisible whole; so does life. A part of a quantum is not something less than a quantum; it is nothing or sheer nonentity: the same holds true of life. The quantum is perhaps the most easily symbolised as a wave or combination of waves, which can only exist as a complete periodicity, and whose very concept negatives its existence as partial or truncated. In other words, it is a specific configuration and can only exist as such: the same holds true of life.

The quantum does not fall completely within the deter-

ministic causal scheme; the same seems true of life. Significant, also, is the fact that quantum phenomena underlie
secondary qualities such as colour and the like, which the
older science in its mechanistic scheme ignored, but which
are specially associated with life and consciousness. Apparently the quantum does not fall completely within the
causal deterministic scheme: the same is true of life. Life
is not an entity, physical or other. It is a type of organisation; it is a specific principle of central or self-organisation.
If that organisation is interfered with we are left, not with
bits of life, but with death. The nature of living things is
determined, not by the nature of their parts, but by the
nature or principle of their organisation. In short, the
quantum and life seem to have this in common, that they
both behave as wholes.

I have before now endeavoured to explore the concept
of life in the light of the more general concept of the
whole. A whole is not a sum of parts, or constituted by
its parts. Its nature lies in its constitution more than in its
parts. The part in the whole is no longer the same as the
part in isolation. The interesting point is that while this
concept of the whole applies to life it is according to the
recent physics no less applicable to the ultimate physical
units. Thus the electron within an atom is no longer a
distinct electron. There may be separate electrons, but
when they cease to be separate they also cease to be. The
eight electrons which circulate in an oxygen atom are
merged in a whole in such a way that they have lost their
separate identity; and this loss of individuality has to be
taken into account in calculations as to the physical behaviour of the atom. The physicist, in fact, finds himself
unable to look upon the entity which is one-eighth of

eight electrons as the same thing as a single electron. At the very foundation, therefore, of physics, the principle or category of the whole applies no less than in the advanced structure of life, although not in the same degree. In the ultimate analysis of the world, both at the physical and the biological level, the part or unit element somehow becomes shadowy and incoherent, and the very basis of mechanism is undermined. It would almost seem as if the world in its very essence is holistic, and as if the notion of the individual parts is a practical makeshift without final validity in the nature of things.

The general trend of the recent advances in physics has thus been towards the recognition of the fundamental organic character of the material world. Physics and biology are beginning to look not so utterly unlike each other. Hitherto the great gulf in nature has lain between the material and the vital, between inorganic matter and life. This gulf is now in process of being bridged. The new physics, in dissolving the material world of commonsense and discovering the finer structure of physical nature, has at the same time disclosed certain fundamental features which it has in common with the organic world. Stuff-like entities have disappeared and have been replaced by space-time configurations whose very nature depends on their principle of organisation. And this principle, which I have ventured to call holism, appears to be at bottom identical with that which pervades the organic structures of the world of life. The quantum and space-time have brought physics closer to biology. As I have pointed out, the quantum anticipates some of the fundamental characters of life, while space-time forms the physical basis for organic evolution. Physics and biology are thus recognised as respectively simpler and more advanced forms of the same fundamental pattern in world-structure.

The older mechanistic conception of nature, the picture of nature as consisting of fixed material particles, mechanically interacting with each other—already rudely shaken by the relativity theory—is now being modified by the quantum physics. The attack on mechanism, thus coming from physical science itself, is, therefore, all the more deadly. Even in physics, organisation is becoming more important than the somewhat nebulous entities which enter into matter. Interaction is more and more recognised to be not so much mechanical as organic or holistic, the whole in some respects dominating not only the functioning but the very existence of the entities forming it. The emergence of this organic view of nature from the domain of physics itself is thus a matter of first-rate importance, and must have very far-reaching repercussions for our eventual world-view.

The nature of the organic whole is, however, much more clearly recognised in its proper sphere of biology, and especially in the rapidly-advancing science of physiology. Here, too, the correct view has been much obscured by the invasion of mechanistic ideas from the physics of the nineteenth century. A crude materialisation all but swamped biology for more than a generation. At the Belfast session of this Association in 1874 a famous predecessor of mine in this Chair gave unrestrained expression to this materialistic creed. All that is passing, if not already past. It must be admitted that up to a point mechanism has been useful as a first approximation and fruitful as a convention for research purposes. But if even in physics it has lost its savour, *a fortiori* has it become out of place in biology. The partial truth of mechanism is always subtended by the deeper truth of organicity or holism. So far from biology being forced into a physical mould, the position will in future be reversed. Physics will look to biology and even to psychology for hints, clues and suggestions. In biology and psychology it will see principles at work in their full maturity which can only be faintly and fitfully recognised in physics. In this way the exchanges of physics, biology and psychology will become fruitful for the science of the future, and lay the basis for a new scientific monism.

A living individual is a physiological whole, in which the parts or organs are but differentiations of this whole for purposes of greater efficiency, and remain in organic continuity throughout. They are parts of the individual, and not independent or self-contained units which compose the individual. It is only this conception of the individual as a dynamic organic whole which will make intelligible the extraordinary unity which characterises the multiplicity of functions in an organism, the mobile, ever-changing balance and interdependence of the numerous regulatory processes in it, as well as the operation of all the mechanisms by which organic evolution is brought about. This conception applies not only to individuals, but also to organic societies, such as a beehive or an ants' nest, and even to social organisations on the human level.

As the concept of space-time destroys the purely spatial character of things, so the concept of the organic whole must also be extended beyond the spatial limits of the organism so as to include its interaction with its environment. The stimuli and responses which render them mutually interdependent constitute them one whole, which thus transcends purely spatial aspects. It is this overflow of organic wholes beyond their apparent spatial limits which binds all nature together and prevents it from being a mere assemblage of separate interacting units.

It is time, however, that we pass on to the world of mind. From matter, as now transformed by space-time and the quantum, we pass step by step through organic nature to conscious mind. Gone is the time when Descartes could divide the world into only two substances—extended substance or matter and thinking substance or mind. There is a whole world of gradations between these two limits. On Descartes' false dichotomy the separate provinces of modern science and philosophy were demarcated. But it is as dead as the epicycles of Ptolemy, and ultimately the Cartesian frontiers between physics and philosophy must largely disappear, and philosophy once more become metaphysics in the original sense. In the meantime, under its harmful influence, the paths of matter and mind, of science and philosophy, were made to diverge farther and farther, so that only the revolution now taking place in thought could bring them together again. I believe, however, their reunion is coming fast. We have seen matter and life indefinitely approaching each other in the ultimate constituents of the world. We have seen that matter is fundamentally a configuration or organisation of space-time; and we have seen that life is a principle of organisation whereby the space-time patterns are arranged into organic units. The next step is to show that mind is an even more potent embodiment of the organising whole-making principle, and that this embodiment has found expression in a rising series, which begins practically on the lowest levels of life, and rises ultimately to the conscious mind, which alone Descartes had in view in his classification. I have no time to follow up the matter here beyond making a few remarks.

Mind is admittedly an active, conative, organising principle. It is for ever busy constructing new patterns of things, thoughts or principles out of the material of its experience. Mind, even more than life, is a principle of whole-making. It differentiates, discriminates and selects from its vague experience, and fashions and correlates the resulting features into more or less stable, enduring wholes. Beginning as mere blind tropisms, reflexes and conditioned reflexes, mind in organic nature has advanced step by step in its creative march until in man it has become nature's supreme organ of understanding, endeavour and control—not merely a subjective human organ, but nature's own power of self-illumination and self-mastery: "The eye with which the universe beholds itself and knows itself divine."

The free creativeness of mind is possible because, as we have seen, the world ultimately consists, not of material stuff, but of patterns, of organisation, the evolution of which involves no absolute creation of an alien world of material from nothing. The purely structural character of reality thus helps to render possible and intelligible the free creativeness of life and mind, and accounts for the unlimited wealth of fresh patterns which mind freely creates on the basis of the existing physical patterns.

The highest reach of this creative process is seen in the realm of values, which is the product of the human mind. Great as is the physical universe which confronts us as a given fact, no less great is our reading and evaluation of it in the world of values, as seen in language, literature, culture, civilisation, society and the state, law, architecture, art, science, morals and religion. Without this revelation of inner meaning and significance the external physical universe would be but an immense empty shell or crumpled surface. The brute fact here receives its meaning, and a new world arises which gives to nature whatever significance it has. As against the physical configurations of nature we see here the ideal patterns or wholes freely created by the human spirit as a home and an environment for itself.

Among the human values thus created science ranks with art and religion. In its selfless pursuit of truth, in its vision of order and beauty, it partakes of the quality of both. More and more it is beginning to make a profound esthetic and religious appeal to thinking people. Indeed, it may fairly be said that science is perhaps the clearest revelation of God to our age. Science is at last coming into its own as one of the supreme goods of the human race.

While religion, art and science are still separate values they may not always remain such. Indeed, one of the greatest tasks before the human race will be to link up science with ethical values, and thus to remove grave dangers threatening our future. A serious lag has already developed between our rapid scientific advance and our stationary ethical development, a lag which has already found expression in the greatest tragedy of history. Science must itself help to close this dangerous gap in our advance which threatens the disruption of our civilisation and the decay of our species. Its final and perhaps most difficult task may be found just here. Science may be destined to become the most effective drive towards ethical values, and in that way to render its most priceless human service. In saying this I am going beyond the scope of science as at present understood, but the conception of science itself is bound to be affected by its eventual integration with other great values.

I have now finished my rapid and necessarily superficial survey of the more prominent recent tendencies in science, and I proceed to summarise the results and draw my conclusions, in so far as they bear on our world-picture.

In the first place we have seen that in the ultimate physical analysis science reaches a microscopic world of scientific entities, very different in character and behaviour from the microscopic world of matter, space and time. The world of atoms, electrons, protons, radiations and quanta does not seem to be space-time, or to conform to natural law in the ordinary sense. The behaviour of these entities cannot be understood without the most abstruse mathematics, nor, apparently, without resort to epistemological considerations. We seem to have passed beyond the definitely physical world into a twilight where prophysics and metaphysics meet, where space-time does not exist, and where strictly causal law in the old sense does not apply. From this uncertain nebulous underworld there seems to crystallise out, or literally to materialise, the macroscopic world which is the proper sphere of sensuous observation and of natural laws. The pre-material entities or units condense and cohere into constellations, which increase in size and structure until they reach the macroscopic stage of observation. As the macroscopic entities emerge, their space-time field and appropriate natural laws (mostly of a statistical character) emerge *pari passu*. We seem to pass from one level to another in the evolution of the universe, with different units, different behaviours, and calling for different concepts and laws. Similarly, we rise to new levels as later on we pass from the physical to the biological level, and again from the latter to the level of conscious mind. But—and this is the significant fact— all these levels are genetically related and form an evolutionary series; and underlying the differences of the successive levels, there remains a fundamental unity of plan or organisation which binds them together as members of a genetic series, as a growing, evolving, creative universe.

In the second place let us see how commonsense deals with this macroscopic world. On this stage commonsense recognises three levels of matter, life and mind as together composing the world. But it places them so far apart and makes them so inherently different from each other that relations between them appear unintelligible, if not impossible. The commonsense notions of matter, life and mind and any relations between them, as well as the world which they form, are an insoluble puzzle. The older science therefore attempted to reduce life substantially to terms of matter and to put a question mark behind mind; and the result was a predominantly materialistic view of the world. The space-time relativity concept of the world has overcome the difficulty by destroying the old concept of matter, and reducing it from a self-subsistent entity to a configuration of space-time—in other words, to a special organisation of the basic world-structure. If matter is essentially immaterial structure or organisation, it cannot fundamentally be so different from organism or life, which is best envisaged as a principle of organisation; nor from mind, which is an active organiser. Matter, life, and mind thus translate roughly into organisation, organism, organiser. The all-or-none law of the quantum, which also applies to life and mind, is another indication that matter, life, and mind may be but different stages or levels of the same activity in the world which I have associated with the pervading feature of whole-making. Materialism has thus gone by the board, and the unintelligible trinity of commonsense (matter, life, mind) has been re-interpreted and transformed and put on the way to a new monism.

In the third place, the iron determination of the older science, so contrary to direct human experience, so destructive of the free activity of life and mind, as well as subversive of the moral responsibility of the individual, has also been materially recast. It was due to the Newtonian causal scheme, which, as I have indicated, has been profoundly shaken by recent developments. Relativity reduces substance to configuration or patterns, while quantum physics gives definite indications of indeterminism in nature. In any case, life through the ages shows clearly a creative advance to ever more complex organisation, and ever higher qualities, while mind is responsible for the creation of a whole realm of values. We are thus justified in stressing, along with natural necessity, an increasing measure of freedom and creativeness in the world, sufficient at least to account for organic evolution and for the appearance of moral law and endeavour. This liberation of life and spirit from the iron rule of necessity is one of the greatest gains from the recent scientific advances. Nature is not a closed physical circle, but has left the door open to the emergence of life and mind and the development of human personality. It has, in its open, flexible, physical patterns, laid the foundation and established the environment for the coming of life and mind. The view, to which Huxley once gave such eloquent and poignant expression, of a dualism implanted in the heart of nature, of a deadly struggle between cosmic law and moral law, is no longer justified by the subsequent advances of science.

But, in the fourth place, another dualism of a wider reach has appeared, which makes the universe itself appear to be a house divided against itself. For while the stream of physical tendency throughout the universe is on the whole downward, towards disintegration and dissipation, the organic movement, on this planet at least, is upward, and life structures are on the whole becoming more complex throughout the course of organic evolution. From the viewpoint of physics, life and mind are thus singular and exceptional phenomena, not in line with the movement of the universe as a whole. Recent astronomical theory has come to strengthen this view of life as an exceptional feature off the main track of the universe. For the origin of our planetary system is attributed to an unusual accident, and planets such as ours with a favourable environment for life are taken to be rare in the universe. Perhaps we may even say that at the present epoch there is no other globe where life is at the level manifested on the earth. Our origin is thus accidental, our position is exceptional, and our fate is sealed, with the inevitable running down of the solar system. Life and mind, instead of being the natural flowering of the universe, are thus reduced to a very casual and inferior status in the cosmic order. A new meaning and a far deeper poignancy are given to Shakespeare's immortal lines:

> *"We are such stuff*
> *As dreams are made on; and our little life*
> *Is rounded with a sleep."*

According to astronomy, life is indeed a lonely and pathetic thing in this physical universe—a transient and embarrassed phantom in an alien, if not hostile, universe.

Such are some of the depressing speculations of recent astronomical theory. But in some respects they have already been discounted in the foregoing. For even if life be merely a terrestrial phenomenon, it is by no means in an alien environment if, as we have seen reason to think, this is an essentially organic universe. In its organic aspects the universe is on the way to life and mind, even if the goal has been actually reached at only one insignificant point in the universe. The potencies of the universe are fundamentally the same order as its actualities. The universe might say, in the words of Rabbi Ben Ezra—

> *"All I could never be,*
> *All man ignored in me,*
> *This I was worth to God."*

Then, again, the very possibility of perception, of knowledge and science depends on an intimate relation between mind and the physical universe. Only thus can the concepts of mind come to be a measure for the facts of the universe, and the laws of nature come to be revealed and interpreted by nature's own organ of the human mind. Besides science we have other forms of this inner relation between the mind and the universe, such as poetry, music, art and religion. The human spirit is not a pathetic, wandering phantom of the universe, but is at home, and meets with spiritual hospitality and response everywhere. Our deepest thoughts and emotions and endeavours are but responses to stimuli which come to us, not from an alien, but from an essentially friendly and kindred, universe. So far from the cosmic status of life and mind being degraded by the newer astronomy and physics, I would suggest an alternative interpretation of the facts more in accord with the trend of evolutionary science. We have seen a macroscopic universe born or revealed to consciousness out of a prior microscopic order of a very different character. Are we not, in the emergence of life and mind, witnessing the birth or revelation of a new world out of the macroscopic physical universe? I suggest that at the present cosmic epoch we are the spectators of what is perhaps the grandest event in the immeasurable history of our universe, and that we must interpret the present phase of the universe as a mother and child universe, still joined together by a placenta which science, in its divorce from the other great values, has hitherto failed to unravel.

Piecing together these clues and conclusions we arrive at a world-picture fuller of mystery than ever. In a way it is closer to commonsense and kinder to human nature than was the science of the nineteenth century. Materialism has practically disappeared, and the despotic rule of necessity has been greatly relaxed. In ever-varying degree the universe is organic and holistic through and through. Not only organic concepts, but also, and even more so, psychological viewpoints are becoming necessary to elucidate the facts of science. And while the purely human concepts, such as emotion and value, purpose and will, do not apply in the natural sciences, they retain their unimpaired force in the human sciences. The ancient spiritual goods and heirlooms of our race need not be ruthlessly scrapped. The great values and ideals retain their unfading glory and derive new interest and force from a cosmic setting. But in other respects it is a strange new universe, impalpable, immaterial, consisting not of material or stuff, but of organisation, of patterns or wholes which are unceasingly being woven to more complex or simpler designs. In the large it appears to be a decaying, simplifying universe which attained to its perfection of organisation in the far-distant past and is now regressing to simpler forms —perhaps for good, perhaps only to restart another cycle of organisation. But inside this cosmic process of decline we notice a smaller but far more significant movement— a streaming, protoplasmic tendency; an embryonic infant world emerging, throbbing with passionate life, and striving towards rational and spiritual self-realisation. We see the mysterious creative rise of the higher out of the lower, the more from the less, the picture within its framework, the spiritual kernel inside the phenomenal integuments of the universe. Instead of the animistic, or the mechanistic, or the mathematical universe, we see the genetic, organic, holistic universe, in which the decline of the earlier physical patterns provides the opportunity for the emergence of the more advanced vital and rational patterns.

In this holistic universe man is in very truth the offspring of the stars. The world consists not only of electrons and radiations but also of souls and aspirations. Beauty and holiness are as much aspects of nature as energy and entropy. Thus "in eternal lines to time it grows." An adequate world-view would find them all in their proper context in the framework of the whole. And evolution is perhaps the only way of approach to the framing of a consistent world-picture which would do justice to the immensity, the profundity and the unutterable mystery of the universe.

Such in vague outline is the world-picture to which science seems to me to be pointing. We may not all agree with my rendering of it, which indeed does not claim to be more than a mere sketch. And even if it were generally accepted, we have still to bear in mind that the world-picture of tomorrow will in all probability be very different from any which could be sketched today.

CHAPTER XII

FORWARD MARCH!

War was declared in Europe on September 3, 1939. The Union Parliament had been summoned to prolong the life of the Senate. After dramatic conferences over the week-end General Hertzog, the Prime Minister, moved that South Africa remain neutral but discharge her obligation to defend Simonstown, the British naval base. Field Marshal Smuts moved an amendment which because of its historical importance is reprinted here:

"This House declares that the policy of the Union in this crisis shall be based on the following principles and considerations, viz.:

"(1) It is in the interests of the Union that its relations with the German Reich should be severed, and that the Union should refuse to adopt an attitude of neutrality in this conflict.

"(2) The Union should carry out the obligations to which it has agreed, and continue its co-operation with its friends and associates in the British Commonwealth of Nations.

"(3) The Union should take all necessary measures for the defence of its territory and South African interests and the Government should not send forces overseas as in the last war.

"(4) This House is profoundly convinced that the freedom and independence of the Union are at stake in this conflict and that it is therefore in its true interest to oppose the use of force as an instrument of national policy."

The Smuts amendment was adopted by 80 votes to 67. General Hertzog tendered his resignation to the Governor-General. Field Marshal Smuts was invited to form a Cab-

191

*inet. Co-operation between General Hertzog and Field
Marshal Smuts, which had been so fruitful, was at an end.
Two months later, at Bloemfontein, on November 3, 1939,
Field Marshal Smuts justified his action in Parliament in
a speech which stirred and inspired South Africa.*

I FEEL quite overwhelmed by this reception. I came here
under the impression that I was to address a selected
few of my followers. Instead of that I am being accorded
a reception such as I have seldom had before. This is my
first political speech, this is the first political platform I
have ascended since I became Prime Minister again two
months ago. After the events in Cape Town I considered
it my duty and the duty of my colleagues to get down to
doing our job and put right what there was to put right
in our respective offices. In the meanwhile I gave my opponents a free run of the country to make propaganda.

The political position in South Africa after all the
milling and shouting of the past two months is now clearing up rapidly. Just recently there have been two con-
gresses—that of the Hertzog Group in Bloemfontein and
the National Party Congress in Paarl, while a meeting of
the Central Head Committee of the United Party took
place here this morning.

You have seen that General Hertzog has decided to
form a group, the "Hertzog Group," which is going to
secede from the United Party and which is going to take
steps to fuse in a new party with the "Purified" Nationalists. A new Afrikaner Party is going to arise, and it seems
to me that it is going to be that very Afrikaner bloc against
which General Hertzog protested so strongly not so long
ago. He will be the leader—or something like that—of the
new party.

On the other hand, from Dr. Malan's side, it was said at Paarl that they are going to negotiate the formation of a new party and that General Hertzog would be the leader— or something like that—and that the "Hertzog Group" would assist the "Purified" Party. If all this came to pass then the republican movement would be placed in cold storage. It is the bundle of hay to lure the donkey on. But I never took Dr. Malan's republicanism seriously. That cold storage has been put to use before today.

This morning we held a meeting of the Central Head Committee of the United Party, and there the final break came. We decided by a big majority to approve of the decision taken by Parliament on September 4, 1939, to take part in the war. After this, General Hertzog and his friends resigned and walked out. But it all happened in a very good spirit and I moved a motion expressing cordial thanks and appreciation for the work General Hertzog has done for the people and the country in the years that he was leader of the United Party. But now they have left— again a secession!

The majority of the members remained at the meeting and decided to carry on. We are the United South African National Party. The United South African National Party is going to go on with its work in future just as in the past. . . .

Those who are remaining with me I give this advice: Hold fast to the principles of the past six years; maintain the bonds and do not let us break down the work that we ourselves have built up so painstakingly. Let the fraternity and the friendship continue to exist.

General Hertzog said the other day that the United Party is dead. I say: "Long live the United Party!" We are on the right and true road of South Africa, the road that leads to National Unity.

I am filled with deep gratitude at the measure of support I have found in all parts of South Africa. It has far exceeded my most optimistic expectation. I knew the course I advised Parliament to take was a risk and a venture of faith, but the establishment of the United Party was a similar venture of faith. In both cases we saw our duty and sought to fulfil that duty according to our best lights.

The course that Parliament decided to take in September was a risky one because there might very easily have been a landslide in the opposite direction. People want to keep out of war—it is only human to want to keep out of trouble, and I was inviting them to court trouble. My old friends in the Cabinet warned me very seriously against what I was doing. They told me there would be grave trouble if my advice was followed; that we would see the country torn from end to end, and even that we might experience a rebellion far worse than the one of 1914.

But looking back on the last two months you will agree with me that nothing could be more wholesome, more tranquil or more satisfactory than the internal conditions in South Africa today. Since we decided to do our duty as a nation, unflinchingly, all those underground rumblings have ceased. You hear very little of those various subversive tendencies today, and I can state sincerely that a more wholesome and satisfactory state of affairs prevails than for a long time.

General Hertzog has recently been attempting to bury the United Party, and at the same time he is resurrecting from the grave an old and very dead corpse—the so-called British jingo. I heard a great deal of that old gentleman in my South African Party days, but I thought that he and Hoggenheimer and a number of other "spooks" had disappeared. But no sooner does General Hertzog bury the United Party than the British jingo is brought back from the grave.

General Hertzog says he has nothing against the English. I quite believe him. It would be monstrous if it were not so. General Hertzog has a curious idea of what the British jingo is: it is an Englishman who disagrees with him. A young Englishman who votes for neutrality is a real South African patriot, but a young Englishman who votes for us is at once a British jingo and the arch enemy of this country. And, of course, the latter young Englishman was misled by a very evil person in the shape of General Smuts.

Let me say that General Hertzog need not worry very much about the British jingoes. There were no British jingoes in the United Party. If there were, they have long since parted from me and they have denounced me in no measured terms. There may be a few British jingoes in South Africa, but my feeling is that there are many more Afrikaner jingoes. In the United Party we had no British jingoes and the vast bulk of South African English-speaking citizens are just as much South African, stand just as much on a South African basis, as any Afrikaner citizen of this country. Let us drop this racial talk, this nonsense about "spooks" and "goggas," because I find that members of my race are sometimes even more jingoistic and even more dangerous in that respect than the British jingo.

Let us now come to the events which led up to the decision of Parliament to enter the war on September 4. British jingoism had nothing to do with the decision which Parliament made. The question before us as a nation was a much more serious and far-reaching one than participation in the war. It was a choice of the future path that South Africa was to follow. I felt very deeply and the more I pondered over the situation the more I realised that South Africa stood at the cross-roads, and that this country was to make a choice which would influence her future for many years to come.

The question was: With whom were we going to stand in the future of this dangerous world? Who were going to be our friends—our old and tried friends of the British Commonwealth, or were we going to go the other way and make Germany our friend?

That question is not raised directly by the question of neutrality, but it underlies the question. We could not decide on neutrality without asking ourselves where it was going to lead us. To me it is quite clear that the real choice before South Africa was whether this was going to be a country which would, in future, develop along the lines of freedom, according to the ideals of government which exist within the British Commonwealth, or whether we would gradually fall under German or Nazi influence and in the end find ourselves in a situation where we never wished to be. There is no longer a question of isolation in this world. This so-called isolation is a complete illusion. The world is becoming so intertwined that it is impossible to talk of isolation.

Night by night this country is being attacked and bombarded with propaganda from Germany, in a way far more dangerous, subtle and insidious than any attack by armies.

Night by night the soul of the people of South Africa is being sapped and their convictions undermined by that broadcast from Zeesen. There are other broadcasters going about this country from platform to platform and they are even more dangerous than the announcer from Zeesen. No, we were at the cross-roads, but we took the right turning. In the years to come, when the situation has cleared up, the people of South Africa will be grateful to the Parliament of this year for deciding to sever relations with Germany and keep this country moving along the same lines as those upon which we have been progressing so well in recent years.

Now I return to the address which General Hertzog gave here within the last few days, and I shall reply to the accusations he made. Speaking of the happenings which led to Parliament's decision on the 4th of September, when, General Hertzog says, "Smuts lay in wait for a good chance to break," it is not necessary for me to deny that accusation, for the whole history of what actually happened denies it. I must say that I was more than surprised when I read this, but if there was this suspicion, if this was in the heart of General Hertzog, did he really trust me in those six years we worked together?

I am human. I must admit it was a shock to realise this after all the trust I had placed in him from year to year, after the support I gave him, after the blood and sweat I gave to see the United Party through its difficulty. I do not boast when I say that the United Party was, in a great measure, my work—my best work for South Africa, my pride and honour. It was the ideal for which I sacrificed everything, for which I sacrificed my personal interests. After I had done all that, why should I break down my own work? Am I fitted for a lunatic asylum? Again I ask you, why should I look for an opportunity and lie in wait to jump out? It never occurred to me. I did everything I could to ensure long life to the Party. There was only one wish I had for my old age—to see that the Party should remain as strong as a rock for South Africa, and after I had disappeared the generation who would follow would have an impregnable foundation on which to build. I prayed God to prevent a break.

General Hertzog talks about small incidents such as flags, anthems and oaths. Everything I did was designed to keep the United Party together. I smoothed those incidents over. General Hertzog said I objected to the singing of "Die Stem." That is false. His memory must have failed him, for if he remembers correctly he will acknowledge that I gave him whole-hearted support in his suggestion to have "Die Stem" and "God Save the King" played at the opening of Parliament.

But the question before us at the beginning of September was not one of flags or anthems. It was a question which went to the very roots of our national life. It was the question of the road South Africa should follow in future. I saw we had now reached a point where I would have to give away everything which I regarded as right for the people of South Africa when General Hertzog came to us with a ready-made plan of neutrality. We had reached down to bedrock.

General Hertzog had consulted his friends and decided to stay neutral on certain lines. He did more. Before he spoke a word to me or one of my colleagues to find out what we thought, he had an assurance that the Nationalist Party would support him in a policy of neutrality. Here are the facts: General Hertzog spoke to me about this for the first time on Saturday, the 2nd of September. I met him in his Chambers with Mr. Havenga and Mr. Pirow. Their policy of neutrality was laid before me and I immediately said: "Impossible." I told them that I found it impossible to subscribe to it. We argued about it for the rest of the morning, and I tried to show them why I thought it was an impossible policy for South Africa. When we could not arrive at an agreement I asked General Hertzog, in view of the seriousness of the situation, to call the Cabinet together. And so the Cabinet was summoned and the matter laid before them. For the whole of that afternoon and again that night we discussed the matter. And all this time General Hertzog had in his possession the assurance of the "Purifieds" that they would support him. General Hertzog did not tell me or a single one of my colleagues anything about the fact that he would rely on the support of the "Purifieds" in his policy of neutrality.

On Saturday night we agreed to meet again. Parliament had been summoned for Monday morning and there was not much time left. Before the Cabinet meeting on Sunday afternoon, General Hertzog again had the assurance— this time in black and white—that the "Purifieds" would support him. Even at that final meeting he told us nothing about that promise from Dr. Malan and his party. I myself heard about it a week later, and for me it was a great shock. . . .

We asked General Hertzog on the Sunday afternoon why he was in such a hurry and advised him that it would be better to call together the Caucus of the Party. But this was also abruptly refused. It was refused because General Hertzog was assured of his majority in Parliament, because he had the letter from the Nationalists in his pocket. The accusation I make against General Hertzog is that he did not tell his colleagues about this letter and that at this critical moment he went over the heads of his own party members. It is being said that General Smuts and his friends set a trap. If there was a trap, I ask you, "Who set it?" No, my conscience is clear. There was no intrigue on our side. But General Hertzog had the promise of support from the "Purifieds" in his pocket.

I expected something quite different. I thought when I saw which way things were going, that General Hertzog wanted to get rid of some of his Cabinet colleagues; that he would then re-form his Cabinet—a thing which he was quite entitled to do—and then go to the country. He would have had a new Government and he would have consulted the people. But instead of that he went to Parliament because he was assured of a majority. They had counted. But they counted wrongly. General Hertzog told me and other responsible persons that he was assured of a majority. But then came the Monday, the debate in Parliament, and the defence of Hitler, and then came the thunderbolt that smashed General Hertzog's secret plans.

I want to make it clear to the people of South Africa that our hands were clean throughout the entire occurrence. General Hertzog and his advisers made mistake upon mistake. I told you what he could have done, but then I am only a dull fellow. General Hertzog leaned on certain "slim" people in the Cabinet who advised him. There was even an attempt to drag in the Governor-General. But everything went wrong. All these miscalculations came to nothing, and the worst of all is that General Hertzog has given over his faithful followers into the hands of

the Malanites, in the same way that he is now giving himself over to Dr. Malan. . . .

Now we are being told that this is the "hereniging" of
Afrikanerdom—something which has been born of blun-
der upon blunder. I want to keep the name of the United
Party clean. Mr. Pirow is going about making accusations.
General Hertzog has made accusations. I think it right to
the public of South Africa that I should say these things.
I am sorry that I have to talk like this of General Hertzog.
I respect him, even though I ask for nothing in return.
General Hertzog has rendered great service to this country. It grieves me to see that in his old age he is busy destroying the great work which he did in the past six years,
and I deeply regret that he has become a tool in the hands
of Dr. Malan. I do not accuse him. He was misled by colleagues about him, and especially by one who gives out to
be a hundred per cent Afrikaner. But upon this man the
people of South Africa look with the deepest suspicion.
This counsellor of General Hertzog was General Hertzog's
downfall, and today he is busy seeking favour with Dr.
Malan.

It is now being said that that decision taken by Parliament was a blot upon the history of South Africa and her
sovereign independence; also that by going into this war
we have bound South Africa to England finally. It is being
said that the British connection was responsible for the
war declaration and that it must be done away with. It is
exactly the same as the case of the British jingo. It all boils
down to this, that if you vote with General Hertzog you
are a good Afrikaner; if you vote against him you are a
British jingo. If Parliament had decided for neutrality it
would have been the best, sovereign, independent Parlia-

ment South Africa ever had. It decided against, and so it was dubbed a Parliament that besmirches the honour of South Africa.

Years ago, when Britain left the gold standard, I counselled South Africa to leave it too. I warned the country of the terrible losses it would suffer if we did not. What was the answer I got? They said: "Look at that British jingo; Smuts is only for the British connection. If England does a thing then we must also do it." The same arguments which are being used about neutrality today were used against me about the gold standard. My advice was not followed, because it was the "British connection." And what happened? South Africa received a blow, a setback, from which it has not yet fully recovered. You here in the Orange Free State know that hundreds and thousands of farmers are still going bent carrying the burden imposed on them by that mistake.

The argument that it will be a blot on us and that it is the British connection which is responsible for these things, does not weigh with me any more. I have heard it too often and I have seen too much of the harm it has done. And now that Parliament by its own free will has decided in the interest of South Africa to go to war, it suddenly becomes a blot on the name of South Africa and there is all this "hoehaai" and chasing about.

You know that for years Dr. Malan asked us to lay down a policy of neutrality. What was the answer General Hertzog and I gave him? We told him that we could not lay down such a policy in advance. It was for Parliament to decide when the situation arose. That was stated over and over again.

On September 4 General Hertzog made his appeal to

Parliament. I was in duty bound to set forth my own point of view, and after one of the most serious debates I have ever heard in the Parliament of South Africa, this sovereign body, without any interference from England, decided that it was in the interests of South Africa and for the good of this country's future that we should take part in this war. The appeal was made to Caesar, and Caesar gave judgment. But now the nation must be brought into confusion and must be torn in two because General Hertzog lost the day. We shall hear a good deal more of the personalities, to which I have referred, in the days to come. Abuse and personalities have ever been the weapons of those who have a weak case to plead.

The charge against me, according to General Hertzog, is this: That a year ago (in September, 1938) when the Sudetenland trouble was afoot, we discussed the matter in the Cabinet and we decided that in this particular matter, the Sudetenland problem, we were certainly not going to take part in any resulting war, but that we were going to remain neutral. You will recall what the Sudetenland question was about. It affected a certain small section of the German population on the fringe of Czechoslovakia, who were dissatisfied and complained of being ill-treated. The peace of Europe seemed to be endangered on this account, and nobody wanted to have Europe plunged into a war because of the demands of the Germans there. We certainly had no interest in the matter. We had no good reason at the time to suspect Hitler of his evil intentions. He alleged that he was trying to right the wrongs of his people and save the German minority in Czechoslovakia. Mr. Chamberlain and the French and British Governments conceded that Hitler had a case, and they did not want war.

At that time and in those circumstances we said that if war should come in Europe over this dispute, South Africa would be neutral. I agreed that this was the right course to take, but I must emphasise that our decision was confined to a particular case. It had nothing to do with any other problem that might arise. We never defined or formulated a policy of neutrality for the future. If we had, why was it not made public? When Dr. Malan challenged us in Parliament to lay down a policy of neutrality in advance we would have said: "We have decided on a policy of neutrality. Here it is!" But we did nothing of the kind. Instead, General Hertzog kept on saying that Parliament would decide in the interests of the country. The policy we decided upon in September, 1938, was confined to the case of the Sudeten Germans and went no further.

Now, what happened subsequent to the Sudeten affair? Six months later Hitler launched his attack against Czechoslovakia, which is not a German country but an entirely different country and had nothing to do with the Germans. They were the historic enemies of the Germans for a thousand years and more. Great Britain and France and all the other countries saw that Hitler's intentions were no longer merely the righting of the wrongs of the Germans, but that he was going to annex a country with an entirely alien population. When this took place a complete change of view came over the people of Europe and of the world.

Mr. Chamberlain had all the time been working persistently for peace. Only the other day we had a statement from our former High Commissioner in London, Mr.

Charles de Water, who, in a farewell message, explained that he had spent ten years in Great Britain and had identified himself with the life of the people there. He added: "I can testify to this country's patient and persistent efforts to keep the peace of Europe." That is what our own representative in London, who is in close touch with the people and the Government there, has testified to have been his experience.

When Hitler made this move against Czechoslovakia, the British Government saw that it had to make another effort for peace. They made a treaty with Poland. They knew that after Czechoslovakia the next victim would be Poland, and so Poland was given the guarantee that if she were attacked Britain would help her. Thereafter Germany was repeatedly warned that if she attacked Poland and continued the march for domination, Britain would be at war with Germany.

Did that stop Mr. Hitler? Oh, no! Hitler, knowing that it meant war with England, attacked Poland.

To my mind it is perfectly clear, and it would be clear to any sensible person, that Hitler's move was in effect a declaration of war against England. No other construction can be put on the matter. That was the construction also which the British Government put on it, and it became a case of life and death. Today we see even more clearly than we did at the outbreak of war that this is a struggle to the death between Hitler and Great Britain and France.

During the last general election, on many a public platform, I expressed my opinion that if ever Great Britain were involved in a war and attacked, and her existence and future were at stake, I did not see how we in South Africa could remain neutral. I made that statement deliberately as my conviction, explaining that our interests and those of Great Britain were so intertwined that an attack on Britain would have consequences so far-reaching that we in South Africa could not face them. After the general election I was challenged on that statement in Parliament. I repeated it with General Hertzog sitting next to me, but he neither contradicted nor objected to it. In fact, several Ministers, who have now sided with General Hertzog, told me that they agreed with me. They agreed that if Britain came into that danger we could not be neutral. Is it not as plain as a pikestaff that this danger is there? Can we fold our hands and say that this is a case similar to that of the Sudeten Germans? Can we say with General Hertzog that this is simply a case of Danzig and the Polish Corridor when the whole world may be in flames? I think it is very definitely a case that falls within my accepted formula, that when Britain is in vital danger this country cannot remain neutral.

Germany declared war on Poland, knowing that it would mean war against England and the democratic nations. The declaration of war against Poland was thus also against England. It is now a question of a life and death struggle for England—it is a world war in which our interests are deeply involved. If Germany wins, then not only England but South Africa as well is lost. We will first become a Nazi country, and then our independence is lost. In spite of General Hertzog's arguments that Hitler's aim was not world domination, the majority in Parliament realised this. No; it was not a question of Danzig and Poland. The honour and freedom of South Africa were at stake.

If this country had remained neutral I shudder to think

what the situation would have been in South Africa and what a setback there would have been in the relations of the people. I shudder still more at the blot that would have been put on the fair name of South Africa. We would have had, and we would have deserved, the contempt of the world. We would have been fair-weather friends. Great Britain, who gave us our sovereign status, who was our market, who was our friend, whose navy defended our shores—we would have deserted her in the hour of danger to remain the friend of her enemy. We would have deserved the supreme contempt of every sensible person in this world.

By what we have done we have not only looked after the interests of this country, but we have saved the honour of South Africa. In years to come, when all these political questions are forgotten, but the great dominant facts of history are penned, it will stand out that South Africa was not a false friend, but a country on whose word and friendship reliance could be placed. Those members of Parliament who did their duty on the 4th of September will deserve the thanks and gratitude not only of our generation but of many generations to come. There is no blot on our sovereign independence. We have acted as a free but honourable people. Dishonour and sovereignty do not go well together.

There is talk today of the Boer War, of concentration camps, and attempts are being made to make our flesh creep about what happened in the old times. But let us think rather of what has happened since. Let us think also of the fine treatment, the generosity and the helping hand we have experienced from Great Britain ever since. We render the people of this country no service by continually harking back to what happened in the distant past and forgetting what has happened since.

By this act of Parliament we have served South Africa's interests in the fullest and noblest sense of the word. But it is right that I should point out that we also served the material interests of this country. Today we are at war, but you see no signs of it. We have the protection of the British Navy and our produce of all kinds is being convoyed overseas to the markets of Europe by the British Navy. Would that have happened if we had remained neutral? South Africa is selling her products not merely at normal prices but at prices better than before the war. Let me just refer you to our wool, maize, dairy produce and now, I understand, also citrus fruit.

In every way possible Great Britain is putting herself out to keep South Africa's farmers going, knowing that she is dealing with a generous, faithful and friendly people and not with false or fair-weather friends. It is true that these products also help Great Britain, but it should not be forgotten that she could easily obtain produce from other countries of the world. Indeed, although Great Britain already had more wool than she needed from Australia and New Zealand, she undertook to buy on the South African market at the same prices as she was paying there because she realised that South Africa's was a friendship which was worth having. I want our friends who attack the Government's policy to sit down and think out for themselves what it would have meant for the country if we had declared for neutrality and if these advantages had been withdrawn from us. We would have had no protection on the seas, no transport, no communications and no markets, and then what would have happened to us in this country?

No, I think we are going to have good times. So far from having brought trouble on this country as things look at present, it seems that we have brought this country to a new era of prosperity, to a new forward era in our industrial development. In the meantime we are going to prepare our own defences. South Africa is not in a position to send armies to Europe, but we must get ready for all eventualities. You noticed that only a few days ago Molotov, the Prime Minister of Russia, said that if peace is not declared now, the war might spread over the whole world.

Our defences are a matter of the greatest importance, which rest in my own hands, and I will take the work and responsibility upon myself. Since nobody can say how far the war will spread, and whether Africa itself will not be in the flames eventually, our defences must in addition to the defence of our coast, also keep in mind African dangers so that we may be ready to meet those dangers when they arise. We cannot wait until the enemy has reached our borders. While we will keep to the terms of the Defence Act we must be prepared—if need be with volunteers—to meet the enemy beyond our boundaries and to halt him there.

It is, of course, a matter for military experts to decide where this can be done best and most effectively. Considerations of transport, of the best positions for defence, of the speed and nature of the attacking air force and mechanised transport, must all be kept in mind. What the military experts under all these circumstances consider right will be done and the necessary steps to that end will be taken.

We must be prepared and ready to go to the assistance of the British Colonies in Southern Africa in case of danger to them and to us. They are in many instances our advance guard, and their population originates to a great extent from the Union itself. Even our neighbour, Mozambique, must be able to rely on our assistance in the hour of danger. If they make an appeal to us, then we must help to protect them in the interests of the Union itself.

As regards the British Colonies, from Kenya to the south, we naturally have the greatest interest in them—in times of war as well as peace—and we must stand by their side like an elder brother on the African Continent. The Great North Road—the Road of South Africa—stretches north and does not terminate at our boundary. Our interests, many of our future markets, are situated there. Our countrymen in ever-increasing numbers have migrated to these territories. In war, as in peace, we stand by our friends of the British Commonwealth in the North. This is the policy which was preached to them in the past, and it is still our policy.

I say nothing of the defence of South-West Africa. In this respect I can only repeat what General Hertzog said in Parliament as Prime Minister when he was attacked by Dr. Malan and his side. "We will defend South-West Africa just as we will defend the Union." We are waiting at present to see whether General Hertzog, too, is going to swallow his own words and accept the "Purified" policy of surrender.

My final message to you is this: "Have courage and forward march as the United Party under the tried principles which guided us since 1933." In the last general election the people, with an unprecedented majority, gave their approval to those principles. This is still our mandate, the mandate for which we will fight until the next general election comes in four years' time. I feel convinced that the vast majority of the people stand by us and we are advancing full of courage. We hear suddenly of a hundred per cent re-union of the "Afrikanerdom." The lion and the lamb will lie down together—and where will the Hertzog lamb end up then?

I only want to say this: A marriage which is born from fear and anxiety and not from love is generally a failure. A movement which pretends that the whole of Afrikanerdom is included, but from which the whole English-speaking Afrikanerdom almost unanimously holds aloof, together with such a large portion of Afrikaans-speaking Afrikanerdom in the United Party, is not a safe basis on which to build up the people of South Africa.

Build the future of South Africa in accordance with a greater plan and stronger foundation than those of the tottering combination of "Purifieds" and United Party members who have been sifted out. And now, faithful friends of the United Party: Forward march, and have courage! There is big work for us to do and a greater victory awaits us.

CHAPTER XIII

GREATER SOUTH AFRICA

During the first war session of the Union Parliament in April, 1940, Field Marshal Smuts flew to Johannesburg to open the Show of the Witwatersrand Agricultural Society. He made an appeal for the Pan-African outlook, for that big vision which was the theme of his first lecture in Kimberley in 1895 and has since been the aim of all his statesmanlike work for South Africa and for the world.

AFTER introductory remarks suited to the occasion, Field Marshal Smuts said:

There are a couple of other matters I wish briefly to emphasise today. The first is the interdependence of agriculture and industry in the economic life and progress of the country. The parallel and equal development of agriculture and industry is, in the view of the Government, essential to our future economic expansion. Hence the determined effort not only to keep agriculture going through the black period through which it has been passing, but also and at the same time to protect and watch over the interests of manufacturing industry in every reasonable way.

It is generally recognised that a great opportunity has arrived for us to push forward industrial development in this country. The great world crisis now upon us may prove a unique opportunity for forwarding our industrial development.

The war must inevitably largely throw us back on our own resources. Much that has been imported will now have to be manufactured locally. Much that has been exported will now, with restricted sea transport, have to be worked up and processed and consumed in this country.

It is an ill wind that blows nobody any good, and this world blizzard may mean much for the economic progress of South Africa. It is for this reason that the Government have decided to ask Parliament to establish an Industrial Development Corporation which will be able to help to finance and guide our industrial development and prove for industry the sort of boon that the Land Bank has proved for agriculture.

If this institution is wisely run it may, and one hopes will, prove an enormous stimulus to industrial development at this opportune moment in our industrial prospects. We have the resources to a large extent; we have also the markets. We want the enterprise and finance which will give this country an industrial shove-on such as it received in the last Great War.

It must not for a moment be considered that the claims of agriculture and industry conflict. On the contrary, we are coming more and more to realise that the health of agriculture in this country is intimately bound up with industry, and that industrial development is the rock on which agricultural stability must in future be largely built. A flourishing industry supplies the markets and the prices required for a flourishing agriculture.

The unprecedented agricultural depression which set in in 1929 was due not so much to over-production in agriculture as to industrial collapse and lowered purchasing power, which made it impossible for agriculture to obtain the market prices on which alone it could live and continue to function. And by the same token agriculture in this country has everything to gain and to look forward to from a sound policy of industrial expansion.

Besides, the health of our people of all classes and colours is intimately bound up with the state of our agriculture, and today we have many serious problems confronting our various control boards and the nutrition council, which is shortly to be established. They must all realise that production and consumption are part of the same wide problem of which nutrition is also a vital part.

A healthy people and healthy workers form the only sound basis for national prosperity, and this can only be achieved when we have worked out an unassailable agricultural policy for our land which will enable all sections of our population to obtain the quality and quantity of food they require to maintain health and physical fitness.

The other matter I wish to mention takes us somewhat farther afield. During the last two months there has been much discussion in Parliament of the north—of that part of Africa which stretches beyond the Union up to the Equator at least.

That discussion was concerned with our war effort, the defence of the Union, which, under modern conditions of warfare, may have to be conducted far beyond our border, and the vital interest which the Union has in the defence of the British territories to our north against any external menace.

We are happy to have in our midst today a visitor from the far north—General Sir Archibald Wavell, Commander-in-Chief of the British Armies in the Near and Middle

East. We all hope that the impressions which he will gather on this fleeting visit will hearten him in the great task which awaits him in the north.

I am not going into that military question here; but the question of defence is part and parcel of a much larger issue of African policy. To the Union of South Africa all Africa south of the Equator at least, and especially the British territories, are a matter of economic interest and concern; and the Union can only realise its true destiny, even within its own borders, by keeping that larger African point of view clearly before itself. This is no question of jingoism or African Imperialism, and it does not in any way affect the several sovereignties or European loyalties or relationships of the several communities which inhabit our southern continent.

It affects the economic interests and development of us all and, in a large cultural sense, the destiny of us all as co-workers in the cause of European civilisation on this continent. And so I come to stress once more, on a great agricultural-industrial occasion like this function, the African viewpoint—the Pan-African idea, if I may call it so. In times such as these through which we are now passing, we are naturally compelled not only to take stock of our own natural resources but also to inquire in how far the neighbouring States can supply us with those goods and materials which formerly we procured from across the oceans. It also behoves us to see whether, arising from the dislocation of world trade and shipping, we can supply our neighbours on this continent with some of those goods from which they must now be debarred.

The time, therefore, would appear to be both ripe and opportune, as never before, for developing and fostering trade between the Union and her neighbours. In this matter I feel that your society can do a great deal. In fact I think that you can rightly claim that you have already led the way in cementing the bonds of friendship and in paving the way to closer relations between the Union and her neighbours.

For instance, the Prime Minister of Southern Rhodesia in 1936 honoured the Union with a visit for the sole purpose of opening this Show. East Africa, through its agricultural society, has on more than one occasion honoured the Union by inviting our Cabinet Ministers to open the great agricultural show held in Kenya at Nairobi, in what is considered by many to be the finest agricultural showground in Africa. For many years past our good neighbours, the Portuguese, have been an outstanding feature in this ring in front of us, whilst various products of the countries north of us have been displayed here from time to time to the mutual benefit of all concerned.

This broad outlook on the part of your society has everything to commend it and has far-reaching possibilities. In fact, I see in it the germ of a Pan-African Show in the not-distant future, not to mention a Pan-African agricultural movement with all their attendant benefits. May we not look forward to the periodic holding of such shows in the Belgian Congo, in Mozambique, in Kenya and in the Rhodesias? All these countries at present hold outstanding agricultural shows at their main centres which, in these days, are becoming more and more easy of access both by road and by air. It may at present seem a dream, but great dreams have a knack of coming true and the Pan-African idea is more than a dream. Perhaps our society may consider the matter and even sponsor the idea so far as Johannesburg is concerned.

More and more the countries north of us are looking to us for guidance in various directions, especially in matters of mining and agriculture, because they are naturally anxious to benefit from our riper and more varied experience. We, on the other hand, have much to learn from our neighbours, and we have much to gain from contact with them. More and more it is being realised that we have to work out an African viewpoint not only in agriculture, but also in many other directions. Our schools and universities might do much to encourage the study of these countries—the languages, the conditions and the requirements of the peoples north of us. In this connection I would like to congratulate the University of the Witwatersrand on the steps which it has already taken in this direction. For instance, on my holiday last year through East and Central Africa I came across the professors of geology, geography and civil engineering leading a party of some 30 students through the wilds and wonders of the Belgian Congo. These contacts made by the youth of this country with the realities of the north must not only leave lasting impressions on their minds, but must broaden their outlook in African affairs and make them more useful citizens, both of the Union and of Africa as a whole.

On that same holiday trip I found that the great copper mines in Northern Rhodesia were run largely by engineers and expert miners who had had their training and experience on the Rand.

Again, each year sees more and more leaders of thought in the countries north of us establishing contact with us, while frequent requests are being made by the neighbouring Governments for the services and advice of our professional officers. The transport and postal conferences between us and the other African States in recent years have led to much closer relations, while at this moment a number of our veterinary officers are collaborating in Tanganyika and Northern Rhodesia with officers of the northern States in combating the dread menace of rinderpest. The recent visit of Union parliamentarians to the north is also not without significance, and I am sure has done much to cement the bonds of friendship and understanding between ourselves and our northern neighbours. These contacts are only natural and to be expected because we have a host of common problems which will require all our combined wisdom to tackle. Human, animal and plant diseases know no political boundaries, and locusts roam at will over most of Africa.

Now is the time for us to readjust our outlook on African affairs and to develop a new conception of our relations with our neighbours. We must demonstrate and bring home to all where our community of interests lies, and we must broaden very much the basis of our co-operation with other African States. We cannot stand aloof, we of this richly-endowed South Africa. If we wish to take our rightful place as leader in Pan-African development and in the shaping of future policies and events in this vast continent, we must face the realities and facts of the present and seize the opportunity which these offer. All Africa may be our proper market if we will but have the vision, and farsighted policy will be necessary if that is to be realised.

Think for a moment of this huge Africa, in which we

live and of which we are a part. Politically, it is composed of countries in all stages of political development, from complete independence to complete subjection to European sovereignties. Self-government is the goal of most of these territories, and they are more and more seeking and learning to stand on their own feet. Their outlook is changing and they are making contacts one with another, chiefly through commerce, trade and the tourist traffic, which promises to become one of the most lucrative industries on this continent.

Roughly, this continent contains 4,000,000 Europeans and 150,000,000 non-Europeans living in a climate which is mainly tropical. We in the Union, however, are the most fortunate of all in that we occupy the great tract of temperate grassland where the climate and natural conditions are the most favourable for white settlement and where, moreover, the mineral deposits are most abundant. The British Government has just announced its intentions to devote £50,000,000 to colonial development and most of it will come to the African Colonies. Surely we as the elder brother on this continent should also share in this development and do what we can to help in the general opening up of the resources of this vast continent and the markets it will afford to our industries.

The mode of life of this immense population tends more and more in the direction of that of civilised man, which means that the commodities required for higher standards of living will be demanded in ever-increasing quantities by one of the great reservoirs of humans still largely undeveloped. Consider what the teeming millions of Africa mean in productive and consuming capacity, for the native can no longer be regarded merely as an aid to production. He is becoming more and more a consumer of the products of civilised industry.

How far, then, can Africa itself go towards meeting this growing demand? What are her natural resources in her vegetation, in her soils, in her mineral treasures, in her mineral fuels, in her wild life, in her recreational assets, in her manufacturing industries, and in her human material? What part can the Union play in this development and in securing its fair share of the common market? Those are important questions for us. Everything that we can think of except perhaps natural petroleum, seems to be supplied by the African continent. Can we not then visualise some scheme of interchange and inter-communication to turn Africa into more of a co-operative whole? Could we not aim at more direct interchange both by overland and by sea communications? Could we not do very much more to make the different constituents of this continent more conscious of one another and more understanding of one another?

We might well begin by encouraging the tourist traffic and by propaganda relating to all aspects of life in the various countries south of the Equator. In this connection, I may point out that much good work has already been done by the various publicity associations and tourist organisations in our own territory and in those of our neighbours. In this sphere also the various automobile associations have played a great part in opening up Africa to the public and much credit is due to them. All this must sooner or later make the peoples realise the ideal of African solidarity and the strength that would come to all if this huge land mass could somehow or other co-ordinate its large policies and especially its economic interests into a comprehensive scheme.

It is not beyond the power of practical politics at the present time to make quite a substantial start in this direction, especially if our commercial and industrial leaders will realise their unique opportunity and thus lead the way. Let us, therefore, briefly glance at our trade relations with our neighbours—South-West Africa, the Rhodesias, Portuguese East Africa, Kenya, Tanganyika, Uganda and the Belgian Congo. The value of imports from these territories amounted in 1938 to approximately £3,250,000, while our exports to these countries were to the value of nearly £4,250,000. This in itself is sufficient to show that contact is already well established between these territories and ourselves. There is, however, one great possession in this block of Africa with which as yet we have made little commercial contact—Angola. Surely this fair and rich land, with Lobito Bay as one of the major African ports, offers a field for trade and closer industrial co-operation.

The countries north of us are naturally able to produce those tropical crops, such as tea, coffee, cocoa, cotton, sisal, palm kernels and oil, copra, rubber, ground nuts, which we can never aspire to grow in any commercial quantity, but all of which are essential for our secondary industries. Apart from this, vast and almost untouched timber resources await development in the west in the basin of the Congo and, to a lesser degree, in the east in Portuguese territory, Kenya and Tanganyika. Extensive natural resources suitable for the manufacture of paper also exist in all parts of Central and Southern Africa. The commodities of timber and paper pulp which in the past we imported from distant Finland and other Scandinavian countries to the value of over six million pounds will now naturally be denied us for some time to come. Will it not be possible to tap the supplies which lie at no great distance from the South African coast ports?

As illustrating the possibilities of opening up new markets in Africa many of you will probably have noticed a recent announcement by the Minister of Agriculture for Southern Rhodesia that Rhodesia had secured a contract to supply the Gold Coast with 100 tons of bone-beef a month for consumption by native mine workers. We can only admire our neighbour's enterprise in this venture and wish her still further success in opening up Africa to herself.

Some optimists have spoken of a United States of Africa and some have adumbrated the policy of a Monroe doctrine for this continent. So far as the present and near future are concerned these ideas belong to the region of Utopia. What, however, is practicable and calls for our serious consideration is the opening up of communications and establishment of contacts, the pushing of trade and commerce and collaboration in hammering out and co-ordinating general lines of policy and in developing common and mutual economic interests. In short, the African idea should become a practical force in the shaping of the destiny of this continent. And the Union of South Africa, in its own interests as well as those of its African neighbours, should take an active part as a good neighbour in furthering that idea and that policy.

CHAPTER XIV

THE CRUSADERS GO NORTH

In July, 1940, South Africa sent its first contingent of troops North. This was the advance guard of the fine volunteer army which had been created and trained under Field Marshal Smuts. As Commander-in-Chief, Field Marshal Smuts later in the year visited the South African troops in the North. This chapter is composed of his speech to the troops when they left South Africa and the broadcast address he gave on his return.

I HAVE looked forward to an opportunity to say good-bye to you before you leave for the front. I therefore welcome this occasion to bid you a very heartfelt farewell. I do so personally, because as an old soldier I know what your service as soldiers in the far north may mean to most of you. I do it also in my official capacity as head of the Army and of the Government. In all these capacities I express to you the gratitude of the people of South Africa for the choice you have made and the service you are prepared to offer your people and your country. More no man can do than offer his life for his friends. That offer, the highest and most solemn offer a man can make, you are making. We are proud of you. You have done so freely and willingly. You are volunteers of your own choice. No compulsion of law has been laid on you. You go forth as free men and serve your country in that highest duty of the citizen—to defend his country, even unto death, if necessary.

Speaking to you today on this solemn occasion of parting, a parting which for some of you will be final, I can but wish you Godspeed from the bottom of my heart and say: God bless you, God bless your great enterprise. From personal experience I know what awaits you. I know what war means—seven years of my life have been spent in wars. They were among the hardest years of my life, but they were also full of the richest experience that life can give. I would not exchange my war experiences of the Anglo-Boer War and the last Great War for all the gold of the Rand.

You are going to face danger, hardship and sacrifice—perhaps death itself—in all its fierce forms. But through it all you will gather that experience of life and enrichment of character which is more valuable than gold or precious stones. You will become better and stronger men. You will not return the same as you went. You will bring back memories which you and yours will treasure for life. Above all, you will have that proud consciousness that you have done your duty by your country, and rendered your contribution to its future security and happiness. You will not be mere items in the population; you will come back as builders of your own nation, of its best traditions, of its lofty national spirit and of its national pride. Your children will be proud of you. A nation is never proud of its "hands-uppers," its fence-sitters, its players for safety. We South Africans reserve our respect and pride for the bitter-enders, for those who go all out; who take their life in their own hands for country and people. And in the free choice you have made you will take your place in that select company of whom South Africans are instinctively proud.

You are going north to meet the enemy where he can be found, not where he comes to find you—in your own homes. That, too, has been the tradition of South Africa. We did it in the last war. Many of you will revisit familiar haunts in the north. But to most of you that will be a new world, full of great interest of all kinds. You will see the vastness of this continent, its immense variety, its richness and grandeur of scenery, its magnificence in every respect. You go to it now as the strategic rampart and defence lines of South Africa. But in the years to come your service there will forge links between north and south which will inevitably open up wider horizons and establish larger interests for South Africans. From every previous war South Africa has emerged a greater country, and this war will prove no exception. Your work will carry further the tradition of Briton and Boer alike.

But we are endeavouring to do more. In taking our part in this war we are not merely defending ourselves, our country, our future. We are also standing by our friends in the Commonwealth of Nations in all loyalty and good faith, as we know they will stand by us. But we are doing more: we are also safeguarding that larger tradition of human freedom, of freedom of conscience, freedom of thought and freedom of religion which is today threatened as never before in history by the Nazi menace. That tradition is the spiritual rock whence we were hewn. We have fought for our freedom in the past. We now go forth as crusaders, as children of the Cross to fight for freedom itself, the freedom of the human spirit, the free choice of the human individual to shape his own life according to the light that God has given him. The world cause of freedom is also our cause and we shall wage this war for human freedom until God's victory crowns the end.

In conclusion, just one word-more. Wherever you may be or whatever you may do, remember that you are South Africans and that our name and honour are in your care. Keep it safe and high. Farewell, my friends; and may God bless and prosper the Right.

———————

Field Marshal Smuts' broadcast address to South Africa on November 4, 1940:

Last Saturday I returned from a visit to our troops in the North, and as relatives and friends of the men, and the public generally, may be interested in my impressions, I take this first opportunity to give this broadcast talk.

For some time I had looked forward to this visit, but circumstances were against me. But quite recently my kind colleagues in the Government had been urging me to take a brief holiday for which no time had yet been found since the beginning of our troubles. I therefore decided to kill two birds with one stone and to make this suggested holiday the occasion for a visit to the troops. And so on the Saturday before the last, I left by air for the North.

Not that this visit was exactly a holiday! In one week I flew more than 7,500 miles and all my time was taken up with a ceaseless round of activities. But the interest of the thing carried me through and the visit has been to me a real refreshment of the spirit. . . .

I met our Air Force Squadron in Khartum, where I heard high praise of their fine work. Their spirit was high and their health good. They had taken heavy toll of the Italian Air Force in Abyssinia. In Kenya I visited practically all the places where South Africans are taking part in the campaign, and came into touch with all the units and ranks of our personnel in all parts of the country where they are stationed or operating. I give a few impressions of general interest.

Everywhere I was pleased to find that our troops had made an excellent impression. Their conduct was exemplary and they were a credit to South Africa. They enjoyed the goodwill and abounding hospitality of the Kenya people, and everywhere people were glad to receive them in their homes. Indeed, the people of Kenya are forming an extensive organisation to provide recreation and home reception for our troops when they are on short leave from the front. South Africa has every reason to be grateful to the people of Kenya for their kindness to our boys and girls. I say girls because we have a number of our young women doing clerical and hospital work and other forms of auxiliary war service in connection with our army in the North; they are suitably housed under the supervision of South African women.

Physically, our troops make a most favourable impression, and are probably in advance of any force we have ever sent from this country—fit and well, and in stature and muscular development well above the average. I doubt whether anywhere in the world troops of a finer physical type can be found. In height and breadth they are so striking that I have heard a British General call them tanks among men! How could it be otherwise when as volunteers, and not conscripts, they represent the flower of our Union manhood. The provision for their health and physical welfare in that exacting climate is the best South Africa can give with her hard experience of the past to guide her. Long training both here and in East Africa has produced a fitness and hardness of a very high standard.

The feeding of the men is of the best, as they repeatedly assured me. But I would impress on the public, as I have already impressed on my wife as Chairwoman of the Gifts and Comforts Organisation, that everything should be done by our public at home to supply our troops at the front with those comforts and knick-knacks which help so much to keep up the spirit in the wilds and far away from home and sustain their interest and morale under difficult conditions. Their morale is at present very high. One could not meet these fine men without feeling proud of them. Their officers speak most highly of them, and, with proper leading, they will prove themselves equal to the exacting demands that are certain to be made upon them, and add fresh laurels to our high military reputation.

Looking at these sons of the fathers whom I was proud to lead in the same historic field a generation ago, I could not but feel high pride and emotion to see that they were worthy of the rock whence they were hewn. They sometimes brought a lump to my throat—how proud one feels of South Africa when one sees how much people are prepared to give up at home and to do in far-away lands and under hard conditions for the honour of their country and the security of its future.

I have spoken of our boys in East Africa. Let me also

add a word about that wonderful country, that wonderland, which so many old warriors, who listen to me tonight, remember so well from their experience of the last war. Two impressions stand out in my mind in reference to this visit—the greatness of that world and the goodness of man. As I flew hour after hour over those endless forests and great lakes, over the Great Rift Valley studded with a jumble of high mountains and extinct volcanoes more magnificent than any to be found elsewhere, I had an overwhelming impression of the vastness and power of Nature and of the forces that had shaped the past of this continent with unrivalled lavishness and grandeur. In this gigantic world the human element seems dwarfed to utter insignificance, and one bows one's head in wonder before a sublimity so overwhelming. Indeed, no words can express the impression of the physical grandness which that world of East Africa produces on one's mind.

The other impression comes nearer home, touches our hearts more closely, warming them and raising them as no mere external greatness of Nature can do. I am free to confess that the sight of our boys in East Africa kindled a deeper emotion in me than even that awe-inspiring natural scenery. How grand is Nature! How good is man! The sight of those young men, with their happy, eager faces, with the thought of what they had given up to serve their fellows and to make this a safer world for the spirit of man to dwell in securely—that sight, that thought, made me realise that their souls were worthy to match this glorious setting of Nature, that the goodness of man was a worthy match for the greatness of Nature.

They are the happy warriors of the New Order, the champions of that spiritual order of the universe which in the end is more deeply founded and more secure than these ancient hills and craters. The New Order will not arise under the swastika, which is the symbol of past tyrannies and the moral enslavement of the human spirit. It can only arise under the sign of the Cross, in the spirit of service and self-sacrifice, which has carried man from his brutal, bestial past to the height of his spiritual vision. Not in mastery, but in service, not in dictatorship, but in freedom lies the secret of man's destiny.

This is what these young South Africans stand for, for what I trust South Africa will stand for till the very end.

CHAPTER XV

AN APPEAL FOR NATIONAL UNITY

*On New Year's Eve, 1940, Field Marshal Smuts broad-
cast to the South African nation a message of hope and
confidence for the New Year. He expressed the belief that
South Africa would reject the challenges of reaction and
the principle of racial domination.*

WE HAVE come, my friends, to the end of the darkest
year in modern history. During it seven nations
have fallen under the Nazi scourge—a new black plague
that sears the souls of men, and withers civilisation at its
roots. Seven nations that were free are no longer free.
Seven peoples that cherished liberty have been enslaved.

That has been calamity enough; but we cannot measure
what it has meant, and what it still means, in the sum of
human suffering and in the destruction of the treasured
fruits of human endeavour.

It has been a dark year; but there have been great
flashes of light—that have illumined the darkness when
the night has been blackest. These flashes of light, fitful
and spasmodic at first, have now become one broad continuous beam, flowing down the path to victory. This is
the spirit of free men; this is the beam of light that flashes
through a world of darkness when the flint of human courage is struck.

A new year unfolds before us. We no longer have any

illusions. We know that we are facing a most formidable and implacable foe. We know that there is no scruple that he will not callously ignore; no ruse, no deceit, no treachery that is too low for him to use.

We know that we must bring into action all the material and spiritual resources that we can muster, and we know that there are dark and critical hours ahead of us; but we know, too, that we are on the path of victory. The tide has turned.

Elsewhere I have spoken about the probable developments of the war in the year 1941, but to my own countrymen I would say that we have ample grounds for confidence. We see today the unrivalled resources of the United States of America being turned to our assistance. The people of that great democracy have realised that we of the British Commonwealth are fighting their battle for them, and that if we fail our defeat will be their defeat and their humiliation. We can rest assured of a steady and increasing flow from America of material help, to supplement the moral sympathy that has always been with our cause. In this and in the growing spiritual and material power of the whole British Commonwealth, lies the assurance of victory. We in South Africa have not felt the blast and torture of this war. We are, nevertheless, playing our part. Some of our sons have given their lives in the cause for which we fight. We, as a young nation, whose freedom is new and infinitely precious, pay that tribute to the principles through which we gained our freedom and our nationhood, so that we may still live our lives as we ordain, and still direct our own destinies according to the common wisdom of our people.

In the new world that will emerge out of all the suffering and devastation of this war we shall need wisdom. Of my countrymen I would ask: "Wherein lies wisdom? Does wisdom lie in national disunity? Does it lie in the tribal spirit which seeks to set the interests and the culture of one race above the interests and the culture of another race; or does true wisdom lie in national unity and in the free, liberal spirit of tolerance and co-operation?"

This war will give the clearest answer to these questions. Indeed, the answer becomes more obvious with every day that passes. Human wisdom is asserting itself. The conscience of humanity is revolting against the selfish reactionaries in Europe and elsewhere who have tried to impose upon mankind the tribal cults and shibboleths of a barbaric age.

The spirit of human progress is fighting the barbarism which would throw the world back into a slavery and subjection unparalleled since the dark ages. If this war means anything at all it means surely this: that civilisation is determined to uphold, and will uphold, the principle that racial domination, racial exclusiveness and top-dogism are in conflict with the whole trend of human progress and enlightenment. The world will not tolerate the challenge of reaction.

That is the message the Old Year passes on to the New Year; it is a message of hope and confidence; and that is the message that I would give my countrymen tonight: South Africa must and will reject the challenge of reaction.

If we South Africans are to play our part in shaping the new world, and if we are to get the best for ourselves and for our country out of the lessons of this war, we must not be out of touch or out of sympathy with the ideas and principles that victory will establish beyond challenge.

Larger sympathies, wider understandings and new visions of service and of sacrifice are being forged in the white heat of war; and out of this great furnace will come, highly tempered by adversity, the unity of spirit and of purpose needed for the regeneration and reconstruction of the world.

We, too, must have that unity of spirit and of purpose, and we, too, must once again reject—as we are rejecting— the narrow prejudices and selfish sectionalism that would make a mockery of our constitutional freedom and our claims to nationhood.

The call for national unity is clear and insistent. National unity is needed for the war; it is needed, too, for the victory that is assured. The New Year will bring us close to victory; and it will, I trust, take South Africa far along the path of unity and internal peace, to progress and prosperity.

I wish you a happy New Year.

CHAPTER XVI

INVESTING IN FRIENDSHIP

In a review of the war situation given in a national broadcast from Cape Town on April 26, 1941, the Field Marshal expressed the view that Britain is building up the moral capital with which the New World Order will be floated when victory is won.

I HAVE been asked to broadcast my impressions of the present war situation and, in view of certain current misconceptions, I readily do so.

Some people appear to be depressed by the turn of events in the Balkans. The sudden and unexpected collapse of Jugoslavia after a brief resistance, and the overwhelming of Greece after her heroic defence against terrible odds, make them fear for the future of the Allied cause. They also note that British forces have once more retired before the superior force of the enemy. They forget that in the last war the position of the Allies in that quarter of Europe was far worse than it is today. Then, both Rumania and Serbia were overrun and crushed; both Bulgaria and Turkey were active allies of Germany, and a large German and Turkish army threatened Egypt and was only beaten off from the very banks of the Suez Canal. Even so, the Allied cause moved to a grand victory in the end.

My friends who fear for the future because of what is

happening in this or that part of Europe make a great mistake which is perhaps pardonable in the circumstances. There is such a rush of events, the canvas of the world war is so overcrowded with incidents, that people are apt to become confused, to lose their sense of perspective, and fail to put events in their proper values and relations in the vast framework of the war. Incidents of relatively minor importance and forming really only mere episodes in the vast struggle come to be looked upon as crucial. In that way we become men of little faith. To view things in their proper perspective in the whole war situation is not only to take the true view but also to have that strong faith which will see us through the perplexities and doubts that beset us in the conflict.

This war will not be settled in the Balkans, and the commotion and confusion which Germany has stirred up there will in the end only contribute to her own undoing, whatever present successes she may appear to achieve. What before was for her a large and valuable supply base has been turned largely into a scene of bloodshed and chaos. The sudden resentment and hatred of so many more millions have been turned in full blast upon her. It is not this sort of victory that will make her win the war. Nor is this the theatre in which this war could in any case be won. Perhaps she has only turned to this theatre to hide her discomfiture in failing to carry out her promise of an early invasion of England and to encourage her people with minor successes at the other end of the continent.

That Britain went to the assistance of Greece and other small countries at whatever cost to herself is to her lasting credit. That she failed in Norway, Holland and Belgium is no blame, no dishonour, and her helping hand stretched to them in the hour of her own sore plight. Britain is investing in friendships as Germany is investing in hatreds in the process of the war, and Britain is thus building up the moral capital with which the real new world order will be floated after the peace. As has often happened before, Germany is thus winning the victories and losing the war.

To keep the developments of this war in a proper prospective, one has always to bear in mind what I consider to be the real crux of the situation. It is this, that Hitler began the war, that he is the aggressor and must continue in his aggression to the very end. The rôle of Britain is essentially a defensive one. If Hitler fails in his attack on the fortress of Britain itself he will have reached that end—his end—and will have lost the war.

To succeed, Hitler will be compelled sooner or later to attempt the invasion of Britain. Compared to this fundamental issue all the rest are merely incidents. Victorious diversions to the Balkans or other parts of Europe will not finally avail him. Hitler may successfully overrun one country after the other in Europe, but unless he overruns Britain he has lost the war.

Of course, for the defence of Britain and the maintenance of the food and other supplies of her people, her vital lines of communication have to be kept open. These are the North Atlantic, the route round the Cape and, to a lesser degree, the Mediterranean. These are her life-lines. She may temporarily even lose everything else, but if she defeats the invasion and keeps these lines of communication open she will have broken Hitler and will recover all she may have lost for the time being. If Britain and her sea power survive the attack Hitler is lost, and not even the prospect of a stalemate will be left him. His Empire will go the way of that of Napoleon, who also won most of the European continent only to lose everything in the end. That is the crux of this war, the truth which dominates everything else.

We have been elated over the victories in East and North Africa and in the Mediterranean. We may have been depressed by the setbacks in the Balkans and elsewhere. In relation to this fundamental issue of the defence of Britain they are but side issues and incidents. In spite of his spectacular diversions in various parts of Europe Hitler has so far failed to face this real issue. When he does face up to that issue he will be up against his real fate. And if he funks it he is equally lost.

In thus again emphasizing what has often been said before, and what I consider the real crux of the war situation, I do not mean to belittle the importance of what has been done in Africa and in the Mediterranean. As the leader of the South Africans I would be the last person in the world to do so. The intrinsic importance of our achievement in East and North Africa and in the Mediterranean basin is very great. For one thing, the bubble of Mussolini has been finally pricked. Most of his fleet is at the bottom of his "mare nostrum." His African Empire lies in ruins and Haile Selassie is marching to reoccupy his throne. One of the two Axis partners is hopelessly bankrupt and becomes a liability to the other. That is the way Austria went last time, and Germany followed in due course. The victories in North Africa and the Mediterranean basin may play a similar rôle in this war; and although not of decisive importance in themselves, may in the total defeat and virtual elimination of Mussolini mark the beginning of the end. Germany will henceforth stand alone in the company only of her victims, who in agony and hatred writhe under her extortion.

The African victories have put the Axis on the scrap-heap. Hitler, in effect, has lost his one and only ally and gained only victims. We, on the contrary, have in effect gained a new ally—the most powerful and worth having in the whole world. With the United States of America and all its goodwill and vast resources behind us we may indeed look forward to the end with steadfast confidence. He has mobilised America for us in a way we never could have done ourselves. If a vast pro-Allies movement is today surging like a tide over the United States, it is first and foremost the work of Hitler. That great good he of all men has accomplished, and in the verdict of history that may yet outweigh the evil he has done. Thus in the moral order of the universe evil always defeats and destroys itself and becomes subservient to the good.

Hitler has roused the American giant from his slumbers—hence the election of President Roosevelt, hence the Lease and Lend Act, hence the firm and unshakable alignment of all responsible American opinion on the side of the Allies. More will follow. America will yet go all the way. This I have for a long time foreseen. To me it has long been evident that only through America's full participation would the way to victory be clear and assured. I have looked forward to this development, not only for the sake of our victory but also for the sake of the peace that was to follow. I could not see a real fruitful peace without America right in it. I could not see America participating in peace unless she had been through the crucible of the war with us.

My friends and I have often discussed the question how

America could be moved and made to see the light. We were convinced that all was at stake that was basic to the American way of life, and if only she could be made to realise this she would not hesitate to act. But she was far away from the European scene. She had unpleasant memories of the last war and the last peace, and she was wedded to her peaceful ideals and her tradition of non-entanglement in European affairs. We saw no one who could move America nor how he was to do it. It never occurred to us that Hitler was to be the missioner to convert America. But—most wonderful among all his wonderful performances—he has done it. And how has he done it? By the simple process of self-revelation—by showing himself as he is, not as he professes to be.

This war has been the revelation of Hitler and his new Nazi order. Since September, 1939, his will to world domination has been written in blood over many free lands. The character of his new order is clearly expressed in the enslavement of the major part of Europe. His principles and practices are thus shown to be a menace to the very foundations of our free ethical civilisation of the West. Hitler himself, through his acts, has supplied the proof for his final conviction. He has at last convinced America. And so, in spite of herself, America is at last girding her loins for the struggle. In due course she will be doing much more. Not in the Balkans but in the West and perhaps in the Far East, the war will be finally fought out. This mortal struggle may be long. It certainly will be hard. But our cause is right and we fight in the conviction of final victory.

CHAPTER XVII

A VISION OF THE NEW WORLD ORDER

On May 12, 1941, Field Marshal Smuts broadcast a prophecy of the future new world order which will arise from an out-and-out Allied victory.

MY SUBJECT is described as a vision of the future. In dealing with it I am, therefore, to be something of a prophet, and to foresee the end of the war and the world-picture as it may be after the war. In view of such a task I trust I may, as a harassed practical man, fairly claim the indulgence of my audience.

I begin with the end of the war. This presents three alternatives—a military stalemate, a German victory, or an Allied victory. I take them briefly in turn in that order.

A Stalemate

Some good people, sickened of the horrors of this war, especially for the civilian population, and the destruction of property and economic life, look forward to, or wish for, as early as possible an ending of the war in a military stalemate. That would, in effect, mean an armistice pending the next great war. A pause during which the rival groups would continue to nurse their wounds and prepare for the deadliest, decisive struggle to come thereafter. My prophetic vision of the future would then have to be set forward to a more distant future, when the world would have had to endure a still more devastating conflict, and there would then scarcely be left any world to prophesy about. I shudder before this prospect and recoil before such a prophetic task. Not only do I consider a stalemate in this war highly unlikely, but I also consider that it may be fatal to the future of the world.

The stage is set and men's minds are keyed up for a decision. No compromise between Hitler's world and the world of the Allies appears likely, and even the most weak-kneed of us had better make up their minds to see this grim business through now, at whatever cost. Let us frankly face the issue. To be or not to be—that is the question before the world at this mortal moment in history.

A Hitler World

The world after a Hitler victory is quite easy to forecast. It would be a continuation of the present Hitler world. That world we already know from the stark, naked facts as they are written not only in Hitler's Germany, but also in the countries which Hitler has so far overrun.

It would be a world more savage than any written of in the darkest pages of our human story. It would be the horror of history. No sane person, outside the ranks of the most fanatical Nazis, could wish for a world in which the present conditions of Austria, Czechoslovakia, Poland and the rest of Hitler's victims are perpetuated. I could understand Prussianism or a soldier's world. But a gangster world such as Nazism, in which one sees the resurgence of all the most hateful elements in poor human nature; in which not only every essential Christian principle, but the finer and nobler human instincts, are trampled upon, and man reverts to the brute—such a world is an insult not only to our ethical feeling, but also to our intelligence. It is in conflict with the principles on which this universe is founded. We can only answer it with the grand and absolute refusal.

I must frankly confess my prophetic soul does not see and cannot face such a world in the future of man whatever vicissitudes may still lie before us.

Some good souls flatter themselves with the thought that a triumph of Hitler would in any case be only a temporary affair; that it would be so inherently bad and unsound that it must lead to an inner revolt and breakdown of itself. So they would placidly fold their hands and reconcile themselves to the prospect of a Hitler victory. They also fall under the "stalemate" category. What a poor and feeble comfort, what a flimsy foundation to build any hope for the future on. I cannot agree to such a way out of our present miseries. The devil is a powerful fellow, and is not to be dealt with in this spirit of appeasement and wishful thinking.

A Hitler world, once well established, may well last a long time. Hitler himself talks of a thousand years. Let his rise in a world of goodwill and appeasement be a lesson to us. If Hitler's creed is, through our weakness and defeatism, allowed to take the place of our Christian human ethics, mankind may have to traverse a dark age before another dawn appears. Remember the disappearance for ages, perhaps for ever, of a feeble Christianity of earlier centuries before the onslaught of Mohammedanism in the Middle East. Hitler's creed is a new religion, a pagan or devil worship, and its victory once achieved may well affect the course of history. Let us not flatter ourselves with the facile thought that evil may reform itself from within and be converted to the good. Evil is there to be fought, and this particular evil of Hitlerism we can and shall fight to its utter defeat.

And so it is that the world I look forward to is one which will emerge from an out-and-out Allied victory.

An Allied Victory

How will that world look, viewed from our perspectives of today? Here, too, I think that present groupings and tendencies point the way to the future, and help me in my task as a prophet. I shall state the gist of my prophecy as briefly as possible.

It seems to me that the day of the small independent sovereign State has passed. That is the sign of the times. In the absence of a mighty world organisation the sad fate of the small independent States of Europe in our day is likely to be their fate more and more in the future. Hitler's victorious course so far has at least proved that much. Philip of Macedon and Alexander the Great proved the same for the Hellenic world. The Greek City State of ancient history and the small independent nation State of today were and are anachronisms in the circumstances of their respective times.

We are unmistakably in for larger human groupings in that holistic process which fundamentally moulds all life and all history. On this theme I could write a book, but here I must forbear. I need only point to what is actually happening today. Already the free Democracies representing the forward movement in our western civilisation, are grouping themselves together under the pressure of the times. That pressure is irresistibly forcing them together in a great world organisation, the outlines and pattern of which we are already beginning to see more or less clearly. In this association there appear various degrees of affinity.

In the inner circle, which now forms the heart of the resistance to Hitler, is the British Commonwealth of Nations. I need not dilate on the particular links which associate this world-wide circle freely together, but their association is undoubtedly a precedent and a prototype of the larger World Association now in the process of formation.

Closest to this inner circle of the British group is the United States of America, which has the same ethic of life and the same political philosophy. Both have, in addition, the strong link of a common language and literary culture. The two thus form a very natural group.

An outer circle of free democracies is represented by the victims of Hitler, nearly all of which are now in alliance with the British group. A few other States would also fall naturally into this association, but I cannot here go into details. Here we have a world-wide, more or less natural grouping, based on common ideals of government and welded together by common interests, common adversity or common danger. At the peace they would naturally form themselves together into a world society, under a distribution which would provide for effective action by the society in all important matters affecting future security and reform. In this way an efficiently functioning organ of the world community would arise, capable of binding the component nations in the paths of peace and ordered progress and arranging its relations with other States not members of the association.

This new world society would follow positive and constructive policies for the future, and not concern itself particularly with the past and with penal or revengeful action towards old enemies. And in this way, in due course, the world may forget its bitter wrongs and once more move into paths of peace and friendly economic relations among the nations. The mistake of the League of Nations in attempting too wide and universal a membership on too loose and nebulous a basis of organisation and duties would thus be avoided and the Association would grow practically out of existing friendships and affinities, and might expand later into the wider international society of the future. We should not attempt to do at one stroke what could only be accomplished in a long process of time and experience.

The crux of this next great step in the organisation of our world will be the attitude of the United States of America. I wish to speak quite plainly on this point. I feel convinced that the United States of America, in abandoning the League of Nations to its fate, after taking the leading part in its foundation, helped to pave the way for the world war which is now devastating Europe and into which she will herself inevitably be drawn. Great is thus her responsibility for the world situation of today, although, of course, I do not deny the greater responsibility of others. She has her share of responsibility for the past; she has an even greater responsibility for the future. Her unique position in the world, her vital stake in the issues in dispute, the dangers which face her also in a world in chaos—all these considerations place a heavy duty on her in this matter of world organisation.

Isolationism is as dead as the absolute sovereignty of the national State. Security, reform, better ordering of our world community—all call for an effective common authority. Thus only can our world be made reasonably safe for peace and liberty—the twin ideals of Democracy.

In that common world authority America must play a leading part. The failure of the League since 1932 is probably the main cause of the present world war. America's sporadic efforts to help from the outside proved unavailing. As a member of the League her rôle would probably have been decisive. I must therefore conclude that, just as world organisation is essential, so America's membership in such an organisation is no less essential. She holds the key. Let her use it, and open the door through which the world can escape from chaos and suffering.

Such in brief outline is my vision of the future after the war. I may be asked what about the other States, our present enemies and those in league or in sympathy with them? Do I abandon them to outer darkness? Will there not then be the opening for rival groups which may sooner or later clash again? I hope this possibility will be avoided by our avoiding all ideas of revenge and penal retribution for a past in whose mistakes we all have our share. Let us try to be helpful in spite of bitter memories. Especially let us give a helping hand in economic reconstruction. Let us thus quietly begin to pick up the threads of a common life again, and let time do its own healing work.

First and foremost we shall be called upon to put our own house in our own democratic circle in order, and ensure as far as possible against the sort of dangers which have now twice overwhelmed us in one generation. Leave the rest to time, to the workings of ordinary prudence and sympathy and reviving generosity, and do not let us attempt more than is wisely possible for the immediate future after the war. Time is a real force, a great healer and a great builder. Let us leave it its place and its function in our vision of the future.

CHAPTER XVIII

THE OFFENSIVE PHASE

The historic speech delivered by Field Marshal Smuts in London to members of the Houses of Parliament on Wednesday, October 21, 1942.

I AM very sensible of the great honour you have done me today. I appreciate this vast audience and the affectionate welcome you have given me, but more, I appreciate today the presence of the chairmanship of my old leader, "L. G."

Words fail me to express my feelings on an occasion like this, but I am here today to address you on the war. The Prime Minister has led me to this; he brought me here, he created this occasion. I feel now like a sacrificial lamb being led to the slaughter, but I rely on your sympathy and support to see me through.

This is a great occasion for me, and I am deeply conscious of the exceptional honour you are doing me. In my experience it is a unique occasion. It is no small thing to be called upon to address the members of this Sovereign Parliament of the United Kingdom, this Mother of Parliaments and free democratic institutions, this Senate of Kings, to use the phrase once applied to the Roman Senate.

I appreciate this honour, which I have not deserved, and which but expresses your goodwill and interest in me and in the country and young nation I am privileged to represent.

I know you have singled me out for this distinction largely because I happen to be the last surviving member, still active in high office, of the War Cabinet of the last war. I was the youngest and the least of that notable band, and no doubt for these good and sufficient reasons I have been spared, perhaps overlooked, by the subsequent storms and the years.

And now that I reappear on this scene after many years you are interested in this somewhat mythical figure and curiosity from the past.

I know the subject of War Cabinets is a minor matter of controversy among you, and I shall therefore avoid invidious comparisons between then and now. But you will at least allow me to refer to the two leaders in the two supreme crises of our sorely tried generation.

I am very proud to be honoured by the presence here today of my old leader, Mr. Lloyd George, but for whom who knows what might have happened in the mortal crisis of twenty-five years ago. Today, in this greater crisis, we gratefully remember his imperishable service and thank God for the gift and saving grace of his great historic leadership. He stands out as the supreme architect of victory in the last war.

No less have we been blessed with distinguished leadership in this vaster struggle of today. I sometimes wonder whether people in this country sufficiently realise what Winston Churchill has meant and continues to mean, not only to them but also to the Allied peoples, the United Nations, and to brave men and women everywhere in the world.

His words and foresight, his courage and energy have been an unfailing inspiration to all of us. He remains the embodiment of the spirit of eternal youth and resilience, the spirit of a great undying nation in one of the greatest moments of history. Let us recognise with gratitude that we have been nobly blessed with wonderful leadership, both in the last war and in this.

I have spoken of the two great actors, the two greatest actors, in the drama, the continuing drama of our age. I call this a continuing drama because I view this war as a continuation of the last war, and the whole as perhaps another Thirty Years' War, which began in 1914, was interrupted by an armistice in 1918, improperly called a peace, was resumed with greater ferocity in 1939, and may continue (who knows?) till 1944. The intervening armistice was a period of feverish rest or unrest and dreams and illusions.

I have referred to two great actors in this drama of our age. There is a third and greater actor to be mentioned. I refer to the British people and the spirit that animates them and the young nations around them in the British Commonwealth of Nations.

One occasionally hears idle words about the decay of this country, about the approaching break-up of the great world group we form. What folly and ignorance, what misreading of the real signs of the times! In some quarters what wishful thinking!

It is true that this greatest human experiment in political organisation, this proudest political structure of time, this precedent and anticipation of what one hopes may be in store for human society in the years to come, this Commonwealth, is being tested as never before in its history.

But is it not standing the test? Is not this free and voluntary association, is not this world-wide human co-operation today holding together more successfully than ever before under the most searching test?

Knowing the dangers and temptations we have had to face, the stresses and strains imposed on us, nothing has been more remarkable to me than the cohesion of this vast structure under the hardest hammer-blows of fate. We have suffered, we are poorer, we shall be poorer still. We have had heavy setbacks and an exceptional run of bad luck.

Is it a wonder that in the fourth year of this war there may sometimes come moments of disappointment, of fatigue, and occasionally even a sense of frustration? But still this great Commonwealth remains the heart of the defence against the most terrible onslaught ever made on human rights and liberties. It stands unshaken by the storms and setbacks.

The people of this island are the real heroes of this epic world-wide drama, and I pay my small tribute to their unbending, unbreakable spirit. I have been absent from this country for almost ten years, and coming back now I can see for myself the vast change which the trials and sufferings and exertions of the war period have wrought.

I remember this smiling land, recovered and rebuilt after the last war, where a happy people dwelt securely, busy with the tasks and thoughts of peace. And now I have come back to a country over which the fury of war has swept, a country whose people have had to face in their grimmest mood the most terrible onslaught in its history.

Many of its ancient monuments are damaged or gone for ever. The blitz has passed over cities, ports, churches, temples, humble homes and palaces, Houses of Parliament and Law Courts. Irreplaceable treasures of one thousand years of almost uninterrupted progress and culture and peaceful civilisation have disappeared for ever.

War, the horror people still call war, but in its modern scientific form something very different from what passed under that name before, war has come to this favoured land and attempted its worst. Much has gone which is lost for ever.

But one thing is not lost—one thing, the most precious of all, remains and has rather increased. For what will it profit a nation if it wins the world and loses its soul? The soul remains. Glory has not departed from this land.

I speak not of outward glory, of what your Gallic neighbours called "la Gloire" in their past revolutionary fervour. I speak rather of that inward glory, that splendour of the spirit, which has shone over this land from the soul of its people, and has been a beacon light to the oppressed and downtrodden peoples in this new martyrdom of man.

Let the enemy say "Gott strafe England." "God bless England" has been the response from the victims of this most fiendish onslaught in history.

But for this country—the stand it made from 1939 onward, its immeasurable exertions since and up to now, its toil and sweat, its blood and tears—this world of ours might have been lost for one thousand years, and another dark age might have settled down on the spirit of man.

This is its glory—to have stood in the breach and to have kept the way open to man's vast future. And when, after a long absence, I see today this flame of the spirit above the flame of the blitz, I feel that I have come to a greater, prouder, more glorious home of the free than I ever learnt to know in its palmiest days.

This is the glory of the spirit, which sees and knows no defeat or loss, but increasingly nerves, nourishes and sustains the will to final victory.

I have singled out for emphasis the spirit and service of this country because they have been the most important, indeed the crucial factors hitherto for our Allied cause. But the spirit of resolution and endurance and sacrifice is not confined to Britain.

Other Allied nations, each in its own degree, share in this spirit. When we survey the world heaving today in its agony we see everywhere the same spirit lighting up the sombre scene.

Think of China and its five years of suffering at the hands of the Japanese war lords, busy with their so-called "co-prosperity sphere" in Asia. Think of Russia and its unbroken spirit amid the hardest blows and most cruel sacrifices of this war.

Look at the wonderful resurgence of the brave little nations of Western Europe, whom no adversity, no defeat, dangers or chains can hold down. Think of the heroic guerrillas of Serbia and other small nations. Look at the new glory of Greece which has so effectively dimmed the tinsel grandeur of Mussolini's Rome—truly a new Hellas has arisen to fulfil the poets' great vision.

And looking further afield, watch the young nations of the British Commonwealth at the job. Last and greatest of all, see America in her invincible might under one of the greatest of leaders, marching to the flaming ramparts of the world in East and West.

And shall we forget France, not dead, but like Lazarus

only sleeping, and waiting for the dawn to shake off the torpor which has temporarily overcome her historic genius?

No, the spirit of man is neither dead nor decadent. It will never bend the knee before the new slavery.

The light of freedom which has guided our slow and faltering advance through the ages still shines in the night which has overtaken us. The glory is still with us, and we shall follow it with all our strength and devotion to the new dawn which surely awaits our race.

But a rough and terrible passage lies before us, and it will call for all our combined resources, all our concentrated will and effort, all our highest leadership to carry us to our goal. There is no place for complacency or wishful thinking.

The mortal struggle is on, and it will become more cruel and desperate as the end draws nearer. For it is indeed a struggle of life and death between the contending systems and ideologies which now divide mankind.

I, therefore, pass on to the war situation. For the first three years of the war our rôle had necessarily to be a defensive one.

That rôle was imposed on us by the intensive secret preparations of the enemy for six years before the war, by the false sense of security he had sedulously fostered among us, and by the mood of appeasement which had thus been created.

That advantage no premature offensive could possibly have overcome. We could barely maintain our self-defence against the terrible odds.

In those cases where we were in honour bound to take the offensive in support of other small peoples we have suffered reverses which still further weakened us. Let us, however, never regret the help we did our best to bring Norway, Holland and Greece in their hour of need.

In these common sufferings which we shared with them the United Nations were born. But these efforts were indeed beyond our resources at that time, and we suffered discouraging reverses. Only in Africa could we successfully assume the offensive, but modesty prevents me from dwelling on that theme.

Then came the most deadly catastrophe of all when France fell. It was an awful moment in history. The sudden fall of a great nation and world Power is a phenomenon almost unknown in history, and this particular blow was as unexpected as it was deadly.

The enemy looked upon it as also for us the end, and this infatuation of his providentially saved us. Instead of immediately turning on London he persevered on his planned course to Paris, and gave us the opportunity to recover our breath and prepare for the blitz against London. And what a defence it was!

Surely never in history did the future hang on so slender a thread, and was the outcome so painfully and prayerfully watched by so many millions over the whole world! Providence saved us there, and let us admit that the Devil helped him. Such is always the ultimate function of evil in this world.

The defeat of the Luftwaffe in that supreme crisis saved not only London and Britain but, I firmly believe, the whole Allied cause and the future of the world.

The fall of France was followed by two other events, both of the greatest importance for the subsequent course of the war. The first was another fatal mistake of Hitler.

Baulked in his air attack on London, he saw that it was unsafe to attempt an invasion of Britain before first clearing his rear in Russia. The magnitude and duration of Russian resistance have surprised not only Hitler but probably everybody else.

Probably no such losses on both sides have ever been suffered in the history of war. If the Russian losses must be terrible it is equally true that the German army is bleeding to death in Russia.

The appalling blood-letting which is necessary for Hitler's ultimate defeat is being administered by the Russians, and they alone can do it. In spite of their losses in men and material and territory, the Russians show not the least sign of giving in, and the bitter defence will go on to the bitter end.

This impression is confirmed by all the best inside information. Hitler has done his best to avoid Napoleon's example, but history may yet record that the course he actually adopted was even more fatal than was Napoleon's retreat from Moscow.

The course for the Allies to follow is clear. Whatever help in whatever form we can give to Russia to sustain her in her colossal effort should be given in the fullest measure and with the utmost speed. She is bearing more than her share of the common burden.

The second result of the fall of France was the almost total loss of the entire Allied positions in the Far East. Vichy opened the door to Japan in Indo-China, and through that unexpected opening the flood poured into Siam, Malaya and Burma.

Indo-China was the back-door to Singapore, a back-door which we never dreamt would be opened by our ally against us—an event for which the defences of Singapore made no adequate provision and which made its fall inevitable.

And when Singapore fell the whole Dutch Indies and the other island groups in the Far East were doomed, and it has only been possible to stop the flood at the very shores of Australia and New Zealand.

People who have not followed or understood the inevitable, the terrible logic of events have blamed the Allies for these tremendous setbacks and the ill-disposed have taken the loss of Singapore as a proof of decadence, and a sign of the approaching downfall of the Commonwealth.

As a matter of fact it was merely a consequence of the downfall of France, and no more.

We mourn these our losses; we mourn especially the temporary loss to Holland of her great Empire in the Far East, which has been a model of colonial government; we deplore our diminished opportunities at the moment of helping China in her stout defence.

But these things will pass. For Japan just as surely as for Hitler's Germany the writing is on the wall. All that will remain of this spectacular Japanese success will be "Japan for the Japanese."

For Japan has infallibly sealed her own doom. Pearl Harbor was at once a challenge to America, to western civilisation and to the principles of good faith on which it is basically founded. In the long run Japan will not be good enough as an associate even for Germany. There are degrees in infamy.

Not that I deplore Pearl Harbor! From our point of view it was a heavy price, but well worth paying for the immense gains that have accrued. It was what the chemists call a catalyser.

It suddenly crystallised, precipitated and solidified American opinion as nothing else in the world could have done. At one sudden leap America was in the war.

These are the steps that have marked our climb out of the abyss into which the fall of France had all but plunged us:

First, the defeat of the German Luftwaffe over London.

Second, the treacherous attack of Germany on Russia, in spite of the peace treaty between them.

Third, Pearl Harbor and its sudden and timely effect in carrying America 100 per cent into the war while Admiral Nomura and Mr. Cordell Hull were talking peace at the conference table.

We have much to be thankful for, but not least for the colossal mistakes of our enemies. Will a fourth blunder be committed? Will Japan, in spite of her peace treaty with Russia, launch a treacherous attack against her also in Siberia? Time alone will show.

We have now reached the fourth year of this war, and the defence phase has now ended. The stage is set for the last, the offensive phase. Let me set your minds at rest at once; I am not going to discuss the future offensive strategy of the war.

The amateur strategists can do that with greater freedom and less responsibility in the Press. I only wish to emphasise that one phase has ended and another must now begin.

The final alignments both of the Allies and our enemies have been made. Resources have been developed and mobilised on a very large scale, ours still on the increase, those of the enemy on the decline.

Our manpower is still growing, that of the enemy is getting depleted, while he makes ever heavier drafts on his suffering vassal peoples. The spectre of want, hunger and starvation is beginning to stalk through the subject countries, the spirit of unrest is heaving and rising.

The explosive limits of endurance are nearing. We are approaching the point when both on the war fronts and on the home fronts in enemy countries the situation is ripening for far-reaching developments.

So far, time has been in our favour, and has, on the whole, been kind to us. In spite of heavy setbacks and many disappointments, we have had the necessary time to prepare to parry deadly blows, and to assemble and consolidate the forces and resources on which we rely for the Allied victory.

Once the time has come to take the offensive and to strike while the iron is hot it would be folly to delay, to over-prepare, and perhaps miss our opportunity. Nor are we likely to do so—of that I feel satisfied.

On this point it would be unwise for me to say more and thus to set going unnecessary and perhaps harmful speculations.

I would only point out to you that today is Trafalgar Day. It reminds us of that dark hour, the darkest in the Napoleonic War, when your great national hero, the embodiment of the heroic offensive spirit of this people, sought out the superior naval forces of the enemy and dealt them that fatal blow which not only saved England from invasion, but turned the whole tide of war, and finally saved Europe from being overwhelmed by the insensate domination of one man.

This anniversary is not only a reminder, but an inspiration to us to go forward and do likewise. I am sure it will not be lost on us and our gallant Allies. For us, too, the great offensive moment is ripening.

I now pass on to another point and wish to emphasise the deeper significance of the struggle on which we are engaged. It is no ordinary political issues that are at stake, and the outcome of this war will not be immaterial to the future character and trend of our civilisation. In spite of the specious promises of a New Order and the alluring appeals to the idealism of youth, actual events have in the last three years revealed the true nature of the Nazi ideology. We know beyond all doubt what Hitler's New Order means.

Persecution, domination, suppression, enslavement of the free spirit of man, aye, extermination—those are the dominant features of the new creed as practised in the occupied countries. It is written in the blood and tears and nameless suffering of vast numbers of innocent men and women of all ages and conditions.

It is in contrast to this that I have emphasised the heroic spirit of the suffering Allied peoples now under Hitler's heel, because I feel that this is the heart of the matter. This at bottom is a war of the spirit, of man's soul.

Hitler has tried to kill this spirit and to substitute for it some ersatz thing, something which is really its negation. He has instilled into German youth a new racial fanaticism.

He has sought strength in the ancient discarded forest gods of the Teuton. His faith is a reversion to the pagan past and a denial of the spiritual forces which have carried us forward in the Christian advance which constitutes the essence of European civilisation.

He has trampled under foot the great faith which has nourished the West and proved the greatest dynamic of all human history and made Western civilisation the proudest achievement of man.

He has trampled on the Cross and substituted for it the Crooked Cross, fit symbol for the new Devil worship which he has tried to impose on his country and the world. Nietzsche's Superman is substituted for the Man of Nazareth as the new leader of the human race and the human advance.

He has stamped on the human virtues which we had learnt to cultivate under the symbol of the Cross. Decency, sympathy, mercy are not words found in his new code.

He has trampled on the spirit of liberty which has become the accepted political creed of the modern world. He has started a new era of martyrdom for the human spirit, an era of persecution such as mankind has not known since its emergence from the Dark Age.

The suffering he has inflicted on Jews and Christians alike, the tide of horrors launched under his Gestapo regime over the fair West, constitute the darkest page of modern history. He has outraged and insulted and challenged the very spirit of humanity and tried to found a new barbarism.

After what has happened since 1939 in the Occupied Countries and elsewhere, both in peace and war, there is no more doubt about the meaning of it all. The real issue has now been made clear. There is a challenge to all we have learnt to value, and to prize even above life itself.

Behind all the issues of this war lies the deeper question now posed to the world: Which do you choose—the free spirit of man and the moral idealism which has shaped the values and ideas of our civilisation, or this horrid substitute, this foul obsession now resuscitated from the under-world of the past?

This in the last analysis is what this war is about. At bottom, therefore, this war is a new Crusade, a new fight to the death for man's rights and liberties, and for the personal ideals of man's ethical and spiritual life.

To the Nazi fanaticism we oppose this crusading spirit, which will not sheath the sword till Nazidom and all its works have been purged from this fair world. And in that spirit the United Nations will march forward to victory and to the world which will follow that victory.

I therefore come to the question: What is the sort of world which we envisage as our objective after the war? What sort of social and international order are we aiming at? These are very important questions, deserving of our most careful attention if we mean not only to win the war but also the peace.

Our ideas on these matters twenty-two years ago were much too vague and crude, and at the same time much too ambitious, with the result that when they came to be tested by hard experience they proved wanting, and their failure helped to contribute to the present conflict. With that experience before us we ought this time to hammer out something more clear, definite and practical.

A great deal of thought is no doubt already being given to these matters, and one may hope that we shall approach the peace much better informed and equipped than we were last time.

Certain points of great importance have already emerged. Thus we have accepted the name of "the United Nations." This is a new conception much in advance of the old concept of a League of Nations.

We do not want a mere League, but something more definite and organic, even if to begin with more limited and less ambitious than the League. "The United Nations" is itself a fruitful conception, and on the basis of that conception practical machinery for the functioning of an international order could be explored.

Then again we have the Atlantic Charter, in which certain large principles of international policy in the social and economic sphere have been accepted. That too marks a great step forward which only requires more careful definition and elaboration to become a real Magna Carta of the nations.

Again, we have agreed on certain large principles of social policy, involving social security for the citizen in matters which have lain at the roots of much social unrest and suffering in the past.

We cannot hope to establish a new heaven and a new earth in the bleak world which will follow after this most destructive conflict of history. But certain patent social and economic evils could be tackled on modest practical lines on an international scale almost at once.

Then, again, we have accepted the principle of international help underlying the Mutual Aid Agreement. The helping hand in international life is thus already a matter of practical politics, and could be suitably extended after the war. This, too, is a far-reaching innovation, pointing the way to fruitful developments in future.

All these are already indications of considerable advances to a better world and a richer life for mankind. To these we may add much of the social and economic work of the League of Nations, which remains of permanent value.

Much of the League organisation could thus continue to function for the future well-being of mankind. In sober resolution, in modest hope and strong faith, we move forward to the unknown future.

There is no reason why we should not hopefully and sincerely attempt to carry out for the world the task which now confronts us as never before in the history of our race. An American statesman has called this the century of the plain man, the common people.

I feel that in this vast suffering through which our race is passing we are being carried to a deeper sense of social realities. We are passing beyond the ordinary politics and political shibboleths.

It is no longer a case of Socialism or Communism or any of the other isms of the market place, but of achieving common justice and fair play for all. People are searching their own souls for the causes which have brought us to this pass.

May it be our privilege to see that this suffering, this travail and search of man's spirit shall not be in vain.

Without feeding on illusions, without nursing the impossible, there is yet much in the common life of the people which can be remedied, much unnecessary inequality and privilege to be levelled away, much commonsense opportunity to be erected as the common birthright and public atmosphere for all to enjoy as of right.

Health, housing, education, decent social amenities, provision against avoidable insecurities—all these simple goods and much more can be provided for all, and thus a common higher level of life can be achieved for all.

As between the nations, a new spirit of human solidarity can be cultivated, and economic conditions can be built up which will strike at the root causes of war, and thus lay deeper foundations for world peace.

With honesty and sincerity on our part it is possible to make basic reforms both for national and international life which will give mankind a new chance of survival and of progress.

Let this programme, by no means too ambitious, be our task, and let us now already, even in the midst of war, begin to prepare for it.

And may Heaven's Blessing rest on our work in War and in Peace.

CHAPTER XIX

THE EMPLOYMENT OF SOUTH AFRICAN FORCES

Field Marshal Smuts was Prime Minister and Minister of Defence when the question of employing South African forces beyond the Continent of Africa was debated on January 27, 1943, in the Union House of Assembly.

THE PRIME MINISTER, J. C. SMUTS: I move—

That, in view of the progress of the war and the prospect of the early completed expulsion of the enemy from the Continent of Africa, this House approves the employment, on the basis of voluntary recruitment, of South African forces beyond this Continent.

Mr. Speaker, I am sorry at the end of the day to take the House out of the calm and non-contentious atmosphere of agriculture into the stormy waters of a war debate, but we do not get away from the war; it remains our great, our dominant issue, both in this country and all over the world. This motion means a modification, it means a step forward in our war policy. Some would say a step backward, but it involves a modification of the war policy on which we have been acting since the 4th September, 1939. On the 4th September, 1939, we entered into the war under a certain reservation under which the Government was limited not to send any expeditionary force overseas. The third paragraph of that resolution reads as follows:

The Union should take all necessary steps for the defence of its territory and South African interests, and the Government should not send forces overseas as in the last war.

This promise the hon. member for Vredefort (Mr. Conroy) refers to in his amendment, that "the Government should not send forces overseas as in the last war." If this motion is passed, Mr. Speaker, it will mean that we are deleting in fact this limitation which is imposed on the Government, this bar against sending forces overseas. That is one change, and the other change is the introduction of the principle that in no case will there be compulsion. Whatever forces are sent out of Africa overseas will have to consist of volunteers.

That, as hon. members know, has been the policy, the declared policy of the Government from the beginning, but it has never been a formal resolution of Parliament, and I think that now that we are taking a step forward, now that we are taking a step further in the prosecution of our war policy, it would be wise to limit the Government formally by a declaration of Parliament in order to prevent and to see that no forces are sent overseas which do not consist of volunteers. Now when eventually this motion is passed, certain steps will have to be taken by the Defence Department. We shall, for instance, have to submit to our forces and to the public generally who want to volunteer, a new attestation. The attestation which has so far been signed voluntarily by the public is an attestation for service in Africa, and that attestation, therefore, will not hold in respect of men who are sent overseas out of Africa. We shall therefore have to amend that attestation and submit a new one which will free us of this condition of service in Africa, and will make it possible for men to volunteer for service beyond this continent. It will also be necessary to make another change in the attestation. As hon. members know, we limited ourselves in the original attestation which has been in force for four years or the period of the duration of the war. We acted on the assumption that the war would probably be finished in four years, that that would be the maximum period. In all probability now it will not be finished in four years, and it is quite possible that at no distant date the attestation will therefore become ineffective, the four-year period will have expired, and men will no longer be bound to serve. Under the circumstances we shall have to submit to the public and to the men now in the forces, this attestation to serve for the duration of the war. I do not anticipate, Mr. Speaker, that we shall have any difficulty in getting the necessary forces for the purpose. Hon. members must bear in mind that in any case it will always be necessary for us to keep fairly large forces in the Union, for local defence and for contingencies. One never knows what may happen in a war. We shall want a large number of men here in any case, who will not be sent even out of the Union, and beyond that we shall have fairly substantial forces within Africa, even if Africa is cleared of the enemy—base troop forces for contingencies will always have to be kept there, and it is only the balance, it may be a fairly large balance, which the Government will be free to send beyond this continent. What I mean to say is this. It will not be necessary for the purpose of the war or carrying on the war, that every man should volunteer under this new attestation. A substantial number will probably serve the purpose. I also want to add this, that strict instructions will be given to the Defence Department, and through the Defence Department to our officers, to make this principle of volunteering real and effective, and not through official influence to exercise any form of compulsion, any form of persuasion. . . .

It is clear, sir, that when volunteering is laid down as a principle of Parliament, it will have to be kept in the spirit, and instructions will go forward from the Defence Department to the various organisations concerned with recruiting, that no undue influence should be used, no undue persuasion should be used, but the men should have a free choice in regard to the decision they are going to make. As I say, it is not necessary for every man, we do not need every man, to make this new attestation, and to volunteer for service beyond Africa. I have heard also a great deal about "blou-eed." Well, Mr. Speaker, there is no intention whatever to depart from that first flash which has become a symbol of honour in South Africa. If there is one symbol, one colour which all over the world is today the distinction of fighting South Africa, a symbol of honour, a symbol which expresses what is best in South Africa, it is this Orange flash, and that token of honour I am not going to trifle with. We do not want any other colour, whether men have volunteered merely for service in Africa or beyond, they will all be distinguished by the same colour. . . .

Let me just pass over now to some of the reasons which have led to this change I am proposing. Naturally, when we entered the war on the 4th September, 1939, everything was very obscure, nobody knew really what was going to happen. Here in this House and all over the country we were making a leap in the dark, and nobody knew what the future would be. Since then much has happened. Our first duty in those first days of uncertainty, the beginning of this war, was the defence of South Africa, of the Union. So that resolution that I have referred to put it in this way, the Government should take steps for the defence of the territory and the interests of the Union. We confined our interests to the Union from whatever direction our interests might be menaced, and so, as a matter of fact, we limited our activities, the scope of our war activities, to this Continent. We formed a Defence Force on the principle of volunteering, we sent men North to East Africa on a purely defensive basis. They were not equal to cope with the very much larger, stronger and more powerfully organised and equipped forces of Italy which they had to face in East Africa, and for a long time there was this purely defensive attitude. After that, as hon. members know, and as the world knows, this force went forward with their allies, they dealt with Abyssinia, and they achieved one of the outstanding achievements of this war in its earlier phases. I do not think that any two countries put up a finer fight, any two small countries put up a finer fight than did South Africa and Greece against Italy. With our allies we finished that Italian army, which was many times larger than our own in Abyssinia. The men of South Africa proved of what mettle they were made. That First Division, and especially that First Brigade of the First Division, brought immortal honour to South Africa. One remembers today, Mr. Speaker, the sad event of recent weeks; we remember that the man who led that wonderful First Brigade was Dan Pienaar, a man who has added fame to our Afrikaner people here in South Africa, whose fame as a soldier has gone over the world. When our task was finished in Abyssinia, it was necessary for us to go further, there was no point at which we could pause, the German forces were going into Egypt in order to help Italy, the Italian army there had been badly mauled by Wavell, and it was necessary for us at that stage to go forward. The cry came to us for help, and we sent our men forward into the Middle East, and into Egypt, and they had a wonderful career, such as probably no other army has ever had. Our South African forces had in the Middle East great victories, great defeats. We cannot forget, Mr. Speaker, that the Second Division, which had achieved that wonderful victory over the enemy forces in entrenched positions, that Second Division not long after was lost and had to surrender at Tobruk. I mention this simply to show the terrific struggle that took place in North Africa, in the Middle East in which our forces took part. After that disaster at Tobruk, the men in this country came forward and helped us to reconstitute the Second Division. The First Division was still there. They went forward right on to Kassala, and although they did not take any great part in that battle, which led to another smashing defeat for the British army and for our army, and to the capture of Tobruk, the First Division had the credit, at any rate, of a masterly retreat from Kassala over hundreds of miles to the El Alamein position. At that El Alamein position they had the honour of stopping Rommel. After that long retreat that might have been sufficient to break the spirit of any force, they stood their ground at El Alamein, and checked the victorious march of Rommel, which might possibly have reached

Alexandria. At the next phase, when the turn of the tide came, this First Division of ours, the division that had been through Abyssinia, and all the heavy fighting for two years in the North, were the first to break through the entrenchments, the minefields and that wonderful fortified line of Rommel's, and contributed in a very high degree to that astonishing defeat which was finally dealt to Rommel's armies. In three months Rommel's army had been driven back over hundreds of miles, and today practically with the exception of one small corner in that tip of Tunisia, the whole of the African Continent is free of the enemy. It is a wonderful achievement. It had its ups and downs for three years, for three years it was a battle against heavy odds, it was a defensive action that had to be fought against chances that were often very heavily against us, but after three years the turn has come, and this Continent is now on the point of being cleared, and cleared finally, of the enemy. Meanwhile, while this was going on, this great battle was going on which has led to the practical clearing of Africa, we also took part in the expedition to Madagascar. It may be said, Mr. Speaker, that we stretched a point, it has indeed been said that we stretched a point, and we went beyond the limitation imposed on us. We did send an expedition overseas, but it certainly was not any such expedition as was contemplated in the original motion. What really was referred to in the original motion was the sending of armies as we had done before to take part in the battles in Western Europe. This was a different case, and there was this to be said for our action that Madagascar was a point of a more vital threat to the Union than probably any other place. If Madagascar had fallen into the hands of the enemy, into the hands of Japan, it would have been a far more serious threat to the Union, a nearer and more vital threat than would have been East Africa and Kenya if that had fallen into enemy hands. Whatever argument one may use about the situation, there is no doubt that we served the interests of South Africa well in clearing our frontiers and the Indian Ocean and preventing Madagascar from becoming a submarine base, which might have had a very serious effect on the British position here in the Union. That is the position we have reached now; with one small exception we have cleared the African Continent, we have succeeded far beyond our highest expectations, we have taken part in operations which I hope are going to have a very far-reaching effect in the final issue of this war. I think the time has come when it is no longer necessary for us to keep this very large force inactive on the Continent of Africa. It is now possible for us to go forward and it is probably also our duty to go forward. It is necessary for us to clarify the position, and by a resolution of Parliament, to release the Government and the country from that limitation which was imposed on us not to send expeditions overseas. I may say this, Mr. Speaker, that in removing this limitation, it is certainly not the intention of the Government to send our forces to far distant theatres. It is quite clear that we cannot stop where we are, we cannot, whilst the war is going on in the Mediterranean, whilst theatres quite close to Africa are becoming the principal scenes of the war, it is impossible for us to keep our forces inactive on the African Continent. There is no intention of sending forces either to America or the Far East, but there is an intention to take part in neighbouring theatres close to Africa, where the war is now probably going to take place, and where most likely the war may be fought out in the months to come. It is for this purpose, and for this reason, that the position has changed completely, the clearing of Africa that has been effected and the opportunity that has now occurred for us to extend our activities beyond this Continent to neighbouring theatres, that the situation calls for this amendment to free us of the limitation and the conditions which had been imposed on our action. In the first instance we had to look to Africa, South Africa and Africa first was the sound strategy from our South African point of view. But I personally have always held the view that even from the larger point of view, from the point of view of our whole war strategy, the African Continent was much more important than many other military thinkers thought it was. The African Continent, the clearing of the African Continent, might have a far greater effect than merely securing the safety and the defence of African territories. If we could clear Africa we might use Africa as a base for wider operations. That view I have held, I held it strongly. There were great differences of opinion about it, but that view is today the prevalent view.

An Hon. Member: You did not say so on the 4th September.

Smuts: No, because it was not necessary, that is the point I am making, the whole situation has changed. Nobody knew on the 4th September what the future would be.

Mr. C. R. Swart: You expected that change to come about.

Smuts: Nobody could say; there was no prophet who could say on the 4th September what the ultimate strategy of this war was to be, but it is quite clear that once we could clear this continent we would not only render South Africa safe, secure the safety of our own country, but we would have a base from which to operate for the final victory in this war.

When Africa is cleared, as it will be within a very short time now . . .

AN HON. MEMBER: Are you sure of that?

SMUTS: We cannot be sure of anything, but I do not think I venture far afield in making that little prediction. When Africa is cleared, not only will our position here be fairly secure, but we shall be in a position to secure that victory on which our safety ultimately completely depends. It is no use merely thinking that we are safe while the war is going to be lost in the world. We are going to be in it to the full and to the end. I think it would not only be a mistake, but it would be a crime, and it would be impossible for us at this stage to sit back and to say we have achieved our end, "Africa is cleared; go home, boys." It would be a crime for us to do so, and I am sure, Mr. Speaker, that nothing would be more deeply resented by our men, by our army in the North and elsewhere, than to sit in North Africa, to remain in the desert, whilst the battle for victory is going on further north. They would resent that extremely, and I think if the choice were put before our men, they would say, "Certainly not, we are for going on, and we are going forward." I say that much has become clear since the 4th September. Much which then we did not understand, much on which we were then divided, is today clear. It is, for instance, beyond all dispute what the measure of Germany's ambition was when she went into this venture.

At that time we did not know. The argument that many people honestly and sincerely used was that Germany intended simply to remedy certain anomalies in the Treaty of Versailles. Today, after three years, events have proved that Germany had very different objects, the idea of dominating the world, of overriding all countries at all costs. That has been proved by events, and no argument is necessary any more to make that clear. It has also been proved, perhaps much better than anybody realised three and a half years ago, that Germany was a much more powerful country, much more powerfully organised, much more highly armed and prepared for the conquest of the world, which was the real object. These are things which have now become clear, and I think that if any justification were ever sought for the rightness of our action, if any proof were needed that this country in that dread hour decided rightly, that proof is given by the course of events of what happened. We have not looked for safety in neutrality like so many other smaller countries—we know that our only salvation lies in final victory. Things have proved how right we have been in the line we took. In fact, the German menace has proved of such supreme effect, far beyond any calculations of that time, that but for certain events which have happened Germany might have won the war. Many of our friends opposite had made up their minds that Germany would win, they made their plans on that, and they had a good deal of reason for it, because the German power was far greater, far greater than most people had thought. They had some justification for their anticipations which, thank God, have turned out wrong.

Mr. Louw: You mean, thank Stalin.

THE MINISTER OF JUSTICE: What a wise word was spoken there.

MR. LOUW: And you will live to regret it.

MR. C. R. SWART: The anti-Christ fighting for Christendom.

SMUTS: I certainly take off my hat to Stalin, to those heroic Russian armies which have sacrificed themselves by the millions, and who have been used as an instrument for saving freedom for this world. I take off my hat to them.

DR. BREMER: Very amusing indeed!

MR. LOUW: You will lose your shirt to Stalin.

SMUTS: I say this in response to my hon. friend—no, sir, it is not only Stalin, it is not only the coming of Stalin which turned the tide, it is also the coming in of America, and does my hon. friend object to that? After having spent so many years in that great country does he still object to America coming in to help us?

MR. LOUW: She was pushed in.

SMUTS: I am sure that my hon. friend does not prefer the company of Japan.

MR. LOUW: Neither of China.

SMUTS: A great change has come over the situation, and it is only the lack of faith and vision among many members opposite that made them make the wrong calculations as to the future. Things are changing. Three years of the hardest struggle and the greatest sacrifice which the world has ever seen. South Africa has made her sacrifices, too, very heavy sacrifices. Three years of the heaviest sacrifices, mostly in defensive warfare, mostly in hanging on. But the tide has turned. The advance of that great army, the German army, has been checked, it has been turned back.

Japan has been checked and turned back in the Far Pacific. Germany is moving back. A great change has come over the scene. Africa practically clear where we were in the greatest jeopardy not so long ago, and what is perhaps most significant of all, the supremacy of the air which is the decisive factor in this war, that supremacy has moved from Germany on to the Allies. Well, I notice from the papers this morning that a conference has taken place at Casablanca. That conference, judging from the statement, deals no longer with problems of defence, it is the problems of offence, the problems of how to arrange our offensive strategy for victory, and it shows the enormous change that has come over the scene. . . .

I think any man who today surveys the scene after three and a half years of war sees something very different from what there was on the 4th September, or the month that followed. Today we look upon a scene where although the struggle may still be fairly long, although it may go on into next year, and hard and bitter blows may still be struck, we can look forward and look forward firmly to victory, and we shall be in the right company in the end. . . .

Looking back now, if we ask ourselves what the position would have been, not only the position of South Africa, but what the world position would have been if South Africa had made the other choice on the 4th September, 1939? . . .

The position would have been this as I see it. In the first place Africa would have been in danger. Instead of being a practically free Continent as it is today, or will be tomorrow, Africa would have been in the greatest danger, and that would have applied to every State on the

African Continent. Africa would have been in just the same danger, if not in greater danger, than Europe, where all these small neutrals have been submerged and wiped out. That would have been the position. And what is more, this Cape route would have been a battle front. . . .

We might have tried to be neutral but we would have converted· this Cape route into a battle front which would also have cut us off completely from the world. . . .

Now, with the resources which we have developed, with the Allies we have, with the air and sea power which we have, we are keeping the seas open and we can get our stuff to the markets. . . .

We can get such supplies as we still want and we can carry on this country—not without difficulty or hardship, but we can carry on this country on a basis perhaps as favourable as any country in the world. Under the guise of neutrality we would have been cut off. This Cape route would have cut us off completely. . . .

And what is probably of as great, if not of greater importance, we would have been one of the hated countries in the world. . . .

We would have been hated by our friends—yes, we would have been hated by our friends in Holland and by any other country. I should like to know what the position of South Africa would have been. What would have been our affiliations, our associations, our friendships in the world if we had made the wrong choice and had been left in the stew in which our friends wanted to leave us—when they wanted neutrality for this country in the present and future, we have been saved and we are now in a position, we shall be in a position at the end of this war—and we can see what that end is going to be—we can look

forward to a safe future for this country. We can look
forward to progress and friendships and alliances which
will guide our young footsteps to the greater future ahead
of us. We chose the difficult path, and we are still choos-
ing the difficult path. In the motion which I propose we
are still making the bitter choice, the hard choice of going
forward, when we might be sitting still. But I am sure that
in making this choice we are saving our future, we are
saving our self-respect and the soul of the people of this
country, and many other things will be added to us; we
shall have our reward. I think the part which the people
of South Africa have played and which they propose to
continue to play to the end will be our title deed to security and prosperity in the years that await us.

CHAPTER XX

FOUR YEARS OF WAR

The text of a national broadcast in South Africa on September 4, 1943, by Field Marshal Smuts, surveying four years of war.

T HE COMPLETION of the fourth year of war marks a very important milestone in its course. It is, therefore, fitting that at this stage we look back for a moment on the long and arduous road behind us, to view the situation as it appears today, and then endeavour to form some idea of what still lies before us. I shall begin with the war as it more directly concerns South Africa and our share in it and then pass on to the war situation in its more general aspects and as affecting the world generally.

I begin with a reference to our decision to enter the war. Who among us will ever forget that beautiful spring day, four years ago, when war suddenly burst on us? It found South Africa quite unprepared for such a crisis— perhaps the gravest and most fateful in our history. It confronted us suddenly and most unexpectedly not only with a first-class political crisis, but also with a most searching and painful moral crisis. The divided soul of South Africa lay revealed in all its nakedness. Amid doubts, hesitations, and harrowing perplexities, we had at a moment's notice to make a national decision which all felt was bound profoundly to affect our future just as it was felt likely to affect the whole world and the future course of history. With heavy hearts and in a deep sense of responsibility we made our choice in Parliament, which many then thought to be fatal and others no less sincerely believed to be the only right course for us to take not only in our own vital interests but also those of mankind at large. The die was cast.

During the last four years a fundamental change has come over the situation. The doubts of that bitter moment are no more. And so now by an overwhelming majority the people of South Africa has approved the decision of Parliament. The events of the last four years, and especially the unmistakable revelation of the real aims and policies of the enemy, have carried conviction home to our people. The course of the war has had another result. Momentous as we then knew our decision to be, the course of the war has proved that that decision was, both for South Africa and the world, of far greater significance than we had any idea of four years ago. In the first ensuing phase of the war Germany carried everything before her. Many neutral countries were brutally overrun, France was forced to surrender, and our Commonwealth of Nations remained the only combatant to oppose the overwhelming might of a victorious Germany. That was the darkest period of the war in which the world and the future of the war were saved from disaster only by the unshakeable staunchness of the British people and the fidelity of the Commonwealth and the Empire to the ideal of freedom for which they stood. South Africa was destined to play her part in this dark hour in which the outcome of the war was to depend very largely on the stra-

tegic position of South Africa and its loyalty to the Allied
cause.

It may now be said without exaggeration that if, during the critical years from 1940 to 1943, South Africa had
not thrown her whole weight with the Allies and kept this
highway of the seas safe for the Allies, the ultimate issue of
the war might have been different. Germany might have
joined hands from the Middle East with Japan through
the Indian Ocean—a disaster which might well have
proved fatal for the Allies.

And it is even more certain that an Allied defeat would
have been fatal to South Africa, even a neutral South
Africa which could expect no greater mercy from the
enemy than many other lost neutrals of this war whose
pre-war record had been so friendly to Germany. We
builded better for our future than we knew. Parliament
decided better than it knew or than anybody then foresaw. And it is partly in the light of this new knowledge,
born of our bitter war experience at that time, that the
people of South Africa has now given its historic verdict
in the recent election. We have much to be thankful for
in our history, but not least for the crowning mercy of
that fateful decision. On that slender thread hung for a
while the future of South Africa and perhaps of the world.
Nothing more providential has happened in our history.
And therefore I emphasise that incident, that decision, for
special remembrance and as a special cause for gratitude
by our people.

Let me now say a few words about our war effort during
that difficult period. Having put our hand to the plough
we did not look back but moved straight forward with the
strength and the stride of a young nation conscious of the

immense task before it. We raised, trained, and mobilised a large volunteer army which could not have been larger or better if conscription had been resorted to. We mobilised and expanded our industrial resources to the limit in order to equip and arm that army. We organised our people so as to maintain and largely increase our civilian activities and expand our productive capacity for civil and war supplies. In spite of very deep and painful divisions among our people we avoided extreme measures and maintained civil order and internal security. Our forces went north beyond the Equator first to take up a defensive line to protect both East Africa and South Africa, and thereafter, when Italy entered the war, to face a much larger and better-equipped Italian army in Abyssinia. They took their full share in the defeat and expulsion of Mussolini's men from that country. Thereafter they moved further north to Egypt and the Mediterranean Basin, and by land, air, and sea made an important contribution to the expulsion of the Axis from the African Continent. The battle of El Alamein, in which they took a glorious part, remains one of the decisive turning points of the war in that it opened the way to the final defeat of the Axis in Africa and to the transfer of the war across the Mediterranean to the European Continent. The African disasters cost the enemy at least a million men, untold quantities of material and shipping, the loss of the Mediterranean and Sicily, and the disappearance of Mussolini and his Fascist regime. The fall of Italy itself is not far off.

I now pass to the wider aspects of the war. Since the first two dark years of war a great change in the war situation has come about and we now look forward to the sure prospect of victory. For this we have in large measure to

thank the almost incredible blunders of our enemies who
have once more illustrated the truth of the old saying that
those whom the gods wish to destroy they first make mad.
Germany, by her unprovoked, treacherous attack on Russia in June, 1941, and Japan, by her unprovoked, treacherous attack on the United States of America at Pearl Harbor in December, 1941, brought as Allies to our side the
two most powerful nations in the world. After that we no
longer stood alone facing a victorious Germany while
other great world powers looked on as neutrals. For, even
taking into account the support which Japan could bring
the Axis, it could not possibly weigh up against the far
greater support which the United States of America, with
its vast manpower and industrial resources, has brought
to the Allied cause. The spectacular Japanese victories in
the Far East will pass and be undone, but the weight of
America and Russia in the war against Germany added to
that of the British Commonwealth must prove decisive.
During the last two years Russia has kept busy probably
two-thirds of the German army and one-half of the German air force and destroyed a large part of both. And
although the result at first favoured the Germans, the
striking Russian recovery, especially since their great victory at Stalingrad—another decisive turning point in the
war—has changed the whole situation. Their armies are
now following up this victory along a vast front towards
the Ukraine. The Russians now have the initiative and
hold the offensive, and although the receding German
front has not yet cracked, it will and must crack as soon as
Allied pressure against other parts of Hitler's European
fortress becomes strong enough. We are now rapidly ap-

proaching that great moment which will open the final phase of the war.

Just as British steadfast heroism saved the world in the first and most dangerous phase of the war, so Russia saved it in the second phase when America was not yet ready and the British army was not strong enough to face the German army on the Continent of Europe. To the Russian army and its immortal bravery both in defence and attack, its unyielding endurance of incredible hardships and, not least, to its magnificent leadership, the world pays ungrudging tribute and will not cease paying tribute as long as the war's annals are remembered. Something has happened there which will affect the future currents of human history.

Unlike the Russians, the Americans needed time to develop their full strength and they had the further handicap of sea transport and insufficient shipping to move their armies across the seas and oceans to the distant battle fronts. But already they have added immensely to the war resources of the Allies, have contributed materially to the countering of the U-boat menace on which Hitler relied finally for victory, and have secured our strategic freedom by opening the Pacific route and helping to reopen the Mediterranean route which has now made it unnecessary for us to rely solely on the Cape route for our long-distance war movements. From now on we possess full freedom of strategic movement across the seas and oceans, and our vastly superior seapower is enabled to exert its full force in the world struggle. Add to this our already decisive air superiority on all fronts, for which American production has been largely responsible, and we see how much America has already brought into the common pool for final victory. We must also remember how much she has already done to halt and push back the Japanese advance in the Southwest Pacific, a task in which the Dutch and the Australians have also taken their honourable share. She has also held the hand of and sustained China in her long agony.

One more touch to bring our war picture up to date: I come now to Hitler's fortress of Europe and the situation in Germany and the satellite and occupied countries. Hitler is accustomed to boast of his impregnable Festung Europa on which he will fall back from his extensive conquests and which he can hold against all Allied attack. Is this boast well founded? Will Hitler, in spite of our mastery on the sea and in the air and Hitler's expulsion from Southern and Eastern and Southeastern Europe, still be able to hold Central Europe indefinitely? Let us, in answer, note some of the salient and admitted facts:

Air attack is already laying in ruins one after another of the great German industrial and munition centres. With our increasing tempo of bombing, most of the great centres of Germany will in another twelve months be in ruins, if not non-existent. If German internal morale broke in 1918 when Germany was intact and had escaped all ravages of the war which she had inflicted on her neighbours, how long will she endure a devastation worse than that of the Thirty Years' War? Hitler's reliance and banking on night fighters to counter this fury of the air will be another vain hope, like the invasion of Britain, or the secret weapon, or the U-boat. The Fortress of Europe will disappear physically before this air onslaught by night and day. And its effects on civilian morale will be even more devastating than its physical effects. Already a nation-wide wail is going up from this blitz which is more than human nature can bear and which even sears the imagination.

But there is even more than the air blitz to point to the doom of Festung Europa. Hitler is already falling back upon and using his reserves of manpower and material resources. The limits of physical exhaustion are not so far off. Occupied and satellite countries are being pumped dry for manpower, raw materials, and food. The suffering subject peoples are writhing and seething with suppressed or open revolt. The fighting forces themselves do not remain unaffected. German U-boat personnel and airmen are no longer fighting up to their old standards. And in Germany Himmler with his Gestapo and SS forces has had to be put in charge—a sure sign of internal heaving and cracking. Apathy, disillusion, and despair are beginning to grip the people who see victory and its conquests going, who have seen Mussolini and Fascism go, who now watch the immense forces of the East and the West marching towards the Fortress of Europe. Internal agitation is growing and it is all the more dangerous because it is suppressed and driven underground by the iron hand of Himmler. Faith in the Führer and belief in his promises of a New Order is going fast.

But there is something more—something deeper still. The Germans are a great people and have for centuries taken a leading part in most of the lines of European advance. They are not all Nazi monsters, moral perverts, or devil worshippers infected with the Satanic virus of Hitler. Deep in the heart of that great people slumbers something which is very precious to our race. What has happened inside Germany, which has been done to innocent neighbouring peoples in recent years, has sunk deeply, scorchingly into millions of German minds. How could it be otherwise where the deepest instincts of our common humanity have been violated and outraged on a scale never before seen in history? There is another and better Germany who must have passed through hell in witnessing this brutal and lawless inhumanity of their people. The degradation of their people under Hitler and his fellow gangsters must be more than decent human nature can bear or stand for long. A deep revolt is brewing inside Germany which must in the end be more catastrophic for Hitler and for Nazidom than even the horror of the air by night. Of all the vast forces gathering for the doom of Hitler and Nazidom, not the least will be the Fifth Column inside Germany, representing revolt in the German soul itself. Let us realise the significance of this and let us remember this when we come to pass final judgment for the crimes that cry to high Heaven.

While the ultimate end is now clear and certain, it is no less certain that it will demand greater efforts from us than ever before. The hardest fighting still lies ahead. Of the four years behind us, three were spent in preparatory measures in warding off defeat and in securing positions for the final struggle. One year more it took us to see the turn of the tide. It will probably take us at least another year to win the final victory. This will be the year of intensest effort and perhaps of heaviest losses. The Fortress of Europe is our main objective and its assault will mean the climax of all our fighting. Let us therefore nerve ourselves for this climax of the war in which we shall be in sight of the greatest of all world victories and the enemy will resist with a corresponding energy of despair. We must assume that final plans for victory have been completed at Quebec and that the time for talking is now past. And indeed there is no further time to lose. If this war, now entering on its fifth year, is not to drag on until the world is completely exhausted and the foundations of our civilisations are endangered, we shall have to force it to a conclusion this year by a concentration of all the means in our power. Time has now become of the essence of victory. Let unity of planning now be followed by unity and speed of action. In that case this will be the last year of this greatest and perhaps last world war.

When the victory has been won we shall be faced with the colossal task of rescuing what is left from destruction. A broken, destitute, starving old world will call for relief, restitution, and the opportunity of being set going again. Let that be our new reparation policy in contrast to the ruinous policy of that name of the last peace. Unless that new policy is followed, our Western society may dissolve in a chaos of suffering and despair. If it be followed in true Samaritan spirit, not only will the self-inflicted wounds of our mother continent of Europe be healed, but a new atmosphere will be created among nations in which the planning of a new world order could be carried out— a world order in which a new human society can arise within the framework of an organised international peace order. That is our double goal; let all our efforts be directed towards attaining it after victory has been won.

CHAPTER XXI

INTO THE FUTURE

The speech made by Field Marshal Smuts at the Guildhall, London, on October 19, 1943.

MY LORD MAYOR, MY LORDS, LADIES AND GENTLEMEN:

I thank you most warmly, my Lord Mayor, for your most kind—your all too kind—words of welcome to me here today. I may say that I am very happy to be with you here today, and I feel deeply grateful to all of you for this great welcome with which you honor me.

When I was in London last year I much regretted that no opportunity was found for a visit to the City and I am therefore all the more pleased to be able to be with you here today and to enjoy your hospitality.

Many ties and memories link me to your great city. You honored me with your freedom as far back as the last war and I am, besides, a Freeman of many of your famous Guild Companies. They have brought me not only honors but many treasured friendships.

And now, after this war, after all you have endured and achieved in this war, these links and memories have a new meaning and value for me. You are today a prouder city than ever before in your long history. Not only your own citizens but freedom-loving people throughout the whole world have heard of London, of this historic and impregnable citadel of freedom. You bear your honorable scars of war. This famous Guildhall itself bears its wounds, its war honors, upon it. But proudly you stand. London stands foursquare as a monument to man's free spirit in the hour of fiery trial. So may it stand forever!

As the city, so stands the nation, united as never before in loyal devotion round the King and Queen, who, in this crisis of fate, are not only the center of national unity but also noble examples of devotion to public duty, examples of the spirit of service and sacrifice to the whole nation, the Empire, and the Commonwealth.

I come to you on this visit a much happier man than on my visit last year and for this I have very good reasons. To begin with I have, as you know, had a successful general election in South Africa. I need not tell you how welcome such an event is to a harassed Prime Minister. Two of my other Dominion colleagues have had similar successes to cheer them on their way. But I think the South African success stands by itself.

In view of the grave constitutional controversies which have raged in South Africa, not only in connection with our part in this war but long before it, we will do right in attaching a special significance to the elections there. By an overwhelming majority the people of South Africa have approved of the war policy and have shown their determination to see it through to the end with all their strength.

But they have done more: they have also affirmed their continuing membership in our world-wide Commonwealth for the future and have once more expressed their firm resolve to stick to their old and tried friends and to shun the pitfalls of neutrality and isolation in this dangerous era through which the world is passing. I need not point out to you the significance of all this. It makes me feel easier about the future than I have felt for a long time. Taking it all round, I think we shall not be far wrong if we look upon this election as one of the major victories of the war.

The local situations in the Dominions have called for elections there. In this country, in Great Britain, no such situation exists; no election is needed to prove that the British people are united to a man behind the greatest leader they have ever had—the leader of whom, it is now amusing to recall, a gentleman prominent in your public life told me only a couple of years before this war that he had no party, no followers, and no hope of future leadership! Such are the ironies of history! I reminded my informant that in the later stages of the last war I had heard from a well-known diplomat exactly the same statement about Clemenceau, the Tiger, and that within a month thereafter he was Prime Minister of France and led his own country to final victory in the war.

You have found a greater man than Clemenceau, and he will lead you to a more conclusive and fruitful victory than that of the last war.

The unbreakable spirit, the unbreakable unity of the British people in their war effort and behind their leaders, is a most heartening sign and a sure guarantee of victory whatever may be the ups and downs before we reach it. Among this people no pep talk is needed, such as Hitler administered to his doubting and bewildered Germans a couple of weeks ago.

I have thought it worth-while, my Lord Mayor, to refer to the political situation in South Africa and elsewhere in the Commonwealth because it did so conclusively deny those prophets of evil who preached the doom of the Empire and who saw in the Statute of Westminster dire forebodings of the dissolution of our Commonwealth of Nations whenever it might come up against a first-class crisis. The crisis did come—and in a worse form than anybody had ever anticipated. But so far from causing a break-up, it has only cemented us more closely in common understanding and in unity of action.

This great Commonwealth of sovereign states spread over the world, forerunner of the future government of man, is today under the most searching of tests more of a reality than ever before just as it is today a greater power for good, a stronger buttress of man's future than it has ever been in the past.

Another special reason which makes me feel happier today is the immense change which has come over the scene since my visit a year ago. I spoke then in a somewhat optimistic frame of mind. I said the defensive phase of the war was over for us, and we were passing over to the offensive which would lead to final victory.

But neither I nor anybody else then foresaw such a vast change as has come over the whole world situation. This great change only strengthens my belief that as we move away from the defensive phase events will more and more take a catastrophic turn. The crises and climaxes will come more sharply and suddenly until the final overwhelming collapse of the enemy.

The situation in mid-October last year looked dangerous in the extreme. Let us for a moment cast our thoughts back to the position as it then was. The only bright spot then was our growing air—and especially our bomber—

superiority with its effects on the enemy home front. In all other directions the scene was somber and threatening. The U-boat campaign was at its climax and was looked upon both by the enemy and ourselves as the most dangerous aspect for us of the whole war situation. In Russia the enemy was deep in the Caucasus and was nearing the Caspian and the Volga. In the east we had been retreating to the frontiers of India. In the Pacific we were desperately defending ourselves in the Solomons and New Guinea.

Worst of all, in North Africa the victorious enemy army, after routing us and capturing Tobruk, was on the border of the Nile delta threatening Alexandria and Cairo. Since Dunkirk and the fall of France, that situation in the summer and autumn of last year was the lowest ebb of our fortunes.

Then, at two points of this vast war front, things happened which transformed the whole course of the war and, perhaps, of history. The battles of Stalingrad and El Alamein marked the real turning points in this war and will rank in history with the other decisive battles of the world.

•The destruction of the German Army at Stalingrad sent a shiver and a shock right through the entire German line from end to end of Russia. Their long line has ever since been bending or reeling back until, now, it rests temporarily and uneasily behind the Dnieper.

The Axis debacle at El Alamein spread over the whole of Italian North Africa until now, with the British and American advance from the west, the Mediterranean has been cleared. Italy has been beaten out of the Axis and the Allied forces are marching on Rome. The Italians are out and the Germans are in retreat everywhere. The passive agony of Europe under the Nazi heel is everywhere changing over to acts of sabotage or guerrilla resistance. The U-boat campaign has, for the moment, been conquered and our shipping losses are less than at any other time in the war though a recurrence of the menace must be expected and prepared against. The Solomons have been cleaned up and New Guinea is in process of being cleaned up.

The change within these twelve months is indeed spectacular and it becomes all the more wonderful if compared with what the enemy had planned to achieve and was almost in sight of achieving. If the enemy had reached the Volga-Caspian line in the north, had taken Egypt in the south, and from both these points had pushed on to join hands with Japan, moving westwards from India and the Indian Ocean, what a mortal blow would have been struck at our prospects of victory! His vision of a Samurai world would have been within his grasp. That was his grand design which was shattered by the Russians at Stalingrad and by the British Commonwealth at El Alamein.

They were the decisive turning points and are now developing to their logical and inevitable conclusions towards the final victory.

The great and increasing American forces, now marching into line, east and west, will play their decisive part in this great battle, but nothing will rob Russia and the British Commonwealth of the glory which is theirs—the honor of having turned the tide of war by ending the victorious course of the enemy at the most critical moments and places of the war, when the enemy was in sight of a colossal achievement. That great moment of history is Russia's and ours.

There is one word more on this subject of war honors which I wish to add and which I think in justice should be said. The Russian contribution to the war is immense and, indeed, has surpassed anything which even the most sanguine had expected of her. We are under no temptation to detract from the credit which is hers—which justly is hers. It is universally recognized with ungrudging admiration and gratitude that Russia—after all her sufferings in the last war and in a bloody revolution since, after the loss in this war of her most valuable agricultural and industrial territories, after the loss also of millions of her brave army and a very large part of her population in a long series of retreats and setbacks—that Russia, after all this, could stage such a comeback and keep it up remorselessly in all weathers is one of the most amazing chapters of history.

Our admiration for all this is unbounded, but our high sense of Russia's service should not make us depreciate our own contribution and make us think less of it in comparison.

From El Alamein onwards, we of the British Commonwealth have done things on the battlefronts which will stand comparison with the contributions of any of the Allies. The conquest, with American assistance, of Africa, of the Mediterranean, and especially the bringing of Italy to her knees, are events of first-rate importance in this war. I doubt whether any other service of greater importance for our final victory has been rendered in this war. No greater events have taken place in this war. The restoration of our vital war communications, the conquest of vital bases for the attack on Hitler's fortress of Europe, the knockout of a great European power, the coming over of the powerful Italian navy to us—all this has followed from our successful Mediterranean strategy. The British Commonwealth, in particular, may be justly proud of its contribution to victory.

Nor have we seen yet the full fruits of what we have won. The Germans have not only lost their reinforcement of fifty or sixty Italian divisions in the field; it may not be long before these divisions, or the bulk of them, will be fighting on our side, goaded and fired by German revenge and atrocities against their people. I say with all emphasis that nothing comparable or of greater importance has been achieved in this war. And it is proper and necessary for a full sense of perspective about the war as a whole that these things should be borne in mind and should be said.

To this must be added our continuous bombing campaign against the enemy industrial centers and communications both in Germany and the occupied territories. Vast destruction has been wrought to the enemy resources and war effort.

Immense manpower has had to be diverted to repair this damage and to move these war industries out of the danger zones. His fighter air resources have had to be diverted to counter this bombing effect and have thus largely been kept away from the Russian war front. Probably some 2,000,000 men have had to be continuously employed on anti-air defenses and other protection against our bombing operations. It may be no exaggeration to say that our air bombing offensive against enemy centers has had, and is having the dimensions and effects of a large-scale additional front.

All this has to be borne in mind if we wish to have a fair picture of our comparative war effort. Nor have we to omit our outstanding contribution on the high seas and in maritime transport for the whole Allied force. All this is generally known and admitted and calls for no elaboration.

We are now in the autumn of 1943; we shall soon be entering upon winter. Looking back now at the hopes and forecasts for 1943 which those of us best able to judge entertained last year, we have already gone farther and achieved more than we had planned to do by next winter.

Certainly my own hopes were more modest than the measure of success already achieved—and still, in fact, to be achieved before the end of this year. We have climbed out of the depths and moved far forward. We may confidently reckon on still further advances, especially in southern and south-eastern Europe. And by the coming winter we shall have closed in upon Hitler's central fortress of Europe and be making our dispositions for the grand assault by our armies next year.

That assault will be our first priority, and while it goes on we shall be increasing our pressure in the Far East and taking all preparatory steps for the assault upon Japan which is our second priority. The fall of Hitler in the West will have far-reaching repercussions in the Far East, and will facilitate and hasten the fall of Japan. Indeed the collapse of Germany may mark the beginning of a cataclysmic turn of events in the Far East also and of the early ending of the war thereafter.

In the assault upon Hitler's Europe next year the

United States will undoubtedly take a leading part—perhaps the leading part. In spite of its already great contribution, its rôle in the war so far has been principally what it was originally intended to be—the arsenal of democracy. Its industrial effort has been prodigious and is still moving to an almost incredible peak. Meanwhile the naval losses at Pearl Harbor have been more than made good and the shipping program has more than replaced all the losses from the U-boat attack since the beginning of the war. Meanwhile, also, vast land and air forces have been forming and training and a considerable addition has already been made to the Allied war fronts in the east and west.

But in view of the intense and prolonged strain and the excessive demands upon the British Commonwealth, American manpower has been rightly looked upon as our grand strategic reserve in the west for the final moves in the war. While, therefore, every ally will go all out to bring about the final climax, the United States, latest and freshest and most potent newcomer into the field, may have to play the decisive part in the concluding act of the great war drama.

Such a rôle in the war would also be the best justification for the all-important part it is likely to play in the peace and the building up of the New World thereafter.

The hopes and prayers of the Old World are with this, its most powerful offspring. For no nation in history has so great and honorable a destiny been marked out by the course of events. None has ever had so high a mission of good and goodwill; on none have such high hopes been built.

One more concluding remark on the war. The time is

short. The time factor in this fifth year of the war has
become all-important, and from now on every moment
counts. Already the moral and physical conditions, especially in the occupied countries, are indescribable, far
worse than at the end of the last war. If Europe is to be
saved from immeasurable disaster we must look upon the
earliest ending of the war as of the first importance.

The longer this agony lasts and the worse it becomes
the more difficult, if not impossible, it will be to restore
the continent to normal conditions after this war. For
carrying on his war Hitler is draining occupied Europe
of all its resources of food, materials, and manpower.
Everywhere the enslaved populations are being reduced
to destitution and despair with the most brutal ruthlessness. Under threats of starvation they are being con-
scripted for war service and labor service, regardless of
age or sex. They are moved about like dumb cattle, far
away from home and friends, shot on the least show of
resistance, shot as hostages even without any allegation of
guilt, while Jews and Poles and other sections of the
population are being systematically exterminated.

The moral and physical sufferings of the victim peoples
surpass all limits of human nature and of past experience
even in the most barbarous times. Even the reading of
authentic accounts of these outrages is more than ordinary
human feelings can bear. A new darkness of ruthless,
monstrous inhumanity, unilluminated by the mercy of
Christ, covers the face of Nazi Europe in this twentieth
century. It must be ended soon if Europe is to be saved.

And there is another reason of a more military character for avoiding delay. Hitler is no longer fighting for
victory, but for time—for something to happen—for the

accidents that so often set the run of events. His only hope
now is to prolong the war on the off chance of something
happening—some new weapon, perhaps some difference
among the Allies, war weariness, some unforeseen development, or what not—coming to his assistance and producing a stalemate or compromise peace.

The answer to all this should be our relentless, ever
increasing pressure exerted, without rest or pause, until
the crack in his defenses comes, and the whole imposing
structure begins to topple. The policy of continuous pressure, begun in the Russian offensive since Stalingrad, and
in our own increasing tempo of attack since El Alamein
in the Mediterranean basin, should be prosecuted cease-
lessly so that the final decision could be forced as soon as
possible next year.

The lines of our strategy are agreed and settled; the
resources for carrying it out will be forthcoming; and we
are not lacking in the genius of great leadership. About
the end there is no longer any doubt, not even in the
mind of the enemy.

It now remains for us to hasten that end by every means
in our power.

It has been rightly said that the peace will be an integral part of the war: that the winning of the war will
be in vain unless the peace is also won. But an even more
immediate task, when the war ends, will be the salvaging
of Europe from the wreck of the war. I have just referred
to the conditions already existing in large parts of Europe.
They will be much worse at the end of the war. The
scorched-earth policy, the inevitable war destruction, the
unspeakable devastation which accompanies the retreat
of the enemy in Russia, Italy, and other liberated coun-

tries, will confront the Allies with a problem almost as great as the war itself.

The mere physical effort of feeding, housing, and caring for the destroyed populations will tax our resources as if it were another chapter of the war. And we shall also have to deal with the psychological aftermath of these conditions in order that Europe may not lapse into anarchy and barbarism. The most pitiable human situations will face us when the blessed "cease fire" is sounded at the end of this war. And our vital public interest no less than our private human feelings will be engaged in grappling with this grave task. It will be vain to think of the world's economic recovery unless that deeper call of humanity is answered. Our whole claim to be a Christian civilization will lay the heaviest duty on us. The good Samaritans will also be the best citizens.

Whatever our reparation policy after this war will be, it will at least begin with this essential work of international relief and reclamation on which the return of the world to better economic and social conditions will depend.

Tentative first steps are already being planned by the international relief and food commissions, but they are but first steps. I have no doubt that we shall take the other necessary steps which have to follow. We shall not repeat the pitiful mistake of the last armistice when we actually allowed the position in enemy countries to become worse, the existing famine conditions to grow and spread until the armistice period inflicted in some respects greater injury and suffering on the civilian populations than the war itself and became a more bitter memory. That mistake is not likely to be repeated in the far more grave situation at the end of this war.

But more difficult problems lie ahead in connection with the peace: the problem of aggression, the basic problem before our race, and the future of our civilized society. It is the last obstacle to be overcome in our long upward climb from our primeval savagery. Here we come up at last against the toughest and, let me add, one of the most heroic instincts of the race—the instinct of the animal in us, of the beast, but of the kings of beasts: the lion and the tiger. The Christian gospel still fights in vain against this earlier, more deeply founded gospel of our race, which is still upheld in some countries and circles as the code of honor and virtue for our society. The blond beast, the superman of nature, still hurls defiance at the Christian code with its gentle virtues.

That last battle in the West—for our western civilization—our race must win, or die. We have reached that stage when the issue has to be squarely joined with the earlier, darker rules of force; and aggression, war as an instrument of national policy, has finally to be adjured.

Its roots go deep into the past and even into the structure of our modern society composed, as it is, of national sovereign states. But even so, the time has come for it to go. Let us make up our minds that it shall go, that no false pride of independent nations, of isolated sovereignties, shall defeat the great hope, ambition, of a peaceful, ordered human society steadily moving forward to the attainment of the high social and spiritual ideals which have been the inspiration of the great spirits of our race.

Let it be our will and firm resolve that this war shall be the last. On that basis alone, on an unshakeable determination, can the future organization for security become effective. Only the will to peace can make our machinery for security function properly. So long as the essential will to peace is there it will not be difficult to establish the machinery. Without the will, the way will not be found. The Atlantic Charter already contains the sketch for our future blueprint for security and our rich and bitter experience will enable us to complete the picture. In that will alone can be our peace, the peace which will lead to the consummation of all we have longed for and fought for in the struggles of our race.

Let the greatest war in human history become the prelude to the greatest peace. To make it such will be the greatest glory of our age and its noblest bequest to the generations to come.

BIOGRAPHICAL SUMMARY

JAN CHRISTIAAN SMUTS, born May 24, 1870, on farm Bovenplaats, near Riebeeck West.

1882: Entered Riebeeck village school; 1886: Victoria College, Stellenbosch; 1888: matriculated third on list; 1891: graduated, B.A.; won Ebden Scholarship and left for Cambridge, where he won double First Law Tripos.

1895: Returned to South Africa, admitted to Cape Bar.

1896: Migrated to Transvaal, practised as attorney in Johannesburg.

1897: Married Sybella Margaretha Krige.

1898: Appointed Kruger's State Attorney.

1901: Appointed Supreme Command, Boer forces in Cape.

1907: Colonial Secretary, Transvaal.

1908: Transvaal delegate to National Convention; urged Union instead of Federation.

1910: Union; Minister of Defence Botha's first Union Cabinet; organised Union Defence Force.

1914–15: Mobilised Defence Force: acting Prime Minister during Botha's absence in South-West Africa.

1916: Appointed Lieutenant-General in British Army and to Command in East Africa.

1917–18: Member of Imperial War Cabinet; offered Palestine Command; formulated plan for defence of London; recommended amalgamation army and navy air arms into R.A.F.; with Milner arranged for unity of command in France.

1919: Peace Conference; with President Wilson formed League of Nations.

1919: Succeeded Botha as Prime Minister.

1924: Leader of Opposition.

1930: Visited U.S.A. to lecture on League of Nations.

1931: President, British Association for the Advancement of Science.

1933: Minister of Justice and Deputy Prime Minister.

1939: Prime Minister and Minister of Defence.

1941: Created Field Marshal.

1942: Visited England to address both Houses of Parliament.

1943: Won overwhelming victory in General Election and re-visited Great Britain.

Date Due

APR 3			
NOV 27 1967			
	PRINTED	IN U. S. A.	